C0-AMU-521

TRACK AND FIELD

second edition

TRACK AND FIELD

Changing Concepts and Modern Techniques

James A. Gordon

Miami University
Oxford, Ohio

PHOTOGRAPH CREDITS

Miami University Audio-Visual Service: 20, 54, 194, 209; Arizona State University, Sports Information Department: 148; Comite Organizador De Los Juegos De La XIX Olimpiada: 223, 225, 226; Des Moines (Iowa) *Register and Tribune:* 84; 1968 *United States Olympic Book,* published by the United States Olympic Committee, 1969, produced by International Olympic Editions, Lausanne/Stuttgart (Germany), Editor Frederick Fliegner: 124, 125, 130, 140, 141, 160, 174, 175, 180, 188, 189; World Wide News: 73; Author: frontispiece, 30, 46, 47, 62, 98, 114, 204.

Library of Congress Catalog Number: 77-165194

PRINTED IN THE UNITED STATES OF AMERICA

To

GEORGE LESSIG RIDER

Gentleman, *Teacher*, and *Friend*

this book is dedicated.

Contents

Preface

This is the second edition of *Track and Field.* It is the purpose of this revision to keep coach and athlete abreast of modern trends and rapidly changing techniques.

In the short period since the publication of the first edition, significant track and field developments have occurred. Fiber glass pole vaulting has become firmly established; the "Fosbury" back lay-out technique has been added to the evolutionary variations of high jumping; innovations in training for the various running events have been introduced.

The XIXth Olympic Games were held in Mexico City during this period. The author attended and gleaned many new insights. Some of the new photographs appearing in this edition are personal ones taken on that occasion.

A re-examination of techniques, continued exploration to find effective coaching methods, and the impact of penetrating research in sports medicine during this time have special meaning for the track and field athlete and for the coach. That meaning finds expression here.

The professional philosophy of this edition remains the same. Track and field coaching is essentially a teaching-learning process. The revision has been designed with this objective in mind. It has been written for coach and athlete. Old, and well-established fundamentals have not been changed; new innovations have been added. An attempt has been made throughout to keep the book basic and compact.

The need to know how and why is one of the most characteristic features of man. It is hoped that the content of this revision will continue to stimulate this urge and motivate readers to go beyond it in their own search for greater understanding in this field.

To Mrs. Robert S. Mann and Mrs. Jean Luechauer, for their capable and generous assistance in preparing the manuscript, and to Milton M. Myers, James L. Morner, and other members of the Miami University Audio-Visual Service, who assisted with the art and photography, I want to express my sincere appreciation and thanks. Also, I most gratefully acknowledge the technical advice of Miami University colleagues, Stanley A. Imhulse, Head Track Coach, and Charles Zody, Field Coach, and of John W. Morris, Track Coach at the University of Houston. I sincerely appreciate too, the contributions of many professional colleagues whose research and writing helped to document the content of this book.

J.A.G.

1
Program Foundations

Track and field is an old sport. Its heritage of basic movement is traceable to primitive man—its more classic forms, to the Games of the Ancient Greeks.

The history of track and field has been evolutionary. Change has been inevitable and with it has come progress. Today, man is running faster and jumping farther and higher than at any time in history. He has overcome, one by one, the barriers in his weight throwing ability. In terms of performance, he is at an all-time high in all events.

Track and field coaching has also changed. Old techniques, fascinating and rich in tradition but swaddled in guesswork and "pet theories," have been replaced by insight and understanding. For the modern track coach, this is an age of science.

The promotion and development of a modern track and field program is a demanding, but rewarding, undertaking. To have a successful program, a coach must take into consideration the factors that will govern its execution. Prominent among these are: leadership, facilities and equipment, competition, cooperation, publicity, budget, and climate.

COACHING

Of all the factors that contribute to the development of a successful track and field program, none stands out more prominently and consistently than enthusiastic coaching. Additional competencies that strengthen such effective leadership are: (1) a knowledge of track and field technique; (2) the ability to recognize, and effectively communicate to the performer, corrective measures for mechanical deviations; (3) a knowledge of physiological responses and the training methods by which they may be altered; and (4) an ability to motivate the athlete. These may be learned through personal competitive experience or acquired by study and observation. All are important. None, however, can substitute for a contagious enthusiasm that makes a love of the sport a part of the personality of the teacher.

The demands placed upon a track and field coach today are heavy. At the college level, one of the most important demands is recruitment of talent. In a setting of highly competitive athletics, recruitment is an especially significant consideration. Without superior talent among the students, a coach cannot expect miraculous results, regardless of his own abilities and enthusiasm. For this reason, the success of many college coaches depends not so much on their ability as teachers as on their ability to recruit superior material. Most college coaches cannot depend entirely upon discovery and development of talent from within the student body as the main source of squad personnel. There are those who still do, and for them the satisfactions of teaching are great—but championships are few and far between. For this reason, many college track coaches today attempt to recruit high school champions, who are already developed, by means of grants-in-aid and similar "scholarship" inducements.

For the high school coach the situation is somewhat different. Here the opportunity for work of a developmental nature is more abundant. Competition is keen, but time for work with the beginner more plentiful. The high school coach is often the builder of future college champions, and our high schools are the setting for some of the finest teaching, real creative teaching, to be found.

The high school coach cannot venture far beyond the running track, athletic field, or gymnasium in his search for talent. He must employ, within the limits of the school environment, every possible medium for discovering and recruiting members for the team. His personal enthusiasm and interest in the young track and field prospect is probably his greatest recruiting asset. Other devices and media used effectively are: (1) participation by athletes on other sport teams out of season; (2) tests of physical proficiency* in physical education classes; (3) intramural track meets; (4) displays on bulletin boards; (5) motion pictures; (6) radio and television programs; (7) assembly programs; (8) community and school newspapers.

A well-balanced squad is the hallmark of a good track and field coach. He gives equal attention to all of the events. As a coach, he guards

* See Speed and Agility, Pulse Rate and Jump-Reach tests which follow.

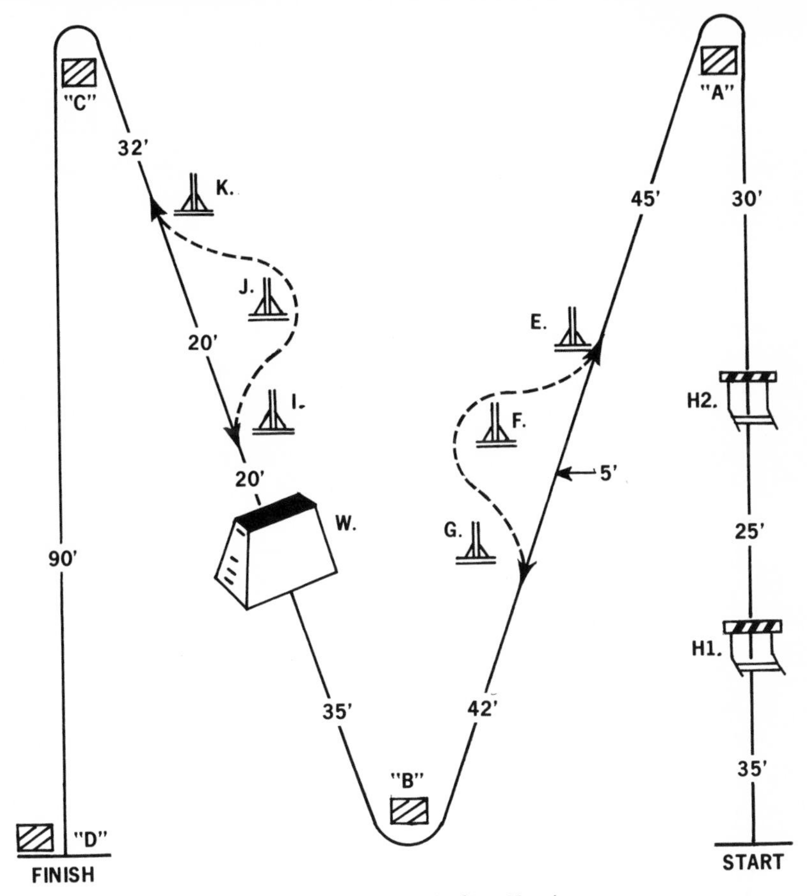

*The Speed and Agility Test**

against the unconscious tendency to favor the event in which he happened to achieve his best record as a performer. In competition his squad is represented by a maximum entry in each event.

The contribution of a track and field coach to the total growth and development of the members of his squad is significant. He is not a trainer of human puppets who follow his every command and demonstrate his worth through their outstanding performance. Rather, he is a leader, an analyzer, a counselor, and perhaps, to some extent, a supervisor. He helps men to do better what they are quite capable of doing well by themselves; he guides them in discovering powers of endurance, skill, and self-discipline beyond what they alone might have realized.

* Adapted by permission from *Conditioning Exercises, Games and Tests.* Copyright © 1960 by U.S. Naval Institute, Annapolis, Maryland.

THE SPEED AND AGILITY TEST

(1) Athlete assumes position on back, head on starting line, arms folded on chest, legs straight, feet together.

(2) On signal, turns over and comes up running for Box "A," clearing hurdles H1 and H2.

(3) As he rounds Box "A," picks up tennis ball.

(4) Runs to Box "B," dodging standards E, F, and G.

(5) Places ball in Box "B."

(6) Runs to Box "C," vaulting over 6-foot vaulting barrier (or equivalent piece of gymnastic apparatus), dodging standards I, J, and K en route.

(7) Picks up tennis ball at Box "C."

(8) Sprints for Box "D," placing ball in box to complete test.

Rating Scale

28 seconds and under	Excellent
28.1–29.5	Good
29.6–32.5	Fair
32.6–35	Average

THE 600-YARD PULSE-RATE TEST

(1) Athlete runs 600 yards at 1:50 pace. (Time at each 110-yard interval to assure even pace.)

(2) At completion of run, rest 1 minute and 30 seconds.

(3) At end of 1:30 rest period, count pulse (at carotid artery of neck) for 30 seconds *to determine potential for distance running.*

Rating Scale

Pulse rate 70 or below	Good
60 or below	Excellent

THE JUMP-REACH TEST

(1) Athlete faces marking board. With piece of chalk in one hand, marks board at point of maximum reach (from toes). This is his reach mark.

(2) From best vertical jump position, jumps marking board at point of highest effort. Three jumps are taken. Best of three jumps constitutes jump measurement.

(3) Compute score by subtracting reach from jump measurement.

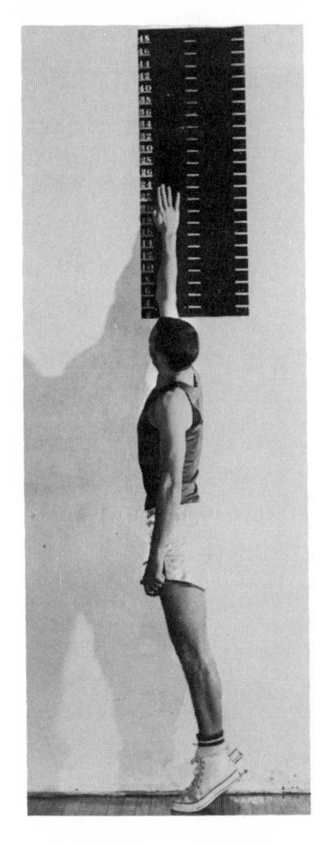

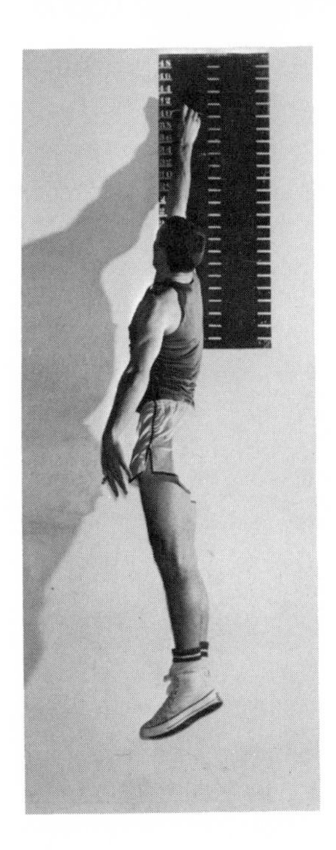

*The Jump-Reach Test**

Rating Scale

28 inches and over	Excellent
27–24 inches	Good
23–20 inches	Fair
19 inches and under	Average

FACILITIES AND EQUIPMENT

Soundly constructed facilities that are well maintained for training and competition are a necessity for long-range program development. An indoor field house is ideal—but not essential. Enthusiastic and imaginative coaches have been highly successful with limited facilities. Effective substitutes for indoor and outdoor tracks have included: corridors, stairways, black-top driveways, parking lots, football fields and golf courses.

* Adapted by permission from *Conditioning Exercises, Games and Tests.* Copyright © 1960 by U.S. Naval Institute, Annapolis, Maryland.

Modern running tracks measure one-quarter mile. Eight 42-inch lanes are provided. Newer tracks are being constructed without a 220-yard straightaway. Most track meets today are conducted in accordance with international rules. The 220-yard dash and, in high school competition, the low hurdle race are run on the curve. The longer, more traditional straightaway is therefore not used. A straightaway long enough for the 120-yard high hurdle race is necessary.

Both old and new tracks, along with all field event areas, should be carefully surveyed and measured to make sure they consistently comply with official rule specifications. Records are frequently lost because of failure to do so.

All-weather materials have been perfected and are almost universally used today in constructing new tracks and resurfacing old ones. Crushed brick, volcanic ash, and pulverized shells are still in use in some parts of the country, but they are gradually being replaced by other materials. These newer materials fall into four general categories:

(1) Fibrous asphalt composition.

(2) Rubber-sand-asphalt hot mix.

(3) Rubberized asphalt cold mix.

(4) Synthetic resin composition.

Synthetic resin material differs from all others. This chemically produced product contains no asphalt. Small installations are laid in sheets. Large ones on track surfaces must be mixed at the track and installed by the manufacturer. The material comes in a variety of colors. It is a tough, durable product with high compression properties. It is a quality installation highly recommended by track coaches who have used it.

The advantages of all-weather surface tracks are significant:

(1) Meets are rarely cancelled because of rain.

(2) The track is ready for use as soon as the snow melts in early spring.

(3) The surface is tough and durable.

(4) Resiliency saves wear and tear on athletes' feet and legs.

(5) Surface of track is smooth, and consistent in texture, which enhances faster times.

(6) Maintenance cost is nominal.

(7) Footing is good. Danger of falls and cinder burns is reduced.

(8) Painted marking is permanent, accurate, and neat in appearance.

(9) Initial cost is relatively low, considering permanency of track and economy of maintenance.

Anyone who is constructing a new track or resurfacing an old one should visit one of the many new all-weather surface tracks now in use in almost all sections of the country. Experts and manufacturers' specialists should be consulted. Controlled tests of materials should be conducted. Specialists recommend that the following criteria be considered in selecting surface materials:

(1) Availability of supply.

(2) Hardness.

(3) Resiliency.

(4) Ability to allow penetration and withdrawal of running spikes.

(5) Ability to resist shearing and twisting from impact of spiked shoes.

(6) Temperature range and weathering quality.

(7) Water resistance or ability to drain.

(8) Cost of installation.

(9) Ease of maintenance.

(10) Service life.

(11) Effect on athletes' legs and feet.

(12) Cohesion of asphalt mixture sufficient to prevent adhesion to running shoes.

The construction of track and field facilities is a highly technical operation in which sound engineering principles must be followed. Surface alone does not make a good track. It must be solidly constructed from the sub-base up. Costly mistakes in track construction continue to be made despite the abundant information that is available. Such errors can be avoided by very little research, some consultation, and basic planning.

When a budget permits, the installation of a running track should be done by experts; this is mandatory if certain compositions are used. If local school employees do the installation, the work should be supervised by a manufacturer's representative or other knowledgeable persons. Methods of construction will vary, but general principles will apply:

(1) A detailed drawing of the proposed track and field area should first be prepared by an engineer. Elevations, drainage, curb location, markings for all events, and location of field events should be indicated.

(2) First, the track area is rough graded. Underground drainage, water and electric systems are laid next.

(3) The track is then laid out and graded to required depth. Local frost line and other environmental conditions should be con-

sidered. State and local highway specifications are of great value in determining the extent of base and base construction.

(4) Curbing is installed as a form for the track. It constitutes the track's official measurement as required by rule. Concrete has been widely used. If steel or wood is used to form the track, wood curbing, which is more economical, may be installed directly on the track surface.

(5) The sub-base is the foundation of the track. It should be carefully prepared and leveled. Roots, sod and mulch should be removed. Depressions should be checked and filled. Weed killer should be applied at this level on all but resin tracks.

(6) The base, which constitutes the next level, is the core of the track. It consists of crushed (½-inch) stone or coarse cinders. Its depth is six inches—never less than four. Old cinder tracks, in some instances, can be stabilized to form this base. It provides proper slope, or grade for the track and assures a uniform thickness of the surface material. It must be graded carefully and accurately.

(7) Leveling material is next laid. Its entire surface should be evenly graded and then rolled. It should be thoroughly dry before subsequent applications are made.

(8) Resilient material constitutes the final dressing. It should be applied in accordance with the manufacturer's specifications. It constitutes the final smooth surface of the track.

(9) Field event approaches are constructed in basically the same way as running tracks. In instances where resin compounds are used, the final surface is laid in sheets.

GENERAL CONSIDERATIONS FOR LAYOUT OF TRACK AND FIELD FACILITIES

(1) For facility of meet management and spectator visibility, attempt to have all races finish at one location.

(2) Set stands for finish judges and timers at least 15 feet from track.

(3) Do not locate jumping pits or runways near the judging area.

(4) Lay out approaches for all jumping events to avoid glare of sun. Locate these events where they may be seen by all spectators. Provide large information boards indicating progress of competition.

(5) Install two directional runways (4 feet wide) for long jump (length, 130 feet) and pole vault (length, 150 feet).

(6) Curbed pit for long jump, filled with mortar sand, measures 9 × 20 feet. Paint markings every 6–12 inches on curbing to facilitate quick measurement. Locate jumping board 12 feet from pit. Anchor on concrete base installed to proper depth at end of runway. Set bolts for this purpose in concrete while

wet. Counter-sink nuts flush with board. Bolts are located at outer edge. Oil-sand composition is used in slot in front of board to determine fouls.

(7) Set pole vault planting box, with provision for removal, in line with middle of runway. Front edge should be slightly below level of runway to allow for safe pole plant.

(8) Concrete standard platforms for pole vault and high jump are set level with runway after runways are completed. To allow for forward and backward movement, platform for pole vault standards should extend one foot in front of, and two feet back into, mound area.

(9) Landing areas for pole vault and high jump measure 20 × 16 feet. Portable foam rubber landing boxes are recommended for the high jump and pole vault. They are shaped to the pit and provide maximum safety.

(10) Provide a three-quarter arc approach for high jump which allows a 25- to 30-foot approach from two directions.

(11) Locate concrete circles for shot put and discus throw with safety and visibility of spectators in mind. Two circles and landing areas for each event are recommended. Level of circle is slightly above grade to allow for drainage. Both areas should be roped off for competition. Stop board for shot put should be installed at end of landing arc. Bolts set in wet concrete hold toe boards in place on circles. Mark landing areas at 2-foot intervals.

(12) On all-weather surface tracks provide holes for two-pin starting blocks at start of all races. Where start of 220-dash is on a curve, install holes for starting block pins so that the blocks may be set for an appropriate angular break for the inside line of each lane.

(13) Provide a warm-up or "bull pen" area adjacent to track for warm-up. Allow contestants on track only for competition.

(14) A public-address system, operated by a knowledgeable announcer, is a must for efficient meet management.

The selection and care of equipment is an important consideration for coach and athlete. Revolutionary changes have occurred in the design and materials of equipment used in the various events. Fiber glass vaulting poles have been perfected; after much controversy, they are being used by most vaulters. Similar synthetics are being used in the construction of padded lightweight hurdles, regulation plastic batons, plastic-coated shots and discuses. Synthetic tracks have already been discussed. These artificial surfaces, if constructed indoors, could well produce a new generation of athletes who could train in all seasons, undeterred by adverse weather conditions.

A variety of new starting blocks have been developed, and the choice of model should be made with care. The single-shaft, two-pin model has advantages: the blocks are easily reversed from left to right according to foot preference; its rubberized face pads are curved; and they shape themselves to the runner's foot as pressure is applied; footing is firm; angle of projection on both blocks is high, so that greater driving angle from ankle to leg is possible.

Shoes are probably the athlete's most important item of personal equipment. They should be selected and fitted with great care. Those that provide maximum foot protection and support should be worn in *practice* as well as in competition because the stresses are greater and injury from strain and over-exertion is more likely to occur. Significant improvement in construction and design of running shoes has been made. European manufacturers have developed a variety of featherweight models that are widely used in this country. Made of kangaroo leather, these "foot-gloves" weigh approximately 1.4 ounces in contrast to the 3.5–4.0 ounce weight of older models. Best identified by three brightly colored strips that wrap around the instep, they provide maximum comfort and reinforcement for the principal areas of foot stress. Various models have been developed for running and field events, and provision is made for changing spikes of various lengths. A wedge type, with flat corrugated rubber sole tapered from ball-of-foot to heel, is widely used and recommended.

New Durene lightweight, form-fitting, warm-up suits have been developed. This Scandinavian adaptation, with turtleneck collar and full zip-up front, appears to be replacing the heavier more conventional models.

Large lettering and wide stripes that circle the runner's chest appear on the newer running shirts. Quarter-sleeve models are sometimes used. Drip-dry nylon appears to be replacing satin as material for running shorts. An entire uniform of this serviceable material weighs less than ten ounces. It washes easily and will dry overnight.

The day of the "dirty" track suit as a badge of athletic distinction has passed. Modern athletic equipment is expensive—its use a privilege. Athletes should be held responsible for its care and cleanliness.

COMPETITION

Competition is the backbone of the track and field program because it provides an incentive for effort and makes it possible to measure achievement. Training is necessary and can be fun. But without competition, interest in a program is likely to wane.

Dual meets constitute the core of the competitive schedule. Relay meets have become a popular phase of early season competition. Both are endorsed because they stimulate interest and development and provide opportunity for participation by large numbers. At the high school level, district and state meets are the climax of the season's competition. At the college level, national championships are usually the setting for the ultimate competition.

Cross-country meets are scheduled in the fall. For schools with appropriate facilities, indoor meets during the early spring months are exciting and interesting for contestant and spectator.

The number of meets scheduled depends upon local school policy. The availability of indoor running facilities, budget, and geographical location must be considered. Schedules should be carefully planned so as to provide a balance of competition at home and away. Midweek meets are necessary in some large cities where more than one school uses the same track. As a regular scheduling procedure, where facilities are not limited, this practice is not recommended. Teams of equal and superior ability should be included on the schedule. Year-round training has become an accepted part of preparation for track competition. For those not participating in other sports, this is a favorable trend. It encourages a certain amount of built-in fitness and allows for gradual development in bringing a contestant up to his peak for the active season of competition.

COOPERATION

Track and field, as well as other sports, should at all times be organized and promoted with the best interests of the total athletic program in mind. While coaching today is highly specialized, a coach's enthusiasm for his sport should supplement rather than detract from the student's interest and participation in other sports. Where an election of sports is to be made, the desire of the participant, rather than of the coach, should be the determining factor. In such instances, an athlete should be permitted to participate in the sport of his choice without undue influence or interference of anyone else. Priorities in participation, if there are to be any, should be afforded the sport in season. A strong total school athletic program makes for strong individual teams. Teamwork and cooperation among coaches, as well as athletes, will prove beneficial to all concerned.

PUBLICITY

Good publicity stimulates interest in all sports and may be used as a medium of promotion and motivation. A coach should cultivate and maintain a close working relationship with the school and local newspapers. Interviews and information that is provided to television, radio, and other news media should be honest, accurate, and well planned. Adequate working facilities and location should be provided for all members of the press and radio staffs who attend meets.

Good public relations are an important asset for the coach. Publicity is only a part. Good public relations begin at home. Personal integrity, respect for the boys, a friendly interest in faculty welfare and that of the entire school—all are essential to creating good public relations.

BUDGET

The track coach should work closely and cooperatively with his athletic director and other school officials in setting up an operating budget. Some otherwise highly respected coaches have lost the support of their superiors because they could not handle money and keep accurate financial records. Estimates of expenditures and income should be accurately and honestly calculated. As in other sports, a budget for track should be sufficient in amount to (a) ensure the purchase of new, and repair of old, equipment, (b) replace old and obsolete track and field accessories, (c) provide for team travel without cutting corners, and (d) cover such incidentals as awards, guarantees, cleaning, laundry, and officiating, if not provided for in the general athletic budget. A good general rule in handling financial matters is "put it in writing" and keep accurate records of all expenditures and receipts.

CLIMATE

Favorable climatic conditions are undoubtedly an important factor in motivating and developing an outdoor track and field program. The advantage of year-round training and competition, uninterrupted by extreme weather conditions, is substantial.

Recently, coaches in areas of cold climate have been finding that year-round training, as long as athletes are dressed warmly, is not only possible and beneficial but also enjoyable for the participants.

Field houses and practice sheds are widely used in areas where cold and wet weather conditions are not conducive to continuous outdoor activity. Their availability is an advantage to teams participating in extensive indoor competition. Indoor running, frequently on short-board tracks with sharply banked turns, requires a unique technique. For this reason, some teams with favorable year-round outdoor training conditions but no indoor track do not schedule indoor competition.

An absence of ideal weather conditions, natural or artificial, may be a deterrent. It should never be considered an insurmountable handicap.

2
Training

An athlete who exercises regularly is capable of greater effort and resists fatigue better than an individual who is sedentary. The progressive process by which he improves his ability to perform muscular work, and to adapt more readily to the stress of fatigue, is known as training. Many physiological responses are altered by the training process: the muscles of the body are strengthened; neuromuscular coordination improves; cardiovascular functioning becomes more efficient so that a better supply of oxygen reaches the working muscles; a greater amount of blood is available for heat dissipation; and pulmonary ventilation is improved, resulting in a more adequate exchange of oxygen and carbon dioxide. Taken altogether, these changes are capable of bringing about an improvement in athletic performance estimated by some to be as great as 100 percent.

Strength is a basic requirement for the performance of all track and field skills. Weakness in muscles limits potential achievement.

TRAINING FOR STRENGTH

There is a relation between muscle size and muscle strength. Muscles grow as a result of repeated work. This is sometimes referred to as the "overload principle." When, owing to exercise, an individual's muscles become larger and therefore stronger, there is no multiplication or formation of new fibers; rather, those that have been undersized because of lack of use grow larger.

Exercises of strength, as in weight training, seem to produce an enlargement of fibers, while those of endurance, such as running, increase the number of capillaries. Gains in muscular strength depend upon three factors of resistance: (1) the amount, (2) the length of time, and (3) the frequency of its application. The manipulation of these variables forms the basis for much of modern track and field training.

Opinion varies about using weights to develop strength. Some believe that only weight men should use them. As one highly successful coach put it, "We try a lifetime to get athletes coordinated, loose, and relaxed in running. Then a lot of us tighten them up through an excessive use of weights." He suggests that four or five chin-ups, push-ups, or isometric exercises are sufficient if taken twice weekly during the period of long training runs.

For those who believe that runners get strength from running, cross-country runs, hill runs, and interval training runs of longer distances replace the use of weights. At the college level, a total of 50 miles a week is prescribed for hurdlers and sprinters. An "880" man runs 70 miles for a week's training. A miler and anyone training for longer distances, totals 70 to 125 miles. Obviously, for the beginner, and less mature high school athlete, these distances would be reduced. Following a preliminary period of easy and gradual conditioning, such trainees might start with total weekly runs of not more than one-third to one-half of the above distances prescribed according to individual differences.

TRAINING FOR ENDURANCE

In track training we are primarily interested in developing cardio-respiratory endurance. Such endurance is the ability of the breathing apparatus to take in large quantities of oxygen and give off large quantities of carbon dioxide. The heart and circulatory system must be sufficiently strong to transport these substances to and from the muscles by way of the blood.

Muscular endurance enables the athlete to continue activity under the stress of fatigue. The primary physiological adjustment evidenced in athletes with endurance is, as previously mentioned, the great number of capillaries in the muscles. There is also an increase in the efficiency of the heart in pumping blood to the muscles. These two results enable the circulatory system to furnish the working muscles with an adequate supply of blood. In a well-conditioned athlete, whose heart is strong and efficient, greater amounts of blood are pumped to the muscles with less effort. Demands for oxygen are thus reduced and the body uses less glucose and other vital food stuffs necessary in the oxidation process.

Running develops cardiorespiratory endurance since it involves prolonged rhythmical exercise of a large number of the body's muscles. It is probable that a good training program continued for several years improves efficiency of the circulatory system and increases the rate of oxygen supply. To develop endurance a runner must extend himself in his training, up to and beyond a point of maximum fatigue. Coaches have found in practice that an excellent device for providing this kind of "overload" is the repeated running of short distances at a given pace with attention on form. The runs are repeated after short "intervals" —before recovery from the preceding run has occurred. Thus, the term "interval training" has developed.

FATIGUE

The relationship of fatigue to a development of endurance is significant but not well understood. The exact nature of fatigue is not known. The things that have been said about fatigue over the years are so many and varied that one is likely to be bewildered in his attempt to analyze it. Much of this confusion is probably due to the fact that coaches, and frequently physiologists, use the same terminology while talking about distinctly different things. For this reason it is probably best to characterize the specific manifestations of fatigue rather than to try to describe it in general terms.

We know that fatigue is a common effect of exercise and is always experienced after exhausting activity. It causes a runner to slow down and to lose his physical efficiency. There is reason to believe that this effect is due to a loss of his capacity to transmit nerve impulses from the brain and spinal cord to the muscles. Some suggest that there is probably a chemical factor involved, but it is not well understood.

Training for endurance is primarily a matter of building resistance to fatigue; it is accomplished by gradually increasing, as condition improves, the amount and intensity of work an athlete is required to perform.

There is a difference between local and general muscular fatigue. Local fatigue is temporary and should disappear approximately one hour after all-out activity. General fatigue persists in spite of rest; it indicates overwork, inadequate diet, presence of disease, or emotional stress.

INDIVIDUAL DIFFERENCES

Much has been written about the importance of individual differences in the process of learning. It is equally important in the process of physical conditioning. In an era when "spartan" training routines are popular, coaches are prone to generalize that what is good for the champion is good for all. Biologically, such is not the case.

The ability to perform muscular work improves in all individuals who engage in physical training. Each, however, has a biological behavior that is special and particular to him. These fundamental reactions constitute, in the whole, a margin of security that allows him to restore his motor abilities to normal—even after violent exertion. The individual's capacities for adaptation and recuperation are important variables to be considered. Therefore a daily amount of training that may be suitable for one athlete may be either too much or too little for another.

Mixed opinion exists about the nature and possibility of "staleness." Some doubt its existence. Others describe it as a "state of mind." Motivation and other psychological factors are related to the question. Probably the observation of a certain veteran coach on this controversial subject—that "You can get a glass just so full of water," was the closest to the truth.

Experiments show that, physiologically, there is a level of exercise which, when frequently repeated, leads to chronic fatigue and "staleness." The effect on the body is characterized, among other factors, by higher heart rates and lactic acid concentrations for a given amount of work than were elicited in previous training sessions.

Individual athletes respond to training at different rates. The "short-swing" type improves rapidly and enjoys several periods of top performance per season before going into a final phase of declining performance. The "long-swing" athlete progresses more slowly. When he reaches his peak he remains there longer. Whatever his type, every athlete goes through a seasonal cycle of rising and falling performance.

There is reason to believe that this "sports performance rhythm" is controlled by the adrenal gland and that it may therefore be "actively influenced" by regulation of the training load. This theory of adrenal gland control is derived from Selye's[1] concept of adaptive reaction of the pituitary-adrenal system to stress. In terms of the theory, an athlete's cycle of training may be divided into three phases: (a) adaptation during which the athlete accustoms himself to training, progresses slowly, but improves his performance; (b) completed adaptation, the period of "best form" and (c) readaptation, during which adaptation is lost and performance decline sets in.

In accordance with this theory, any athlete who tries to "beat" the readaptative decline by overtraining stumbles into a chronic stress syndrome and overtiredness due to the discrepancy between his adaptability and the performance demanded.

[1] Hans Selye, *The Stress of Life* (New York: McGraw-Hill, 1956), p. 64.

The significance of wide individual differences in physiological adaptability to training are well summarized by Brouha:[2]

> The wide individual differences in physiological adaptability to training are striking. It should be fully realized that although anybody can improve his working capacity by training, outstanding athletic performances are attainable only by a comparatively small number of individuals whose physiological mechanisms are highly efficient and precisely integrated. To become a champion implies innate capabilities, mental and physical, that are developed to a superior level by adequate training and permit outstanding performances in a particular field of athletic activity. The variation in capacities and the limitations of any individual who goes into training should be known by those who are responsible for directing physical education and sports activities.

CIRCULATION AND RESPIRATION

Work capacity and related circulatory and respiratory functions are subject to improvement through regular training. With training, the heart is able to circulate more blood while beating less frequently. Thus, the heart, like other muscles, becomes more efficient with training; if it is normal, exercise will not damage it. Of great importance to every athlete before engaging in track and field activity is a medical examination to ascertain fitness for such stress. If he is fit, he will find that training will improve his cardiovascular recovery process after he stops an exercise. The better trained the athlete, the sooner his heart rate and blood pressure return to pre-exercise level.

Respiratory muscles, like other muscles, are developed and strengthened by training. Resulting changes in respiratory responses are progressive. Four to six weeks are needed before maximum efficiency is reached.

The precision and economy of any sequence of motion involved in muscular activity is capable of improvement by training. For any mechanical work performed there is one motion which is most efficient and which is physiologically the most economical in terms of oxygen consumption.

Training is specific. Light amounts transfer from one sport to the other. Heavy amounts for a specific event result in greater efficiency and capacity for work of that particular nature. When an athlete completes a training season for a given sport in excellent condition, then starts im-

[2] Lucian Brouha, "Training," in *Science and Medicine of Exercise and Sports*, ed. Warren R. Johnson (New York: Harper and Brothers, 1960), p. 416.

mediately to participate in another sport, observation shows that a certain period of time will elapse before he reaches his peak in the new sport. After a given point is reached, an increase in the *rate* of work has a greater effect on the improvement of condition than does an increase in its *duration*. Physical efficiency is more adversely affected by an interruption of intense training than by an interruption of light training.

NUTRITION

Track and field participants and coaches have traditionally stressed this aspect of training as much as has any sport group. Hundreds of theories, pet ideas, and superstitions have existed over the years. Many are fast becoming discarded or modified as research reveals scientific facts about nutrition, food supplements, vitamins, and other similar factors relating to diet and energy supply.

What is the best diet for an athlete? Most medical authorities today suggest that normal, well-balanced meals supply everything a high school, college, or professional athlete needs. Nothing is gained by adding more steaks or other items that are high in protein.

Still, many coaches and athletes have their own pet diets and foods, even though most of the reasons they give for them would not stand up under controlled scientific study. All too often these dietary schemes receive credit that should go to skill and endurance, as well as to good coaching.

Examples of theories include the use of vitamins, dextrose, or salt. These diet supplements do no harm and are given for some verifiable effect that they are known to create. Dextrose between meals provides quick energy and occasionally is given as fruit juice or a soft drink during competition. Tests have shown, however, that most of the energy used during prolonged exertion is stored up 48 to 72 hours prior to the exertion. Thus, it might be more worthwhile to avoid heavy workouts a day or so prior to competition in order to preserve this energy. Salt tablets may be used when perspiration is profuse, especially in hot weather. Many coaches prefer to have athletes salt their food excessively rather than risk the possible gastro-intestinal upset that sometimes results from taking salt tablets.

The pre-meet liquid diet has been suggested for the athlete who is so tense that digestion is disturbed. He is too upset to eat either a normal meal or the traditional meal of lean beef, baked potato, salad, toast, and tea several hours before competition. The solution to this type of stress is, of course, for him to learn to take competition in his stride. He must gain a sense of proportion so that he realizes that sport is sport and that excess tension does not make one a better athlete.

The major limiting factor in muscular work is the amount of oxygen that can be delivered to the interior of the muscle cell. In fact, the superiority of the athlete lies in his ability to meet the demand for oxygen. Carbohydrates can be converted into energy when oxygen is lacking temporarily. Thus dextrose supplies quick energy but only for a short event such as the 100-yard dash. Some athletes appear to get a lift in their performance when sugar, in one form or other, is given immediately before competition. However, most investigators seem to agree that its effect on a high-strung athlete is largely psychological and improved performance more probably depends on energy reserves and training than on the extra carbohydrate consumed.

The health of well-nourished athletes cannot be improved by a superabundance of vitamins. Their use by track and field contestants, unless there is a personal deficiency diagnosed by a physician, is of little value and otherwise costly.

A well-balanced and nutritious meal the night before competition, because of the time required for the digestive system to convert it into energy, is probably the most important one as far as the athlete is concerned. As important as its content is the time it is eaten.

The same is true for the last meal before competition; here too, individuals differ. Some can eat a short time before competition without stress. Others require more time for the meal to settle. Most find that they get the best results when the pre-competition meal is eaten approximately three hours before a contest. The meal at this time, adjusted to the needs of the individual and his event, should in most cases be light as well as nourishing. Other than this precaution, the advice of most doctors and nutritionists is, eat an abundant and nutritious diet. During the competitive season eat regularly. Eat what agrees with you and drink plenty of water.

THE TRAINING ROOM

A clean, accessible, and well-equipped training room is a highly desirable facility for track and field training. It should be well supervised and never permitted to become a loitering place for squad members. First aid should be carefully administered in terms of established procedures, while major injuries should be referred to the proper medical authorities. Though it may have therapeutic values in cases of muscular injury, massage is not recommended as a regular part of track and field training.

3
The Training Program

Training for track and field competition is a continuous process. It is sequential in nature. Training activity, adjusted to individual differences, is planned on a daily, weekly, and seasonal basis.

THE DAILY PRACTICE PLAN

Most track and field athletes today, regardless of event, follow basically a three-part daily training plan that includes (1) Warm-up, (2) Instruction and conditioning, and (3) Warm-down.

THE WARM-UP

Physiologically, the warm-up is an important part of track and field training. It is frequently neglected or of insufficient duration, particularly on days of competition when the athlete feels more acutely the emotional effects of stress. The purpose of the warm-up is to prepare the body physically for maximum vigorous activity by gradual loosening of the musculature and stimulation of the circulatory and respiratory systems.

Jogging and slow running, gradually building up in intensity, constitute the major part of the procedure. The nature and duration of the warm-up depend upon the individual—his age, event, and physical makeup. Weather conditions, time within the season, and nature of the activity to follow must also be considered. Most coaches and athletes today consider the warm-up a part of the conditioning process. Calisthenics are used sparingly. Some include them in a modified form while walking off the fatigue of their preliminary run. Regardless of where or how they are used, most agree that the few calisthenics practiced should be selected in relationship to the particular muscle groups used in the performance of a given event. Their general or wholesale use, either because of tradition or for showmanship, is a waste not only of time, but probably also of the athlete's energy. Because of their unique contribution to the development of flexibility, selected calisthenics are recommended by most coaches for the training of hurdlers. These exercises are included in the chapter on hurdling.

Accelerated running, commonly referred to as a "pick-up" or "wind-sprint," is an important part of the warm-up procedure. It consists of a sprint of approximately 120 yards. From a standing start, the runner gradually accelerates his speed for the first 40 yards, runs at maximum speed for the next 40 and uses the last 40 for purposes or deceleration. In addition to completing a warm-up of the musculature, accelerated running stimulates the circulatory and respiratory systems. Adjustment to the demands of fatigue is thus made less difficult during later maximal exertion. It should be noted that individuals differ in their ability to adjust to an "oxygen debt." The amount of accelerated running preparatory to competition, therefore, can best be determined by experience.

THE INSTRUCTION PERIOD

The instruction period is the core of daily training. It is devoted to a practice of technique and conditioning exercises, requiring the personal supervision of the coach. At this time squad members report to him; he may instruct them individually, or in groups by event. Unless he has assistants, the coach during this part of the practice period must budget his time. *He should never neglect one event in favor of another.* Field events should be given as much attention as running events. Hurdlers, unless they are practicing with sprinters, work on technique while awaiting their turns.

A coach should attempt to work personally with team members in each event at least once every other day. Written or verbal instructions may be given on days when he cannot. Members of the squad should be expected to follow them without close supervision. Older and experienced members, in the absence of the coach, may serve as squad or event leaders. There are times during the practice period when a majority of the squad may be brought together for instruction; starting practice is one such instance. Relay racing is interesting and provides another method of group instruction—one whose competition the field event contestants enjoy and in which they can easily be included. Other innovations of this kind may be explored and utilized.

THE WARM-DOWN

Physiologically, the warm-down assists the body in the recovery process. The warm-up might be considered a "winding-up" process—the warm-down an "unwinding." It may consist of a jog of several laps or more, or an alternate jog-walk interval pace, depending upon the intensity of the exercise that has preceded it. Such a letdown provides a better rate of oxygen intake and diminishing of fatigue than would result from a more sudden conclusion of activity.

THE WEEKLY TRAINING SEQUENCE

The object of the weekly training sequence is to bring the athlete up to a peak of physical and psychological readiness for competition. During midseason, competition is usually scheduled every sixth day. Most runners train seven days with a tapering-off session on the day following a meet.

To provide added competition, or make up for postponements, two meets per week are frequently scheduled. These usually fall on Wednesday and Saturday, or Tuesday and Friday. In large cities, where more than one school has to use the same facilities, other combinations, usually with at least two days' rest between meets, are scheduled.

In such cases, further adjustment in the training sequence is necessary. The nature of such modifications depends upon the time of the season, the individual, and his event. If early in the season, the midweek meet is frequently considered a "time trial" or "pace work session," and since training on this day is hard anyway, the meet does not otherwise interrupt the normal weekly practice schedule.

Subject to the above variables, a general rule frequently followed by coaches during midseason is simply to lighten up on the day's regular schedule immediately preceding and following a midweek meet. Others feel that if it is late in the season, the entire squad, and jumpers in particular, should rest completely. Most knowledgeable coaches today seem to agree that in late season it is preferable to err on the side of underworking an athlete rather than overworking him.

The nature, extent, and intensity of each day's training varies with the individual. Some runners find that the best results are achieved by placing major emphasis on a given day on either speed, endurance, or pace. Others include some of each on each day. Some favor over-distance running on the first of a six-day sequence. (Over-distance running is running distances longer than one's competitive event. A half-mile run would be over-distance for a quarter miler. The purpose of over-distance running is usually to develop endurance. Under-distance runs are used to develop speed and knowledge of pace.) Speed work is taken on the second and fourth days. The third is devoted to pace training. On the fifth day, the day before competition, the athlete either rests or takes a light warm-up. Modifications of this pattern are followed. Regardless of the training sequence, there are coaches who believe strongly that all training for runners should be performed at ¾ to ⅞ speed.

Athletes in the field events vary in their weekly training sequence. In the weight events, most train hard every day until fatigue affects their timing. Jumpers tend to taper off slightly the day before competition. Individual differences and the event should be the determining factors in establishing this aspect of training.

THE LONG-RANGE TRAINING CONCEPT

Traditionally, the American system of training has aimed to bring the runner up to a peak condition for each week's competition. Each trial has emphasized all-out performance for a particular time in the season and period of training. Each competitive effort has been an end in itself, and little consideration has been given to the relationship of one to another. Seasonal relationships and continuity have not been a primary consideration, and the American school calendar, with its sharply defined sport seasons, has been an influence. Eligibility rules have limited the years of scholastic and collegiate competition.

In contrast, the "long-range" training concept, as advocated by such coaches as Arthur Lydiard of New Zealand, places emphasis on an overall developmental approach. Post-school running is assumed. Each phase, immediate and long-range, is a prerequisite and foundation for the next. Emphasis is placed on a few "big" races each year. All others are "developmental." Training occurs seven days a week and is year-round. Mileage training, up to 100 miles per week, serves as a foundation for eventual speed running. A 12- to 14-week period of cross-country running and marathon training is included. To offset its duration, variety is essential in this period: variables include differences in terrain, pace, intensity, and competition.

The active track season is divided into two 6-week periods. The first includes controlled speed work. This is supplemented with steady runs of two to six miles. Interval and repetition running at distances of 50, 220, 440, and 880 yards is prescribed. Over- and under-distance pace work, at a steady, easy, and controlled speed, is added to this training. Or, the athlete may run his actual distance, but at a pace slower than he would follow in competition.

During the second 6-week period, a balance of speed running and steady pace running continues. The pace is faster but still adjusted to individual differences. During all of this training, degrees of effort are established on an established time basis. Assignments are highly individualized. Tables of ¼, ½ and ¾ effort, for distances of 220 yards to six miles, are determined by the athlete's previous performance. Conditioning and development is gradual.

At the conclusion of the active season there is no sudden letdown. Each athlete tapers off with a 3- to 6-week period of reduced but regular training, according to his personal nonathletic schedule. During this period he runs approximately one hour per day at an easy pace. On one of these days his total running may cover a distance of twenty miles.

This training concept, with its emphasis on sound running and developmental essentials, is worthy of serious consideration by coach and athlete.

MOTIVATION

Motivation is considered by many to be the key to success in athletic achievement and coaching. In track and field we hear much about "desire" as the unique quality that distinguishes the great from the good athlete. Others believe that the successful coach is one who can inspire his team, or its individual members, to great heights. In short, there is nothing more important to the success of the teaching process than motivation.

Motivation is closely related to the athlete's reaction and response to success and failure. Athletic competition, like classroom competition, provides both the opportunity to excel and the opportunity to be beaten. Being beaten provides an incentive to improvement, as long as some prospect of winning remains; but continual beatings are frustrating and may produce mounting maladjustment and other neurotic behavior.

Motivation is complex and difficult to construct and understand, and there are many popular misconceptions. Nowhere is this more in evidence than in coaching. For some decades coaches have been guided by a theory of motivation, based upon a notion of moral responsibility for success, expressed in the aphorism "where there's a will there's a way." Actually, the implied idea that the lack of desire to achieve is willful, the result of laziness, or lack of enthusiasm runs contrary to everything we have learned in the last 40 years about motivation, individual differences, the need for achievement, and learning. Since it has been found that generalized motivation comes only as the product of prolonged and diverse experiences of success, a more accurate precept might be, "where there's a way, there's a will."

Basic to an understanding of motivation is a recognition of man's unified nature, his oneness or wholeness. The brain does not operate by itself, nor does the body. In the training process, what affects the athlete psychologically affects him physically. No part or element within him is unrelated to his learning and achieving; he reacts as a total personality. This concept has much meaning for the coach of track and field.

Motivation is a means of bridging the gap between teaching and the personal action of the athlete. It is well for the coach of track to understand how people learn and about the drives or impulses which produce this learning. Much can be learned from recent research in sport psychology. Cratty[1] believes that the greatest help afforded by the experimental literature revolves around information outlining helpful ways to elicit maximum skill. He observes:

> Material seems to indicate that the coach may impede motor learning by scheduling practice sessions too close together in time, and/or by over-teaching, thus not permitting a skill to be assimilated. Research on transfer indicates that while so-called coordination drills, though not directly resembling the athletic skill(s) they are designed to improve, may indeed create some kind of general motor learning set. To optimize transfer from practice to competition, one should also attempt to exactly replicate game conditions in practice. . . . To elicit maximum effort from athletes, practice sessions should first of all be as interesting and novel as possible, perhaps varying in content from day to day. More mature athletes may be further motivated by planning their own workouts. Furthermore, if athletes obtain exact knowledge concerning the intensity and duration of a practice session they are less likely to slow down on their initial efforts; if no or incorrect information is afforded, they are likely to save themselves for the most rigorous practice imaginable.

Motivation means a facilitation of learning. Learning in track and field is generally facilitated when the athlete:

(1) Wants to learn and his learning transfers to competition.

(2) Believes his goal is desirable and worth working for.

(3) Understands the means that will have to be employed in achieving his goal.

(4) Understands the sacrifices he must make and the satisfactions he will derive in working toward and achieving his goal.

(5) Judges in anticipation that the satisfactions derived from achieving his goal are worth the sacrifices necessary to attaining it.

(6) Has a model with whom he can identify, who exemplifies or testifies to the worth of his goal.

[1] Cratty, B. J. "Coaching Decisions and Research in Sport Psychology." In *Quest*, a publication of The National Association for Physical Education of College Women and the National College Physical Education Association for Men, Monograph XIII, Winter Issue, January 1970. p. 48.

(7) Is reinforced, as he works toward his goal, by some taste of success; or at least his training is so planned that he does not experience continuous failure which disheartens and discourages.

(8) As he pursues his goal, sees a "point" or "pay-off," which he values.

At that point motivation has tentatively taken hold and may with substantial and frequent reinforcement become more deeply rooted.

Motivation appears to be related to the athlete's attitude toward success and failure. Some perform well in competition while others with at least equal potential do poorly. All may compete poorly on some occasions but there seem to be characteristics that distinguish the good from the poor.

An athlete's attitude toward aggression may be a factor. Competition in sports requires that aggression be focused on the goal of victory. There are great differences in how freely athletes allow themselves to pursue victory. An average competitor may fear aggression occasionally, while a good competitor seems to fear it only infrequently. Consciously or unconsciously, a poor competitor may have learned to fear aggression most of the time.

An athlete in competitive sport must face his goal of winning. To accomplish this he may have to overcome his distaste for "violence" or for "hurting" someone. Coaches frequently refer to the poor competitor as the one who lacks the "killer instinct." All athletes seem to experience this difficulty sometimes, the poor competitor more frequently than others.

Personality is not static but dynamic; a poor competitor may become a good one and a good one may become a poor one. Other factors, such as his coach, the crowd, or non-athletic problems, may help or hinder an athlete's ability to win. For the young athlete experience may be a factor. An athlete must get the feel of winning before he can be successful. In track and field, "nothing succeeds like success." An athlete has to "think he can do it" before he can win. The four-minute mile, the 17-foot pole vault, and the 70-foot shot put are examples of how important it is for athletes to believe that it can be done. Once these records were broken it was commonplace to do so, but before that, they seemed to be insurmountable barriers.

TEACHING CUES FOR THE COACH

(1) Keep instructions simple. Use analogy as a teaching device. It is usually best to proceed from the known to the unknown.

(2) Demonstrate when possible. A good demonstration is worth a thousand words.

(3) Keep the whole skill in mind while working on its parts. This may be done by: (a) observing other athletes perform, (b) observing movies, film strips, and loop film, (c) studying photographs, magic-eye sequences, and films on paper, (d) discussing the event with athletes and coaches and (e) trying the event.

(4) Observe—then teach.

(5) Do not over-teach. A good teacher is not judged by how much talking he does.

(6) Encourage the learner. The first requirement for successful learning is belief in oneself. The second is a teacher who believes in his pupil.

(7) Adjust teaching to individual differences. One man's medicine is another's poison.

(8) Practice of the right skill makes perfect. Errors should be detected and eliminated as soon as possible.

(9) It is easier to prevent the formation of bad habits than to correct them.

(10) Break the event down into component parts to facilitate the mastery of each fundamental. Practice *one thing* at a time. Practice exercises are a means to an end.

(11) In practice, do not concentrate on height or distance at the expense of correct form.

(12) Criticism should be given constructively and quietly.

(13) The kind of training is as important as the amount. Frequent, but short, well-planned practice periods are better than long ones.

(14) In practice, stress skills used in competition.

(15) Do not attempt to compete with the athlete during training.

4
Sprinting

Sprinting may be defined as running at maximum effort for distances of fifty to two hundred and twenty yards.

Study and experimentation have effected significant advances in sprinting techniques since the first scholastic and college track meets were held in the early 1900's. Starting blocks have been developed and are in use universally. Modern running tracks provide a smooth and consistent sprinting surface. Competition among sprinters is keen, and records are at an all-time high.

SOMATOTYPE

Not all men possess sprinting ability with competition potential, and a coach is fortunate to have good sprinters on his squad every year. The truly great ones come at infrequent intervals. Because of their inherent characteristics, sprinters are "discovered" not "made." Any man can sprint, but how fast is another story.

Attempts to characterize the ideal sprint type have been numerous though none have been completely successful. Among the common characteristics of this classic type is a combination of (a) strong, well-developed musculature, (b) quick reaction time, (c) rhythmic coordination, and (d) an ability to relax at maximum sprinting effort. Good coaching does much to bring out these native characteristics. Without them, few have become great sprinters.

Traditionally, sprinters have been classified as (a) short muscular and (b) long-limbed. The musculature of the long-limbed type, of which Olympic champions Jesse Owens and Bobby Morrow are typical examples, appears to lend itself more effectively to relaxation. Assuming a similarity in stride and nervous reaction time, the advantage seems to favor this type. But, the changing characteristics of world record holders, both as to somatotype and sprinting style, would indicate that it is well to keep an open mind in identifying athletes best qualified for this event. Six-foot Bob Hayes, who set a world's record for the 100-yard dash (00:9.1) June 21, 1963, weighed 198 pounds; he was definitely a "power" type sprinter.

THE 100-YARD DASH

There are four parts to the sprinting technique for any of the dashes: (a) the Start, (b) Acceleration, (c) the Stride, and (d) the Finish. In the description of the 100-yard dash, full explanations of the four aspects of sprinting techniques will be included. They apply, with a few suitable modifications, to the other sprints as well.

THE START

There are basically three types of starts used by sprinters. Distinguished according to the placement of feet in the starting blocks, they may be identified as follows:

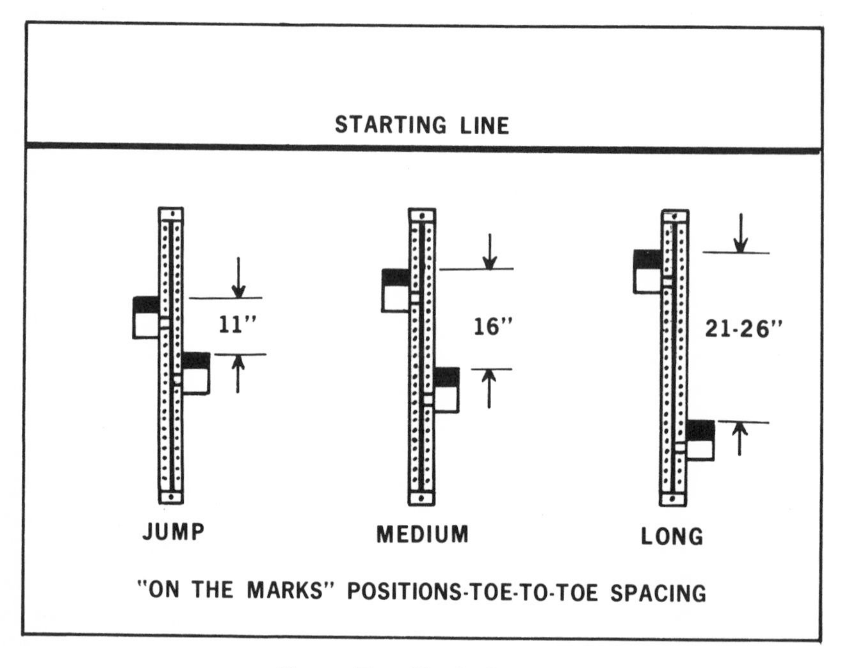

Toe-to-Toe Block Spacing

In observing the preceding diagrams, one will note a difference in (a) the distance between blocks, and (b) the distance of the front block from the starting line. The type used is determined by the physical characteristics of the individual sprinter. Placement of the blocks should be determined by experimentation. Balance and mechanical efficiency in starting action are important guides. Most sprinters find a modified or intermediate placement the most effective in achieving this objective.

Henry[1] attempted in his studies to establish a theoretical description of the "ideal" start and of the influence of foot placement upon its effec-

[1] Franklin M. Henry, "Force-Time Characteristics of the Sprint Start." *The Research Quarterly*, Vol. 23, No. 3 (1952), pp. 317–318.

tiveness. Force-time graphs of the leg thrust during the start were obtained on eighteen sprinters who made four runs each, using longitudinal toe-to-toe spacings of 11, 16, 21, and 26 inches. He reported:

(1) Reaction time is uninfluenced by block spacing and uncorrelated with speed in the sprints.

(2) Leg length is not important in determining the best block spacing and is unrelated to 50 yard sprinting ability.

(3) Use of the 11 inch bunch start results in clearing the blocks sooner but with less velocity than secured from medium stances, resulting in significantly slower time at 10 and 50 yards.

(4) The highest proportion of best runs and the smallest proportion of poorest runs result from starting with a 16 inch stance. A 21 inch stance is nearly as good.

(5) An elongated stance of 26 inches results in greater velocity leaving the blocks, but the advantage is lost within the first ten yards.

(6) With block spacing held constant, speed in the sprint is significantly related to how closely the individual approaches the ideal start (defined as early development and maintenance of full maximal thrust with each leg until the respective blocks are cleared as a necessary result of forward motion).

(7) Although the rear leg develops considerably more maximum force than the front, the latter contributes twice as much block velocity because its impulse has a longer duration.

(8) The experimental results are, in general, consistent with theoretical expectations and apply to sprinters differing in ability and skill.

(9) A simplified form of pressure-chronograph will probably prove useful in teaching sprinting skill.

Setting the Blocks

(1) The sprinter must first determine which foot he prefers to place in the rear block. Most sprinters have a "foot preference." It is best identified by experimentation.

(2) The blocks should be placed as close to the starting line as is consistent with a steady, mechanically efficient and balanced "set" position.

(3) The placement of the front block ranges from 12 to 19 inches from the starting line. The rear from 28 to 40 inches.

(4) The sprinter should make sure his blocks are tight on their frame and set firmly into the track. A mallet or tamp should be used.

Taking the "On the Marks" Position

After placing and adjusting his blocks the sprinter stands behind them and waits for the command of "Take Your Marks." If the *right* foot is to be placed back, he then:

(1) Straddles the blocks.

(2) Comes down to a crouch position placing his hands several feet in front of the starting line.

(3) Places his right foot firmly against the rear block.

(4) Places his left foot firmly against the front block.

(5) Rests the knee of the right leg on the track.

(6) Slides hands back immediately behind and parallel to the starting line. Shifts weight forward until shoulders are directly over or slightly in front of hands. Supporting hands, with thumb and index finger parallel and just behind starting line, are in one of three positions: (1) fingertips together, (2) fingertips spread, (3) fingers bent with knuckles on track. Position used depends upon best support afforded individual sprinter.

(7) Makes necessary adjustments in position to ensure maximum comfort and balance.

(8) Focuses eyes comfortably on the track.

The "On the Marks" Position

The "On the Marks" Position

In this position the sprinter's:

(1) Feet are firmly against the blocks.

(2) Knees are directly in front of his feet and pointing straight forward.

(3) Shoulders are directly over his hands and his arms are perpendicular to the track. Some excellent sprinters position the shoulders 6-8 inches forward of the starting line. Others use a slightly bent or "bowed" arm position.

(4) Hand position is comfortable and steady.

(5) Neck and shoulders are relaxed.

(6) Eyes are on the track—not on the starter.

The "Set" Position

The "Set" Position

On the command of "Set," the sprinter raises his hips to a position slightly above the level of his shoulders. *Both feet must be kept firmly against the blocks.*

In this position he should feel that he can get a maximum *push* from both feet. His arms are fully extended, shoulders square, and eyes focused on or slightly behind the starting line.

In this position the sprinter:

(1) Does not lean too far forward. Shoulders are approximately four inches in front of hands. Forward shoulder position is slightly in excess of four inches, an advantage providing: (a) hands are strong enough to maintain a steady position, (b) leg action is fast enough to maintain balance in first few strides.

(2) Does not "sit back" on his heels.

(3) Maintains a steady hand and arm position.

(4) Keeps his feet *firmly* against the blocks.

(5) Keeps his eyes on the starting line with head and neck relaxed.

(6) Does not "roll" up to his "Set" position.

(7) Does not allow himself to "settle back" once his "Set" position is taken.

(8) Concentrates on the gun. *Does not try to beat it.*

(9) Does not "tighten up" in his "Set" position.

(10) Is physically relaxed, but mentally alert as he waits for the gun.

Starting Action

The action coming out of the blocks is an *explosive drive.* It combines a maximum thrust of the legs, accompanied by a whipping,

Starting Action—The First Step

a. Rear leg drive. Head and shoulders have moved upward. Rear foot drives against block.

b. Right arm drives forward as left foot leaves block. Left leg starts forward in fast recovery action.

c. Note excellent body angle. Body lean is maintained as result of fast and high lift of left knee.

d. Center of gravity moves forward over lead leg.

flinging, alternate action of the arms. The hands are held open and relaxed. The knees are well lifted. The progression of the entire body is straight forward. Studies indicate that the first push comes from the rear foot. The knee of the rear leg is *snapped straight* as a reflex action to the sound of the gun. The sprinter's head, shoulders and trunk are driven forward *before* he comes up into an erect running position. The front foot follows, but the time elapsing is negligible.

Vigorous arm action, which accompanies the explosive push off the blocks, is the key to efficient starting. A shoulder swing is included. A forward and upward thrust of the left arm accompanies the driving lift of the right knee. Simultaneously, the bent right arm is swung backward in a balancing action. The right hand reaches a point next to the right hip.

The entire action provides the lift of the sprinter's body. It prevents his "falling" out of his blocks. This action is continuous and greatly assists the athlete as he accelerates to full sprinting effort.

The first step out of the blocks is important. It must come straight forward and must not be too long or short. Distance varies with the individual. It should touch the track approximately 14–18 inches directly in front of the starting block. A long first step will tend to straighten the body angle too soon. A short step will result in a chopping action which decreases the initial drive off the blocks. When executed correctly the sprinter's first step will be his shortest. The second will be an inch or two longer until full stride is reached at a distance of 10 to 12 strides. The toes must point *straight forward* and both knees and arms drive straight ahead. Toeing in or out will cause lateral sway and shorten the stride. The sprinter's driving power must stay behind his hips. The coach can help his runner to determine the correct distance of the first step by standing in front of him in his on-the-marks position. The coach, whose arms are straight and hands are resting on the sprinter's shoulders, instructs the sprinter to take the "set" position. The sprinter then takes his first step out of the blocks. With the coach's support, the athlete holds this position while he adjusts his foot location. The point from which the greatest forward drive against the coach's arms can be exerted is marked. It constitutes a tentative first-step checkmark. It is a point of reference and adjustment as full-effort starting practice continues. A wall, or other similar support, may be used for this same exercise.

ACCELERATION

The rate of acceleration distinguishes the great from the good sprinter. It may be defined as the time elapsing between the start and the point where the sprinter reaches his maximum stride. It has sometimes been defined as a "shifting of the sprinter's gears." The exact distance varies—even among sprinters whose total times are the same for an event. Maximum velocity is reached in approximately 5 to 7 seconds.

It is estimated that an athlete who can sprint the first 30 yards of a 100-yard dash in 3.0–3.3 seconds is achieving satisfactory acceleration time. A similar time between the 30- and 60-yard marks also indicates good acceleration. A time of 6.2–6.4 for 60 yards is indicative of excellent sprinting ability.

For some sprinters, a more sudden rise out of the starting blocks improves acceleration. A more vigorous knee lift helps others. Vigorous arm action is an asset. Sprinting time can be improved if acceleration time is shortened. To be effective acceleration must be smooth

Acceleration

a—Eyes focus on finish line. Hands open and relaxed.
b, d, f—Excellent body alignment and lean from shoulder to toe of extended leg.
c—Center of gravity is continuously in line with forward leg drive. All parts of body function in proper alignment with pelvis.
d—Relaxed elbows carried slightly away from body.
e—Center of gravity is over lead foot; high right knee action (f) comes from strong drive off rear foot (d).
d, f—Knee lift is high. Arm action vigorous.

and well timed; with concentration and practice, it can be improved considerably. It should not however, be stressed to the point where it is not a *natural* part of sprinting action.

THE STRIDE

Sprinting efficiency is determined by two factors: (1) stride length and (2) rate of stride or stride speed. A combination of these factors determines the sprinter's potential.

It is generally accepted that training has little effect on leg speed. Speed is determined by muscular contraction which is inborn. There is little that can be done to change muscular fiber speed. This leaves stride length as the main consideration.

Most coaches agree that one way to increase stride length is to increase the strength of the sprinter's legs. The stronger and more explosive the force of the driving leg, the greater the stride length and thrust.

High knee action is a factor in developing stride length. The execution of high knee action is often misunderstood. Many believe it comes from a *lifting* action of the knee. Observation reveals that the main force for raising the knee comes from the driving force exerted by the sprinter's rear foot. The greater the force of the driving foot, the higher the knee action. In attempting to lengthen his stride, the beginner frequently commits another error—reaching out too far with his lead leg. Rather than reaching, or "over-striding," a more mechanically efficient action can be achieved by accenting the drive from the rear foot. The front foot then can make contact with the track under the sprinter's center of gravity, a more natural position. This is a much better position from which to add force to the next stride.

The hips play an important role in the sprinter's stride. As the knee is driven upward, the hips roll forward. The more flexible the hips, the longer the stride. In sprinting, all parts of the body must function in proper alignment with the pelvis. This is the key to *body lean.* Body lean is more than lowering the head or bending at the waist, two popular misconceptions. Lean is the direct result of rear foot drive. In its execution, there is a straight line from the sprinter's head to the shoulder, and through his hip to the toe of his driving foot. Contrary to popular belief, the sprinter favors a somewhat erect or flat-backed position. His gravitational line of weight at all times falls through his supporting foot. His feet point in the line of progression and initiate the main force of his smooth, rhythmical, and straight forward action.

Arm action, since it counteracts body rotation caused by leg drive, contributes significantly to the sprinter's stride. The arms set the pace of the sprinter's leg action and provide balance for his over-all sprint action. While there are variations, most good sprinters carry their forearms at an approximate angle of 30–35 degrees to the upper arm. Shoulders are dropped and relaxed. Elbows are carried slightly away from the body. The hands are carried open, loose, and relaxed. In the backward swing of the arm, the hand reaches a point just behind the hip. In the forward swing, the thumb comes chin high, approximately in front of the center of the body. The head and eyes are straight forward. The entire action is smooth and rhythmical, and relaxation at maximum effort is complete.

Relaxation at top effort is the key to sprinting efficiency. It is the hallmark that distinguishes the great from the good sprinter. Much can be learned about relaxation. There are signs and symptoms of muscular tension that the coach can recognize and correct. These can be observed in the sprinter's face, neck, and arms. Clenched fists and raised shoulders are common faults that can be detected.

It is not easy to relax when one is sprinting at top effort. Individual differences play a part, and some sprinters may never learn to relax. Relaxation is psychological as well as physical, and the whole athlete must be considered. Relaxation is a matter of "undoing" as much as "doing." Many of the terms used in teaching sprint action, such as "power," "drive," and "explode," are not consistent with the relaxation concept.

There are coaches who believe that training at ⅞ speed, except in practicing the start, is a means of developing relaxation. Others recommend running downhill in full stride, allowing the athlete to let himself go in a flowing, rolling action. Both have merit. There is probably no one best way to teach relaxation, but constantly reminding the sprinter of its importance is probably a valuable first step.

THE FINISH

The finish is simply a continuation of maximum sprinting effort. The objective is to maintain correct mechanical posture and relaxation regardless of pressure and stress. The sprinter gathers for the finish 15 yards before the tape is reached. His stride is slightly shortened. Body lean is increased. Arms are driven more vigorously as an explosive thrust through and beyond the tape is executed. Some sprinters employ a chest thrust. In considering the use of form variations at the finish, it should be remembered that the principle of action and reaction applies. Ducking under or reaching for the tape with the arms is therefore not recommended. Leaning back in an attempt to run faster should be avoided because it results in a loss of gravitational balance and decrease of speed. The head should be up, eyes on the tape, and the vigorous arm action should continue.

The letdown after crossing the finish line should be slow and gradual. It should be straight forward until a full stop is completed. Walking is continued until breathing returns to normal.

THE 220-YARD DASH

The technique and form in sprinting 220 yards are essentially those used for sprinting 100 yards. The race is started from stagger and run around one turn. Modifications of straightaway sprinting are necessary. A crouch start is employed. All fundamentals covered under the 100-yard dash apply. The turn is run at top speed. The athlete runs as close to the inside of his lane as possible. His stride is slightly shortened for balance, and his body leans at the hips as he runs into the curve. The action of the left arm is vigorous; combined with a slight swing over of the right, it assists in maintaining balance around the turn.

A strong sprinter runs at full, but relaxed, sprinting effort for the entire distance. The one who cannot do so should "free-wheel" the last twenty yards coming out of the turn; this relaxes and helps him maintain balance as he gathers at the top of the straightaway for his all-out sprint and finishing effort. In his attempt to relax, the sprinter must never let down mentally. He must also maintain gravitational balance as fatigue increases. Vigorous but relaxed arm action is employed throughout.

Running 220 yards at maximum effort requires strength and endurance. One who runs it must be in excellent physical condition. In addition to the training he does for the shorter dash, the contestant in this event includes considerable over-distance running. Distances of 150 to 300 yards at maximum relaxed sprinting effort, with repetitions determined by the needs of the individual, supplement the sprinter's regular training program.

TRAINING

Training for the sprinter is highly individualized. It is adjusted to somatotype and needs and should help the sprinter train for strength as well as speed. The distribution of work load and amount of rest needed for competition should be determined by experimentation. His upper body and arms are as important as his legs. *Both* should be developed as a result of training. Practice should be regular and purposeful, and competitive conditions should be approximated, especially in the practice of starts. A daily and weekly schedule, following guidelines in Chapter 3, should be established. Practice drills should include the following:

(1) *Jogging, Stretching, and Bending*: Warm-up preparatory to full-effort sprinting or starting.

(2) *Accelerations* (wind-sprints): Standing start. Emphasize form and relaxation. Should precede full-effort sprinting or starting. Distance 100–120 yards. One-third gather, one-third full effort, one-third letdown. Repetitions: 3–4 times.

(3) *Starts*: Always adjust to weather conditions. Starting practice is limited or canceled on cold days. Accompany them with sprints of 35–40 yards. Sprinter should learn to distinguish between degrees of effort. Number of *full-effort* starts to be taken on any one day varies from 8–10. Always adjust to individual needs and physical condition. Not more than three such periods during midseason. Late season, limit to one—preferably early in week.

(4) *Practice of "Set" Position*: May be included as part of, or separate from, starting practice. Purpose is practice of the 2-second hold in the set position. Regular starting procedure is followed. Commands are given. Sprinter is held in set position until steady and balanced. No start is taken. Faults in set position are checked. Unsteadiness usually traceable to an "On-the-Marks" position which is too close to starting line. Repeat six to eight times.

(5) *Acceleration Practice* (with crouch start): Purpose is practice of acceleration phase of sprinting technique. From regular start, sprint 40–50 yards with emphasis on fast acceleration to full sprinting effort. Starting practice may be concluded with this exercise. Repeat 3 to 4 times.

(6) *Practice of Finish*: Distance 120 yards. Use crouch or standing start. Sprint first 100 yards at three-fourths effort. Drive last 20 yards at maximum effort breaking tape as in competition. Emphasize definite change of tempo at 100 yards with vigorous arm action and maximum drive for the last 20. In midseason repeat should be 3–4 times twice weekly.

(7) *Conditioning*: Under-distance and over-distance sprinting at a prescribed pace. For under-distance practice—repetitions at 50–75 yards. For over-distance—at 150, 300, and occasionally 440 yards. All are performed at *relaxed* but *full* striding effort. Number of repetitions determined by time of season and needs of individual. Sprinters frequently long-jump and hurdle which provides additional conditioning exercise.

(8) *Training Variations*: Appropriate for use indoors with limited facilities.

 (a) *Stationary sprinting.* For purpose of support, sprinter leans against wall with extended arms approximately chest high. Determines body angle from which greatest drive against wall can be exerted. Runs in position emphasizing knee lift. Use erect body position, closer to wall, for fast tempo. To emphasize forward drive and power, sprinter positions feet further from wall and assumes a more pronounced lean.

 (b) *Arm action exercise.* With and without pulley weights. From stationary stride stance, raise arms to proper sprinting position. Swing arms forward and backward simulating full sprinting action. Emphasize use of shoulders. Small weights may also be used in this exercise.

Weight Training Schedule

Number of days weekly: Off-season (fall and winter)—three.
Early competitive season—one or two depending upon needs of the individual athlete.
Mid to late competitive season—discontinued.

Precede lifting with a thorough warm-up. Follow guidelines—Chapter 10.

Exercise	*Amount of weight*	*Number of sets*	*Number of repetitions*
Military press	⅓ body weight	3	5
Bench press	⅔ body weight	3	5
Curl	⅓ body weight	3	5
Toe raise	½ body weight	2	15
Sit-ups	Start with 15 per minute. Increase to maximum of 30 per minute. Add five pound weight held behind neck. Execute 30 per minute.		
Arm swings	5 pound plate in each hand. Swing past hips and forward to eye level.		

TYPICAL WEEKLY TRAINING SCHEDULE FOR SPRINTERS

Midseason—College level

Adjust in duration and intensity for high school athletes. Include members of 440- and 880-yard relay teams. Duration of daily practice period never to exceed *one and one-half* hours.

Monday

(1) Warm-up (previously described)—20–30 minutes.

(2) Run 440 yards—3 times—each in 53–55 secs. Rest interval—10 min. (This distance may be increased to 500 yards as condition improves.)

(3) Run 110–120 yards (on grass) 10 times at ¾ speed.

(4) Warm-down.

Tuesday

(1) Warm-up.

(2) Practice baton exchanges as member of 440-yard relay team, each man running 110 yards 4 times as follows:
 1st time at ½ speed.
 3 additional times at same speed, accelerating the last 30 yards with exchange at full speed.

(3) Run 330 yards—3 times—each in 38–42 seconds.

(4) Warm-down.

Wednesday

(1) Warm-up.

(2) Practice baton exchanges as member of 880-yard relay team, running 220 yards 6 times—each at 25–28 seconds.

(3) Warm-down.

Thursday

(1) Warm-up.

(2) Take 8–10 starts (on grass) accelerating for 30–40 yards with each.

(3) Run 110–120 yards (on grass) 6–8 times at ¾ speed.

(4) Warm-down.

Friday

Warm-up for 20–30 minutes.

Saturday

Competition.

COMPETITION

(1) Check all equipment the day before. Make sure spikes are proper length for running surface. Test shoe strings.

(2) Know starting time for race and report well in advance.

(3) Warm up slowly and thoroughly. Most sprinters do not warm up sufficiently, particularly on days of competition.

(4) Be familiar with operation of starting blocks. Make sure they are properly spaced and firmly set into track. Use a mallet or tamp for setting, not heel of foot.

(5) Take at least six preliminary starts before race, gradually building up to full effort action.

(6) Allow a period of at least five minutes' relaxation before race.

(7) Know starting time of race and be ready when final call is given. Do not depend upon coach for this information.

(8) Know the rules of starting and do not try to "out-guess" the starter. Concentration is the key to good starting.

(9) Keep eyes straight ahead during the entire race. Never give up regardless of position.

(10) Do not let up in preliminaries.

(11) Stay in lane at finish and let down slowly. After the race is completed keep walking for recovery.

(12) Never reconcile to being "second best," regardless of results in any one day's competition. Even the best have "off days."

(13) A race once completed is "water over the dam." Devote energy exerted in worrying about a defeat to correcting mistakes and improving condition.

5
The 440-Yard Dash

The 440-yard dash is a demanding race. It is a test of speed, endurance, judgment of pace, and above all—courage. Until recently, it has been classified as a middle-distance run. Those supporting this belief contended that the physiological demands of racing 440 yards made it primarily a test of endurance. The record book confirmed their point of view. Ted Meredith, who for 15 years held the world record of 47.4 seconds for the quarter mile (the "440"), was a great half-miler. Ben Eastman, of Stanford University, the first man to run the "440" in less than 47 seconds, established a world's record for the longer event.

The year 1932 was a significant and transitional one in the history of quarter-mile running. The Eastman-Carr duels of this year, culminating with the Olympic Games, introduced a new concept of the event. In this memorable series, William A. Carr, a relatively unknown sprinter from the University of of Pennsylvania, with little previous experience in running 440 yards, amazed the sports world by defeating the stronger Eastman each time they met. In their final meeting, Carr established a new world record of 46.2 seconds for 400 meters. Carr's sprinting technique was flawless. Its tireless perfection enabled him to maintain a fast, but relaxed and steady pace for the entire distance. In describing the 400-meter finals of the 1932 Olympiad, Grantland Rice wrote:

The three United States finalists in the 400-meter dash of the 1932 Olympic Games at Los Angeles: Ben Eastman, Stanford University; William A. Carr, University of Pennsylvania; and the author.

> . . . Just 60 yards from the tape Carr came on. There was no sign of extra effort. There was no struggle for extra speed. It was the master painting a masterpiece. He came abreast of the Stanford star and then began to move ahead. Foot by foot opened California daylight. Foot by foot—and still there was no sign of extra effort on Carr's part. Here was flawless form—form that could be extended without a catch or a break because it had no hampering faults.

Those since who have equaled or broken Carr's record have not all followed his racing tactics. Few have matched his tireless style. None have gone back to the sprint-float-sprint concept of running that preceded Carr's day. Herb McKenley (45.9) and George Rhoden (45.8) ran an all-out sprint-type race. Each had sufficient endurance, though slackening his pace considerably, to maintain at the finish a substantial lead built up in the first 300 yards. Arthur Wint (46.2) and Jim Lea (45.8) ran an evenly paced race.

Modern performances, culminating with Lee Evans' brilliant 43.8 seconds for 400 meters in the 1968 Olympic Games, have definitely established this event as an endurance sprint.

SOMATOTYPE

From the foregoing discussion, it should be apparent that sprinting ability has been a common asset of those most successful in racing 440 yards. Most champions, at the college and Olympic level, have been capable of sprinting 100 yards in 9.8 seconds or better. Endurance, essentially a matter of strength, and developed by proper training, has supplemented this attribute. Most coaches today, therefore, look for a strong sprinter as the ideal quarter-mile type.

While there have been exceptions (Carr 5′9″), most record holders in this event have been tall men (Klemmer 6′2″; Wint 6′4″). Height, of course, enhances the length of the athlete's stride, an asset in sprinting so great a distance. Some coaches believe that a tall, heavier athlete generates more momentum than a lighter one. For a distance of 440 yards, this, too, may be a significant factor.

Maturity appears to be an element of importance in this event. Most athletes who have run 440 yards in less than 47 seconds have been at least twenty-one years of age. Otis Davis and Arthur Wint were both 28 at the time of their best performance. Herb McKenley was 30 when he ran 45.9 seconds for a new world's record. Apparently, age enables one to develop size, strength, and endurance necessary for championship performance.

Fatigue in an endurance sprint of 440 yards is maximum and acute. Relaxation is the key to a maintenance of body control under such stress.

For some (e.g., Carr), this appears to be an inherent quality—for others, developed. A sense of timing, which enables one to distribute his energy equally over a given distance, is an asset in developing the staying power required of this event. It is a refinement that distinguishes the great quarter-miler.

STRATEGY AND TACTICS

Strategy, as distinguished from tactics, is the overall plan of the race. Tactics are the skillful maneuvers used to accomplish the overall plan. Each varies with the individual. He must consider the strengths and limitations of his opponent, as well as his own. How far does he sprint at the start of his race? Does he run better when leading or following another runner? When will he meet a challenge? Does he depend upon superior speed and sprinting ability, or is he an endurance type of runner?

The location of the start and the layout of the course are other variables. A race starting from scratch (a straight line across the track) involves a different overall plan from one run in lanes for the entire distance. Tactics also differ. A race run from a spur, or long straightaway, around one turn, differs from one that is run around two turns.

The 440-yard dash is run in lanes for the entire distance. To equalize the distance around the turns, a staggered start is required. This has modified the strategy and tactics of the race. Maneuvers once vital in gaining and maintaining a favorable pole position (lane closest to the curb, or inside, of the track) have been replaced by a new concept of "timing" and "energy distribution." In this kind of race, knowledge of pace and the ability and strength to carry out one's overall racing plan play a prominent role.

If the entire race is run in lanes, the athlete's tactics depend a great deal on his staggered start position. The advantage here lies with the "pace" type of runner. Due to his excellent sense of timing, he will probably run as well in one lane as the other. For a more "competitive" type of runner—one who depends on others in the race to set the pace, this is not always the case. In a six-man race, he will probably run better in lanes 1, 2 or 3 where, being on the inside of the track, his starting position is farther back on the track than his opponents' positions. If he is to run in lanes 4, 5 or 6, however, he will have to guard against extending himself too far at the start (carrying his initial sprint too far) or, conversely, against running too slowly in order to offset this danger. If they draw an outside lane, some quarter-milers run an all-out race. If starting from lanes 1, 2, 3, or 4, a runner should put greater emphasis on pace with a strong finish.

While there are variations, most 440-yard endurance sprinters today employ either an "all-out sprint" or a "unit type" of strategy in their race. They have replaced the traditional sprint-float-sprint concept. Both place a heavy premium on sprinting ability and differ only in their concept of the runner's distribution of his energy.

In the "all-out" plan, a superior sprinter, such as McKenley, runs as fast as he can for the entire distance. His race is somewhat of a gamble. His strategy is simply to build up as big a lead as possible on his opponent and hope to outlast him on the finish.

In a "unit-type" race, a smooth, flawless sprinter, such as Carr, maintains a steady but fast pace for the entire distance. His strategy is to stay within striking distance of the all-out sprinter. His superior judgment of pace and relaxed technique enable him to overtake and pass his fatigued opponent on the finishing stretch.

The "unit-type" strategy, or evenly paced race, is recommended by most coaches. It is followed by many of today's record holders. Because the runner's energy is equally distributed, it is the most physiologically sound. An athlete employing this strategy aims to run both 220-yard parts of the race in approximately the same time. In competition, this rarely happens. Actually, most run their first 220 yards about four seconds faster than the second.

For purpose of pace judgment, some divide the distance into four parts of 110 yards each. Due to the start, the first quarter of the race is somewhat slower that the second. After the start, the sprinter quickly and smoothly shifts into a fast but relaxed "440" pace. At 220 yards his time is usually 1.0 to 1.5 seconds slower than his best time for the distance. It is, however, usually faster than the second 220 yards of his race. Times for the two parts may vary by 1.5 to 4.0 seconds. The first half of the race is a critical one for the unit-type runner; if he runs it too fast, it is virtually impossible for him to finish the 440 yards in good form.

During the third 110 yards, the emphasis is on relaxation. Momentum gained during the first half of the race must be maintained without an undue expenditure of energy. It is here that a pace type runner starts gaining on the all-out sprinter.

During the last 110 yards, the athlete concentrates on holding form and maintaining the strong steady pace he has set throughout the race. While the last 110 yards is usually his slowest, his pace does not slacken appreciably. It is an all-out competitive effort. When the race is close, courage, superior condition, and competitive spirit are the variables that determine its final outcome.

Regardless of how well a runner plans his race, adjustment to the unpredictable elements of competition must be taken into account. The experienced runner is quick to analyze and react to opportunities that will improve his position. He likewise should be ready to adjust to the unexpected tactics of his opponent. The unexpected is more likely to occur when the race is not run in lanes. In such instances, competitive tactics, covered more in detail under the 880-yard run and distance running (Chapters 6 and 7), apply.

TRAINING

Year-round training, with cross-country running in the fall, is a consistent pattern of training for the successful 440-yard runner. All general practice and warm-up methods previously described apply for the "440" man. In all instances, training is adjusted to the age, somatotype, strength, and weaknesses of the individual trainee. For the beginner, the start is slow—the build-up gradual.

In general, the training program emphasizes a balance of exercises to develop speed, endurance, pace, and technique. Various forms of under-distance interval training constitute its core. The pace and the number of repetitions depend upon the experience and condition of the individual. For a beginner, a comfortable rest interval is used, with the speed and number of repetitions gradually increasing. In early season, the number of repetitions is great, the pace slow, and the rest short. When the distance of the repeat is short, its speed is increased and a longer rest period is allowed. In midseason the speed of repetitions is approximately at full effort, with the time of rest intervals increased.

While the 440-yard dash is essentially a sprint race, speed should not be emphasized in training at the expense of endurance. Much of this is developed by cross-country running, year-round conditioning and weight training. As an early season build-up, runs of 660–880 yards are frequently recommended. Over-distance training has value not only for purposes of developing endurance, but also because it assures the athlete of his ability to sustain near-maximum effort for the full 440-yard distance of his race.

TRAINING DRILLS

For Warm-up:

(1) Jog easily and continuously for fifteen to twenty minutes. Rotate arms, shoulders, and head in process.

(2) Walk for five or ten minutes, continuing head, shoulder, and arm rotation.

(3) Repeat three to five accelerations of 100–150 yards with five minutes of walking as a rest interval.

(4) Baton-passing practice may be used as part of the warm-up procedure.

For Speed:

(1) Practice starts with sprinters and other "440" runners, sprinting 50 to 75 yards at full effort. Approximate competitive conditions as closely as possible. Run on straightaways and from staggered starting position around curves.

(2) Short-interval speed and endurance training. Repeat distances of 110–220 yards two to five times (as condition improves) at full effort to one second slower. Rest interval should be three minutes or less, walking or jogging.

(3) To vary practice pattern and perfect baton-passing technique, run same distances as competitive relay laps.

For Endurance:

(1) Long-interval training. Repeat distances of 300–600 yards two to five times (as condition improves) at speeds two or three seconds slower than best 440-yard pace. Rest interval should be twenty minutes or less, jogging or walking.

(2) Speed play (Fartlek), alternate jog, stride and sprint for distance of two or three miles. Include as part of early week training. Vary location of run if possible to include grass surface.

(3) Interval repetitions of 550–660 yards at speed two or three seconds slower than best 440-yard pace. Rest interval should be twenty minutes, walking or jogging.

(4) Cross country and hill running. Long sustained runs (10–15 miles). Pace: Relaxed steady state running.

For Pace:

(1) Short-interval pace and endurance training. Repeat distances of 110, 220, and 330 yards. The 110 yards at full effort, 220 yards one or two seconds slower, 330 yards two to three seconds slower. Rest intervals should be five minutes or less, jogging or walking.

(2) Run 360 yards at desired competitive pace as part of last full-effort practice period for week.

Pace Chart for 440-Yard Dash Training
(in seconds)

Results Desired	110 Yards	220 Yards	300 Yards	330 Yards	360 Yards	440 Yards
60	14.5	29	40.5	45	49	31* 60
58	14	28	39	43	47.8	30 58
56	13.5	27	37.8	42	46	29 56
54	13	26	36.5	40.5	44.4	28 54
52	12.5	25	35	39	43	27 52
50	12	24	33.8	37.5	41.4	26 50
48	11.5	23	32.5	36	39.5	48
46	11.2	22	31	34.5	37.8	46

* The upper figure of two figures is the time in which the second 220 yards should be run, while the bottom figure is the time for the whole 440 yards.

6
The 880-Yard Run

The 880-yard run and the 440-yard endurance sprint have much in common. A new concept of the longer event has evolved. As performed today, a high premium is placed upon speed. While endurance and strength are important factors, they are frequently offset by the important elements of superior technique and excellence in judgment of pace.

Improvement in the performance of this event, as evidenced by Peter Snell's record of 1:45.1 for 800 meters in the 1964 Olympic Games, has been especially noteworthy.

Athletes of unknown ability frequently try this event as their first attempt at competitive running. If run at a reasonable pace, it is not too demanding for the young aspirant. Potential endurance and speed are discovered by coach and athlete without early discouragement. Those with sprinting ability are frequently moved to the 440-yard dash, while those with endurance may switch to the longer races. In either case, the training work done for this event provides an excellent background of early conditioning and development.

SOMATOTYPE

Athletes proficient in this event vary as to build. World record holder, Peter Snell, weighed approximately 171 pounds and stood 5′10½″ tall. An American champion, Arnold Sowell, was relatively small at 5′9″ and 135 pounds. It is probably well to select candidates for this event on the basis of natural speed and endurance rather than by typing them by height and weight characteristics.

Frequently the half-miler with speed also runs a good quarter-mile. Anyone who can do both well will frequently compete as a member of a mile relay team. Others with an abundance of endurance are successful in the 1500-meter and one-mile events. All are capable of maximum relaxation at top effort, smoothness of stride, and accuracy in a judgment of pace.

TECHNIQUE

Most half-milers today use a standing start. This is a rather recent revival of an old technique. Some question its preference over the more conventional, perhaps faster, crouch position. If employed, it should be executed correctly. The most common problem for those unfamiliar with such a start, or who use it incorrectly, is a lack of steadiness in the "set" position. Others fail to coordinate arm and leg action.

Basically, the runner is starting from a standing stride position. His line of progression is straight forward. Such a position is not assumed until the command of "Take your marks" is delivered. At this time, one foot is placed up to, but not on, the starting line. The opposite foot is back. If the right foot is forward, the opposite (left) arm, in bent running position, is forward. The hand of the bent right arm is held at the right hip. Not until the command of "Get set," does the runner come down into a balanced crouch or bent knee position. Here he remains steady, but alert, until the gun fires. His arm action then is just as vigorous as in the crouch start. From this position he sprints for position, coming quickly into full stride.

A smooth, rhythmical stride is the hallmark of those most successful in this event. When correctly executed, it provides for maximum mechanical efficiency and reduction of wasted motion. Beginners are cautioned against extending their stride beyond its normal limit; such a fault sets up a braking action when the feet strike the ground. On the other hand, a short jerky stride is to be avoided. When in proper alignment, the runner's chin, knee, and toe, are on, or very close to the same vertical plane when either foot hits the track.

While a steady and relaxed pace is used for a greater part of the race, most half-milers will "tie up" if they use a long stride for the entire distance. A distinct finishing technique is therefore necessary and a stride adjustment must be made approximately 100 yards from the tape. Success in developing this technique depends upon a sense of timing. The runner's tempo is changed: his stride is shortened and quickened, body lean is increased, arm action is vigorous, neck and back muscles are relaxed; all parts of the body are maintained in proper alignment as the drive through and beyond the tape is completed.

TACTICS

Tactics employed in racing 880 yards and 440 yards are similar. Essentials covered under the shorter distance (Chapter 5) apply. The longer race attaches greater importance to pace and timing. A unit-type race, in which a strong steady tempo is maintained throughout, is favored by most of today's champions. A half-miler employing such tactics for a 2-minute race would aim to run two 60-second quarter-miles. Average time for each 220 yards would be 30 seconds. Actually, most run their first quarter mile faster than the second. Commenting on tactics, Peter Snell observes:

> All I'm concerned with in the half is insuring a fast tempo the whole way. If it's not fast enough, I have to go out and force it. Most half-

> milers can lick me over a 100. My half-mile time is an indication of my stamina. I don't want to be killing myself, however. I still need speed for the straight. There is great confidence in knowing that in a hard half the one with the most stamina is going to be the strongest.[1]

The 880-yard race is run from a staggered start for only the first turn. After the first turn, runners break for the pole because the inside lane is shortest on turns and there are three more turns to run in the "880." Great importance, therefore, is attached to the runner's position in relation to the pole or curb. For this reason, additional competitive factors that are unique in this race should be considered. Among the most important are:

(1) Know the course of the race. Be thoroughly familiar with the start and finish, and the mark at which the break for the pole may be made.

(2) Plan your own race and run accordingly. Do not count on others in the race to set the pace for you.

(3) Be alert to adjust to unpredictable elements of competition.

(4) Be decisive in sprinting for position at the start.

(5) Do not carry your initial sprint too far.

(6) On turns, run close to the pole or lane mark.

(7) Make your break for the pole position gradual.

(8) Never pass, or attempt to pass, an opponent on a turn.

(9) Passing, if necessary before the final sprint, should be done at the start of a straightaway.

(10) When you are running in the lead and an opponent challenges on a turn you can force him to run wide by accelerating your speed.

(11) When running a "following" race, never let an opponent get beyond striking distance (10 yards ahead).

(12) Do not run directly behind an opponent. Position yourself with left shoulder splitting the middle of his back. In this position, you can not easily be boxed in and you are in position to pass.

(13) The best strategy for getting out of a "box" is to avoid getting into one. Once in, decisive sprinting, when an opening occurs, is the best escape.

(14) Be alert at all times to the danger of being "jumped." (Opponent makes sudden spurt, most frequently at 550- to 660-yard mark, momentum of spurt builds up a substantial lead that is difficult to overcome before finish line is reached.)

[1] Gilbert Rogin, "The Fastest Is Faster," *Sports Illustrated*, October 5, 1964, p. 60, © 1964 *Time*, Inc.

TRAINING

Training of the 880-yard runner includes a combination of exercises designed to develop (a) endurance, (b) knowledge of pace, and (c) sprinting ability. The last factor distinguishes the great from the good. All general training principles and procedures previously covered will apply to the "880" man when adjusted to the age, strength, and needs of the individual athlete.

TRAINING DRILLS

For Warm-up

Same as 440-yard dash. Increase distances.

For Endurance

(1) Cross-country. Competitive running during fall season.

(2) Fartlek (speed-play). Two to five miles and over. Increase distance according to age, strength, and improvement of condition. Run on cross-country course or similar terrain, up and down hill. Emphasize "free-wheeling" (maximum relaxed stride) running down hill. Alternate the location of runs, if possible. Establish "circuits" of two to four miles. Include runs that aim to maintain an average speed per mile for a given distance.

(3) Long-interval training (see Table 3).

For Pace

(1) Short-interval pace and endurance training (see Table 1).

(2) Repeat-running exercises:

a. At an established base or desired time for 440 yards (e.g., 60 seconds)

Repeat series:

110 yards in 15 secs.
220 yards in 30 secs.
330 yards in 45 secs.
440 yards in 60 secs.

Decrease base time, following same procedure, as condition improves. Order of timing segments may be reversed, starting with 440 yards and moving down.

b. At three-quarter speed:

Repeat 440 yards, running the second 220 yards in same time as first.

c. At three-quarters of desired *racing speed*:
   Repeat 660 yards. Check splits at each 220 yards for evenness of pace.

d. During midseason, run 660 yards at a pace slightly faster than that desired for next competition.

For Speed

(1) Short-interval speed and endurance training (see Table 2).

(2) Repeat accelerations of 100–150 yards. Run on grass as part of warm-up. Build up to maximum sprinting effort. Stress correct form throughout. Emphasize quickness of tempo in contrast to that of regular "880" stride.

(3) Repeat series at 150 yards. Run first 100 yards at best "880" pace, shifting to best sprinting effort for last 50.

(4) Repeat 100 and 220 yards at best sprinting effort. (This exercise may follow over-distance training.)

(5) Starts and short sprints with sprinters.

Meet Time	Practice Distance	Average Speed	Number of Repetitions	Jogging Interval
Table 1 Short-Interval Pace and Endurance Training*				
1:56	440	:57	Start with two. Increase as condition improves.	A fixed time. Five minutes or less.
	220	:28		
2:00	440	:59		
	220	:29		
Table 2 Short-Interval Speed and Endurance Training*				
1:56	440	:57	Five	A fixed time. Three minutes or less.
	220	:28		
2:00	440	:58		
	220	:29		
Table 3 Long-Interval Training*				
1:56	660	1:24	Two, then three as condition improves.	At least twenty minutes.
2:00	660	1:28		

* Adaptation of Tables by J. Kenneth Doherty. Courtesy *Scholastic Coach*.

Table 4 Pace Chart for 880-Yard Running

(in seconds)

Results Desired	220 Yards	440 Yards	660 Yards	880 Yards
2:30	36	38† 1:14	40 1:54	36 2:30
2:20	33	35 1:08	37 1:45	36 2:20
2:16	32	34 1:06	36 1:42	34 2:16
2:10	30.5	33 1:03.5	34.5 1:38	32 2:10
2:04	29	31 1:00	33 1:33	31 2:04
2:00	28	30 58.0	32 1:30	30 2:00
1:58	27.5	30 57.0	31.5 1:28	29 1:58
1:56	27	29.5 56.5	30.5 1:27	29 1:56
1:54	26.5	29 55.5	30 1:25.5	28.5 1:54
1:52	26	28.5 54.5	29.5 1:24	28 1:52
1:50	25.5	28 53.5	29 1:22.5	27.5 1:50
1:48	25.0	28 53.0	28 1:21	27 1:48
1:46	25.0	27.5 52	27.5 1:20.5	26.5 1:46

† The upper figure of two figures is the time in which that particular 220 yds. of the race should be run, while the bottom figure is the desired cumulative time at that point in the run.

7
Distance Running

Few events on the track and field program have shown as much progress in recent years as has distance running. Records in the longer runs, ranging from two miles to the marathon, all were surpassed within a period of two years. The breaking of the "four-minute mile barrier" in 1954 will go down in history as one of the great athletic achievements of all time. The continuing assault on this record as indicated by the chronological table below is noteworthy.

Americans traditionally have not been great distance runners. Early world and Olympic records were set by Pavo Nurmi of Finland. Roger Bannister, of England, was first to run the mile in less than four minutes. In more recent years athletes from Australia, New Zealand, and France have led the way. In the 1968 Olympic Games at Mexico City, athletes from Kenya, Tunisia and Ethiopia, more accustomed to running at high altitudes, dominated the distance running events. With the exception of Johnny Hayes' Marathon Victory in 1908, and Horace Ashenfelter's Steeple Chase gold medal in 1952, America's obscurity in distance running has, until recently, extended in length to everything beyond 1500 meters and in time through every Olympic renewal since the first at Athens in 1896.

Foreign domination of distance running was interrupted for the first time with the 1964 Olympiad. When the Games at Tokyo hit full stride, United States distance runners suddenly moved to center stage. Robert Schul, "a tall bony American," won the 5000-meter run. Four days before Schul's victory, on the first day of track and field competition, Billy Mills, a "seven-sixteenths Sioux Indian from Kansas," served early notice of America's growing distance-running prowess by a surprising 10,000-meter victory. Distance running, long a neglected and under-developed phase of the American track program, thus came of age.

Time	Name	Country	Location	Date
3:59.4	Roger Bannister	England	Oxford, England	May 6, 1954
3:58.0	John Landy	Australia	Turku, Finland	June 21, 1954
3:57.2	Derek Ibbotson	England	London, England	July 19, 1957
3:54.5	Herb Elliott	Australia	Dublin, Ireland	Aug. 6, 1958
3:54.4	Peter Snell	New Zealand	Wanganaui, N.Z.	Jan. 27, 1962
3:54.1	Peter Snell	New Zealand	Auckland, N.Z.	Nov. 17, 1964
3:53.6	Michel Jazy	France	Rennes, France	June 9, 1965
3:51.1	Jim Ryun	U.S.A.	Bakersfield, Cal.	June 23, 1967

SOMATOTYPE

Individual differences are perhaps more pronounced among successful distance runners than among the contestants in any other event. Athletes of varying builds and descriptions achieve surprising success in distance races. Any athlete who is physically and organically sound can participate, and possibly excel.

Success in distance running comes through hard work over a long period of time. Age and maturity, in terms of competitive experience, appear to be a factor. A keen individual desire for self-improvement is essential. Those who achieve greatness apparently do so for reasons other than just training and natural ability. Of great importance are the characteristics of determination, tenacity, and courage. Training makes great performance possible. But these mental factors must be added to transfer training into the reality of superior achievement.

Modern distance runners have taught us much about technique. But they have taught us more about work and man's ability to endure and adjust to the stress of fatigue. This new knowledge, which indicated that much of a runner's fatigue was psychosomatic, has probably contributed more to the marked progress in distance running than any other factor. The extent to which an athlete approaches the limit of his potential is a matter of interesting speculation. Some suggest that educated mental determination, coupled with physical perfection, will soon be insufficient to win an Olympic title. For such an achievement in the future, it is contended, a peak of psychological near-fanaticism will have to be an element of the runner's makeup.

An analysis of the ability to withstand stress should always take into account the fact that nearly all great distance runners have been mature athletes. Many have devoted full time to athletic training for an extended period of years. To suggest that beginners attempt, without a gradual build-up, to follow a champion's exact training pattern would be unwise, if not futile. Much, however, may be learned from the winner's example. Adaptation to stress over a period of time enables a champion to achieve comparable success within the limits of his individual strength and maturity. Intense training alone did not ensure his success, though it was, of course, a means to that end. Mental attitude, knowledge of pace, and technique are other factors which may ultimately contribute to achievement.

TECHNIQUE

The technique of distance running is highly individualized. No two athletes employ identical form. Observation and research, however, reveal common elements employed by those who are most successful. These elements may best be analyzed as they pertain to the various divisions of the race.

THE START

Most distance runners today employ a standing start (previously described in Chapter 6, on the 880-yard run). The break for position is fast and decisive. Full stride, at a predetermined pace, is quickly effected.

THE STRIDE

The stride, more than any other aspect of technique, characterizes the common identity of successful distance runners. The position of the pelvis is the key. Its forward and backward rotation controls the lumbar spine and the degree of hip flexion relative to the track. When the runner executes his stride, the spine undergoes a twisting motion. Its lower part rotates backward allowing for an extension of the trailing leg. At the same time, its upper part rotates forward with the arm on the same side to maintain equilibrium. An erect, flat-backed position of the trunk enables this action to be carried out more easily and efficiently. The runner's arms, bent at approximately a ninety-degree angle, are carried high.

The hip and knee of the lead leg are in a maximum flexed position at the time of takeoff and then go into partial extension, as the stride progresses, depending upon the individual runner. The entire leg moves strongly backward as the foot hits the track. Resistance and deceleration are thus lessened. The foot is under the body at time of impact. The runner's gravitational line of weight falls through shoulders and hips to the supporting foot. Lateral balance is maintained as the supporting foot falls in the line of progression. The head, in a relaxed and comfortable position, is carried directly above this line. The chest is thrust well forward allowing for maximum respiration. Side-to-side sway of the body is kept at a minimum. The entire action is one of ease, rhythm, coordination, and relaxation.

THE FINISH

While not many distance runners are good sprinters, an ability to sprint at the finish is a distinct asset. Timing is important. The finishing sprint must not be started too soon. The runner must at all times be alert and prepared to meet his opponent's final challenge.

The technique of the finish does not involve much of a change from the runner's normal stride. His tempo is quickened, stride possibly shortened, arm action more vigorous, as he drives through the tape.

Distance Running Technique

a, b—Foot plant is flat. Roll to inside comes through on ball followed by strong push.

c—Palm of hand carried open and relaxed.

d—Posture is erect. Flat back position of lumbar spine is flexed.

e, f—Float phase of stride.

g—Right foot falls in line of progression. Head, comfortable and relaxed, directly above. Body balance good.

h—Lower half of rear leg tucked and high. Runner rolls in squarely over lead foot. Right foot under body. Gravitational line of weight falls through supporting foot.

i—Arms, bent at approximately 90 degrees, carried high. Forearm parallel with track.

j—Full driving extension of rear leg, firm push of rear foot. Chest thrust well forward. Hip and knee of lead leg in maximum flexed position.

k, l—Note hip swing and relaxed arms. Forward and backward rotation of pelvis, and twisting of spine, allow for extension of trailing leg.

TACTICS

Tactics in distance running are basically the same as those employed in running 880 yards. The longer the distance the more opportunity there is for their application. Naturally, the possibility of error in judgment is increased, too. Innovations in tactics have developed. Improvement, resulting from a more careful study of pace, relaxation and sprinting, has been made.

Fundamentally, the athlete aims to run his race according to a predetermined plan. The trend today favors a consistent pace for each lap, and the better distance runners are surprisingly efficient in this respect. Few, however, actually follow this pattern. Most run their first and last laps faster, while others vary throughout the race. Evenness of pace, however, is the aim.

While not a consistent pattern of today's better distance runners, one- and two-man diversionary tactics are occasionally employed. A popular two-man tactic is to enter a runner who is not expected to finish strongly, if at all, with the express purpose of having him set a killing pace. An opponent who will follow is thus weakened for the benefit of the pace-setter's teammate. This "decoy" tactic is well known and is rarely effective against an experienced distance runner.

"Boxing" an opponent is an old and familiar racing maneuver. By quickly taking the lead, two members of the same team may position themselves so that they may force an opponent following in third place either to stay behind, or to tire himself extremely if he runs around both or attempts to pass either. As familiar as this tactic is, it is surprising how many runners continue to be trapped by it.

Another "team" tactic is to rotate pace setters. This tactic was introduced and employed by the Finns some years ago. If three men are entered from the same team, each takes his turn at running in first place every third lap. While it may be diversionary for the opponent, the advantage, if any, of this maneuver, appears to be primarily psychological. To be in position to take his turn, each runner must stay within "striking" distance of the leaders. Weaker runners may thus extend themselves physically, as well as psychologically, more than they would be likely to do if relegated to a following position throughout.

As a diversionary tactic, an experienced runner may deviate from an even pace by running an exceptionally fast 220 or 440 yards at some predetermined point in his race. Bob Schul reported that one of his well-known competitors employed this tactic in the finals of the 5000-meter run of the 1964 Olympic Games. Such a tactic, unless one is clearly superior to his opponent, is a calculated risk. Against an experienced opponent, especially one of near or equal ability, it is rarely successful.

Because it is physiologically and tactically sound, an even pace has proved to be the most consistently successful pattern for distance running. In competition, the athlete's aim is to win. A pace schedule is his guide; it is always subject to modifications as competitive developments make them necessary. Confidence in one's pace schedule is the key. Tenacity to develop and follow it can make the difference between success and failure.

TRAINING

Modern training for distance running is characterized by intense but purposeful work. In most instances it is year-round. With possible modifications it includes cross country in the fall, indoor running in the winter and regular outdoor meets in the spring and summer. During the active season many good distance runners train twice daily, with a morning and afternoon practice period adjusted to the personal and academic schedule of the athlete. Although the amount of work taken is great, its content is highly individualized and flexible. Much of the running is done on golf courses, parks, and isolated highways where hills and pleasant scenery break the monotony of the runner's routine.

The first sub-4-minute mile started a new era in the training of distance runners. Emerging from this era appear to be two distinct but related trends: (1) the utilization of a high degree of intensive running, and (2) an application of physiological and medical principles to the training process.

Regardless of the system employed, modern training for distance running emphasizes four essentials: (1) gradual and progressive adaptation of the runner to physical and psychological stress, (2) adjustment of the training program to individual differences, (3) emphasis on technique as a means of providing for an economy of effort, and (4) the development of cardiorespiratory endurance (ability to sustain activity under the stress of fatigue).

European coaches have played a major role in developing procedures and systems of training which have inspired research and contributed to the marked improvement in distance running technique. Foremost among these, each with a world-class athlete as testimony of the effectiveness of his method, are: Waldemar Gerschler and Rudolph Harbig (Germany), Gaston Meyer and Michel Jazy (France), Gosta Holmer and Gunder Haegg (Sweden), Franz Stampfl and Roger Bannister (England), Percy Cerutty and Herb Elliott (Australia), and

Arthur Lydiard and Peter Snell (New Zealand). Their successes are milestones in the emerging science of training distance runners. A closer examination of the training variation followed by these coaches reveals two common approaches: (1) interval training and (2) continuous (marathon) running.

INTERVAL TRAINING

Most coaches use some form of interval training in their conditioning of distance runners. There are those who believe that interval training is probably the most economical system of training ever developed, giving maximum returns in the minimum amount of time. Interval training was first used by Waldemar Gerschler of Germany and his prize athlete Rudolph Harbig who established world records at 400 and 800 meters. While other locations are used, interval training is usually performed on the track with the athlete running a set distance at a given pace for a specified number of times. Each fast run is followed by a prescribed recovery or rest period.

Effective interval training requires an understanding of four variables:

(1) An exact repeated distance that remains unchanged in any single practice period.

(2) A pace at which the distance is covered.

(3) A recovery interval of time during which restful jogging or walking occurs.

(4) The number of times the distance is repeated.

Concepts of interval training are rapidly changing. Psychologists advocate interval training because they contend it is the only way in which a great deal of quality training can be done in a comparatively short period of time. Physiologists believe that interval training increases the size of the heart and the body's alkaline reserve, creates muscular hypertrophy, and generally accustoms the body to withstand fatigue. Some suggest that to be effective, distances used in interval training should be run within prescribed ranges of time; the middle distance runner should run 100 yards in 16 to 14 seconds, 220 yards in 34 to 30 seconds and 440 yards in 74 to 68 seconds. For the distance runner, times for these distances would be slightly slower. Others believe that after running these distances, the runner's pulse should not exceed 180 beats per minute and not take longer than 90 seconds to return to a rate of 120, at which time the distance should be repeated. Some add a further dimension to the interval training process by establishing three additional guidelines:

(1) The maximum duration of the recovery period should be 1½ minutes.
(2) The maximum duration of a single run should be 1 minute, and
(3) The intensity of a single performance should result in a pulse rate of 140 to 120 at the end of the recovery period.

Coaches have found interval training to be effective because it is flexible. It can be adjusted to the needs of the individual runner at a particular stage of development. An athlete can undertake comparative amounts of work without having to endure the physical and emotional stress of bi-weekly competition. He will certainly develop in stamina, speed, judgment of pace, and resistance to the effects of fatigue.

Variations of interval training have developed. One such modification is referred to as Fartlek, a Swedish term meaning "speed-play." It was developed by Gosta Holmer, the Swedish Olympic coach. It is based upon the running of long distances with untimed variations of pace. It is a stimulating and interesting form of training because the runner is not dominated by a stopwatch or the coach's observation. The athlete can make his training as difficult as he wishes while he still can enjoy his running.

"Repetitive running" includes a fast run followed by a set period of rest. A 2-minute half-miler might run five distances of 660 yards, each at 1:37, somewhat slower than competitive pace. At competitive speed, the distance of repetitive running never extends more than half the actual distance of the event for which the athlete is training.

"Wind-up" training might include a run of three quarters of the competitive distance. After jogging for a full rest interval, the runner would attempt to run one half of his race distance at a speed equal to, or better than, the first half of his three-quarter trial. If the race distance was a mile, the runner's practice would consist of a ¾-mile, an "880," a "440," a "220" and a "110," with each distance carrying a faster pace than the previous one.

Mihaly Igloi of Hungary and Tony Nett of Germany have introduced variations of interval training for distance runners that have met with enthusiastic acceptance by American coaches. The Igloi system attaches great importance to *degrees of effort*, and relies on the ability of the individual runner to determine his own running *pace* and *tempo*. (See page 76.)

Particular emphasis in this system of training is placed on two leg muscles—the *gastrocnemius* (calf) muscle, and the *quadriceps* (thigh) muscle. To be successful in this kind of training, an athlete must learn to identify and work on them one at a time.

The *gastrocnemius* muscle, it is contended, "drives" the runner up on the ball of the foot, and moves his knee forward into the front stride.

It pushes hard against the ground when the rear leg is extended in its natural striding movement. Training action advocated for developing this part of the stride is called the DRIVE.

The *quadriceps*, according to this theory, takes over when the calf muscle loses its force. It raises and swings the leg forward while the calf muscle is resting. The leg is *lifted* and the knee raised somewhat higher than in normal running. This combined action is called the LIFT or SWING.

In planning practice schedules, coaches who employ the Igloi system use combinations of the pace and leg-action variables and abbreviate them. GD stands for "Good-Drive." "Good" defines the pace and "Drive" the leg-action. Combined they mean that for a given distance the athlete runs about half-speed and concentrates on a use of the calf muscle. HL stands for "Hard-Lift." "Hard" defines the pace and "Lift" the leg action. This combination means that the athlete runs the distance at a relaxed three-quarter effort and emphasizes a use of the thigh muscle. Daily and weekly workout schedules that include the use of Igloi principles can be found at the end of this chapter.

CONTINUOUS (MARATHON) TRAINING

Continuous training, more commonly referred to as "marathon" training, refers to running long distances at relatively slow speeds. Foremost among the advocates of this kind of training is Arthur Lydiard, the New Zealand coach who suggests a simple method of conditioning the athlete: running 100 miles a week regardless of the event to be run. After approximately 14 weeks of gradual, but intensive, conditioning, hill training is added to the runner's schedule. This consists of repeat runs of 2 miles, over a variety of cross-country courses, where the athlete can sprint up hills and run down them with a full, but relaxed, stride. As the competitive season approaches, usually 6 weeks before the first race, the runner returns to the even track for interval training at a distance of 220 yards, where he can practice sprint technique and maintain the condition he has acquired through his long distance running.

Lydiard's concept of long distance training is based upon the physiological principle of "steady state." When a runner starts to exercise, there is a gradual but definite rise in his oxygen intake, which reaches a steady level within approximately 2 minutes, depending upon the degree of exertion. If the degree of exertion is increased, another 2 minutes is required for his body to adjust to the new level of activity. If the activity continues at a constant rate, the respiratory rate remains constant. At no time does the body prepare for the work to be done: it adjusts to the new requirements only after the work has begun.

The period during which the runner's body takes in oxygen at a constant rate, after the initial "lag" of 2 minutes, is known as the "steady state." During the "steady state," the oxygen intake is equal to the demands of the runner's body for the duration of his run; when he stops, the oxygen consumption returns promptly to the normal resting level.

The distances covered in "steady state" training are related to the racing event. A miler runs three to five times his racing distance or even more. A three-miler runs 6 to 12 miles, while a six-miler might run 12 to 18 miles continuously at slow speeds. It has been found that the heart rate during this type of training is approximately 150 beats per minute, depending upon the individual athlete. For the high school miler, 8 minutes per mile, or 120 seconds per 440 yards, might be sufficiently fast. A more experienced runner might require a pace of 6 minutes per mile, or 90 seconds per 440 yards, to bring his heart beat up to 150 beats per minute. This training represents the first step in gradually adapting the runner's cardiovascular system to the stress of running and the ability to withstand fatigue. It is not limited to any particular racing distance, and forms the basis for later training at a faster pace related to a specific racing speed and distance. This type of training should not be timed. It can be done on the running track, but for psychological reasons is usually done cross country, on golf courses or on isolated roads.

Arthur Lydiard summarizes his philosophy of "steady state" running: "In theory I am trying to develop my runners until they are in a tireless state. In practice this means I am trying to give them sufficient stamina to maintain their natural speed over whatever distance they are running. Stamina is the key to the whole thing, because you can take speed for granted. . . . It is merely a process of long, gradual conditioning."

PACE TRAINING

Pace is an important consideration in distance running and much attention is given to it in training. In the past, great emphasis in practice and competition has been placed on the use of a stopwatch. More recently there has been less reliance on the stopwatch and more on the personal and preconditioned judgment of the individual runner. When a stopwatch is used, honesty and accuracy of timing is stressed.

Pace-endurance and speed-endurance work make up a major part of the distance runner's short-interval training. In pace-endurance training the number of repetitions is increased as condition improves. In speed-endurance training the speed of the repeated distance is increased.

Bob Schul (U.S.A.) hits the tape to win the 5,000-meter run in the 1964 Olympic Games at Tokyo. Running on a muddy track, Schul turned on his whirlwind sprint on the final lap to lead Harald Norpoth (Germany) and Bill Dellinger (U.S.A.) to the tape in 13:48.8 seconds.—World Wide Photos

Of the two types, opinion appears to favor an emphasis on speed work, particularly as the season progresses. This seems to be justified. Sprinting ability is a unique asset of the great distance runner. Bob Schul's amazing sprint, which carried him, against great odds, to ultimate victory in the now-historic 5000-meter run in the 1964 Olympic Games at Tokyo, is a striking example.

In modern pace training a coach places great emphasis on knowing the runner's "best time" for a given distance. He usually knows this from the athlete's past experience, or in the case of the beginner, by use of a stopwatch; then he uses this best time as a reference. If in early season a coach wishes to establish the pace at which 440 yards should be run he might instruct the athlete to add 15 seconds to his best time for that distance. If it was 50 seconds, his pace would be 65 seconds. His practice style might be further specified by adding GD (Good-Drive), which would mean that the distance was to be run at about half-speed or better, emphasizing the use of the calf muscle. In planning for a longer period of training a coach might indicate that this initial time was to be reduced 2 to 3 seconds each week until his midseason training pace was reached.

In under-distance interval running, the training pace is usually 1 to 4 seconds faster than the projected average racing time. Thus, a 4-minute miler (60-second average per 440 yards in a race) would train at 56–59 seconds per 440 HD (Hard-Drive). A 28-minute six-miler, whose average racing pace is 70 seconds per 440 yards, would train at a pace of 66 to 69 seconds per 440 GD (Good-Drive).

For the knowledgeable coach, the distance runner's training is a highly individualized consideration. Its intensity and amount is adjusted to the strengths and needs of a particular athlete. A continued search for more scientific methods of determining the biological and psychological effects of stress, such as reported by Rompotti,[1] Sprecher,[2] and Selye,[3] is needed. Until others are discovered, the coach is professionally and ethically obliged to institute practices of close observation of each runner, regular check of the runner's body weight, and having the runner diagnose his own progress and needs.

Year-Round Training Schedule

Period	*Training exercises*
End of Spring competitive season through August	Continuous (marathon) training, 9 weeks 100 miles per week, "Steady-state" running; supplement with easy jogging

Weekly schedule for period: Beginner trains on either time or distance basis.

Day	*Time*	(or)	*Distance*
Monday	1 hour		10 miles
Tuesday	1½ hours		15 miles
Wednesday	1 hour		12 miles
Thursday	2 hours		18 miles
Friday	1 hour		10 miles
Saturday	2–3 hours		20–25 miles
Sunday	1½ hours		15 miles

September through November	Thirteen weeks. Cross country running. First 3 weeks, long mileage over variety of surfaces and terrains. Fourth through 13th week: follow training schedules on pages 80–81. Adjust schedule to age and condition.
December	Alternate continuous (marathon) and "fartlek" training. If in eastern part of country and preparing for indoor racing season, include: interval training and hill running.

[1] Kalevi Rompotti, "The Blood Test as a Guide to Training," *Track Technique*, September 1960, No. 1, p. 7.

[2] P. Sprecher, "Visit with Dr. Waldemar Gerschler," *Track Technique*, September 1962, No. 9, p. 282.

[3] Hans Selye, *The Stress of Life* (New York: McGraw-Hill, 1956), p. 64.

January through March	Adjust training to indoor track schedule. If no competition, continue conditioning running. If competition is scheduled, follow training schedules on page 81.
April through June	Outdoor competitive season. First six weeks: follow training schedules on page 81. *Very light* training last 7 weeks. Concentrate on hard racing.

DAILY AND WEEKLY TRAINING SCHEDULES

Daily and weekly training schedules for the distance runner are planned for the individual athlete using guidelines covered in this chapter and in Chapter 3. The training of a distance runner is very much an individual matter. What is good for one is not necessarily good for another. The key to success is a well-balanced program. This includes cross country and hill running, speed-play, long sustained runs, interval running using a variety of short and long distances, resistance running, speed running, and a limited amount of training with weights using the accepted strength-training techniques with few repetitions and heavy weights. There is one common characteristic in all distance-training programs—WORK. There is probably no one best method of training for distance running. All of the respective methods and techniques have strengths. It is up to the coach and individual athlete to select the best of each on the basis of results in terms of performance.

The beginner should be started slowly and built up gradually. For the miler a 5:20-pace might be a good start. For the novice 2-miler an 11-minute pace, or slower, may be advisable. The training schedules which follow should be adjusted to the age, experience, and developmental status of the individual. A coach may find that he gets the best results by having an easy day follow a hard day's training. Regardless of how carefully the week's training program is planned, a coach should check each day on an athlete's condition and plan his training accordingly.

These are early to midseason schedules. These schedules, or a combination of them, should bring the runner up to the competitive season. As he reaches the peak of his training, the extent and intensity of his running should decrease. During midseason a day of light work should follow a day of heavy work. A runner's condition in late season should be carefully observed and complete rest prescribed if indicated by loss of weight, excess fatigue, or mental and emotional tension.

TRAINING CUES

(1) A medical checkup should precede all training for distance running. Periodic blood pressure, hemoglobin, and electrocardiogram tests are advisable.

(2) Select distance running shoes carefully and make sure they fit properly.

(3) Study and understand the physiological basis of your training.

(4) Start training slowly and develop gradually. Adjust the kind and amount of training to age, experience, and individual capacity.

(5) Always train on grass.

(6) Always start hard for the first 10 steps, regardless of the prescribed pace.

(7) Carry your arms about waist high. Let them swing across the body.

(8) Run relaxed and in an upright position.

(9) Keep the lower lip loose and relaxed at all times. This is an aid to total body relaxation.

(10) Keep the chin level (not up or down).

(11) When legs feel heavy, go into a lift action.

DAILY TRAINING SCHEDULES—ONE TO SIX MILES

(College Level)

These Schedules are a Guide:

All schedules must be adjusted to *age* and *experience* of runner and his *level of competition.* Work load, in intensity and amount, may be reduced for beginner and high school athlete. Principles and sequence apply in all instances.

These schedules may be used for cross country and for runners who practice twice daily. *Eight hours should intervene between twice-daily workouts.*

Key to Abbreviations

Pace and Tempo

F = FRESH	Somewhat faster than a good jog.
G = GOOD	About half-speed or slightly better.
H = HARD	Three-quarter effort (emphasis on relaxation).
VH = VERY HARD	Maximum effort with control.
AO = ALL OUT	Maximum effort without control.

Leg Action

D = DRIVE	Accent use of gastrocnemius (calf) muscle.
L = } LIFT S = } SWING	Accent use of quadriceps (thigh) muscle.

Combinations

FD = Fresh-Drive
FD/FL = Alternate driving and lifting action.
(/) This sign means to alternate.
GD = Good-Drive
HD = Hard-Drive
VHD = Very Hard-Drive
AO = All-Out—using natural leg action.
BU = Build-Up—Start out hard; shift into established pace; in last half of prescribed distance, pick up pace every third stride.
GDBU = Good-Drive-Build-Up
(440) = Figure on top of line = training distance.
220 Figure on bottom of line = rest interval.

FL = Fresh-Lift
FS = Fresh-Swing
GL = Good-Lift
HL = Hard-Lift
VHL = Very Hard-Lift
GLBU = Good-Lift-Build-Up

WARM-UP AND WARM-DOWN

An athlete who has not been on a steady training program prior to a start of the regular season should spend extra time and distance in warming up and warming down. If on a given day he feels stiff and sore the warm-up distance should be doubled. Warm-ups and warm-downs listed below should be varied from day to day.

WARM-UP SET (A)

(1) Jog one easy lap (stress relaxation)
(2) 10 × 100 FL/FD
(3) 3 × 250 FL building to GD
(4) Training assignment for day

WARM-DOWN

(1) 15 × 100 FL/FD
(2) 1 × 660 at 1:35
(3) Easy warm-down jog

WARM-UP SET (B)

(1) Run one mile. (1st 440, 3 minutes; 2nd, 2½ min.; 3rd, 2 min.; run 4th 440 alternating 50 yards fast, 50 yards slow, each faster than preceding. Final 50 yards, all out.)
(2) Training assignment for day

WARM-DOWN

(1) 8 × 150 FL/FD
(2) 1 × 660 at 1:35
(3) Easy warm-down jog

Key to Schedule I

A-1

10 × 100 FL
6 × 150 GD
10 × 100 FD
6 × 150 GL

B-1

Jog mile in 8 min.
15 × 150 GL/GD
Jog mile in 8 min.
12 × 150 HD/FL (HD is controlled)

C-1

3 to 6 miles steady run—6:00 to 6:30 per mile
Walk 5 min.
10 to 15 × 150 2 FL, 1 GD, etc.

Key to Schedule I (cont.)

A-2

10 × 100 FL
6 × 150 GL/HD
10 × 100 FD
6 × 150 GL/HD

B-2

No warm-up
Alternately run FL/FD 110's (about 25 sec.) and GL/GD 220's (about 32–35 sec.) until 2¼ miles have been covered

C-2

6 to 10 miles steady run—6:20 to 6:40 per mile

A-3

10 × 150 FL/FD
6 × 100 GL
10 × 100 FL/FD
6 × 100 GD

B-3

1¼ miles of FS/FD and short GDBU's
3 × (2 × 110 GD/FL; 2 × 220 GD/FL; 2 × 110 HD/FL)
Walk 3 min. between sets

C-3

10 to 15 miles steady run—6:30 to 7:00 per mile

A-4

10 × 110 FL
6 × $\frac{220}{100}$ GL/GD
10 × 100 FL
6 × $\frac{220}{100}$ GDBU

B-4

Jog mile in 8 min.
4 × (330 GD; 220 FL; 110 HD)
Walk 3 min. between sets

Schedule I

(Recommended for A.M. workout when practices are scheduled twice daily.)

Week	Sunday	Monday	Tuesday	Wednesday	Thursday	Friday	Saturday
1. —	B-1	B-1	A-3	B-2	B-4	A-1	A-2
2. —	C-1	A-4	A-1	B-3	A-3	B-4	B-2
3. —	C-3	B-1	B-2	A-4	C-2	A-2	B-3
4. —	C-3	A-1	A-2	B-1	A-4	A-2	B-2
*5. —	A-2	B-2	C-1	B-3	A-1	A-4	A-1

* After 5th week adjust kind and amount of work to individual needs.

Key to Schedule II

(SHORT-INTERVAL)

SERIES I. 110-yard interval
(Speed—FRESH to HARD; Leg action—Alternate between SWING and DRIVE)

110-A 6 to 8 × (110 HD, 440 FL; 110 HD, 330 FL; 110 HD, 220 FL; 110 HD, 110 FL; 110 HD)

110-B 4 to 6 (10 × 110 GL/GD). Walk 3 min. between each set.

110-C 1 to 3 × (20 × 110 at 3 GL, 1 FL, 2 AO, 1 FL, 3 GD) (repeat 19 times)

110-D 3 to 6 × (10 × 110 HD) 110 FL after 1, 3, 5, and 9th 110; 150 FD after 2, 4, 6 and 8th 110.

SERIES II. 220-yard interval
(Speed—FRESH to HARD; Leg action—Alternate between SWING and DRIVE)

220-A 1 to 2 × (10 × $\frac{220}{150}$ GD). Walk 5 min. between each set.

220-B 3 to 4 × (6 × 220 HD/FL). Walk 5 min. after each set.

220-C 20 × 220 GD/FL

220-D 26 × $\frac{220}{110}$ 2 HD, 3 FL, 4 GD, 2 FL, 2 HD (repeat)

SERIES III. 440-yard interval
(Start with pace 15 seconds slower than best time for 440 yards. Increase pace 2 to 3 seconds faster per 440 yards every two to three weeks until desired training pace is reached.)

440-A 2 to 4 × (5 × 440 GD). Jog intervals—440, 330, 220, 110. Walk 3 min. between each set.

440-B 20 × $\frac{440}{120}$ GD/GL

440-C 2 to 3 × (10 × $\frac{440}{110}$ 3 GD, 2 HD, 2 FL, 3 GL) 220 between HD's

440-D 3 to 5 × (4 × $\frac{440}{110}$) 1st set GD; 2nd set FL/FD; 3rd set HD; 4th set FL/GD; 5th set GD/GL

440-E 3 to 5 × (440 HD, 330 FL, 110 GD, 440 HD, 330 FL, 110 GD, 440 HD). Walk 5 min. between sets

440-F 3 to 5 × (4 × $\frac{440}{110}$ GD). Jog 660 between sets

SERIES IV. 660-yard interval
(Pace for GD—1:40 to 1:45 Secs.)

660-A 3 to 5 × $\frac{660}{440}$ HD

660-B 10 × $\frac{660}{220}$ GD/GL

660-C 3 × (3 × $\frac{660}{150}$ FL, HD, FL)

660-D 9 × $\frac{660}{220}$ GD, HL, GD. Walk 5 min.; GD, GL, GD; Walk 5 min.; GL, HD, GL.

(LONG-INTERVAL)

SERIES I. 880-yard interval

(This series is considered the "core" of early season cross-country training.) Training distance and pace are coordinated so that intervals may be repeated many times without undue stress on the runner who is not in top condition. It is recommended that the rest intervals be a jog or walk to provide a more rapid recovery at this time of the season. (Recommended GD = 2:12 to 2:16 seconds — or 2:15 to 2:20 seconds.)

880-A 8 × $\frac{880}{660}$ FD/GD

880-B 8 × $\frac{880}{660}$ GD/GL

880-C 9 × $\frac{880}{660}$ GD, HDBU, FL, FD, GD, GD, FL, HD, FL

880-D 10 × $\frac{880}{660}$ GD, GD, GD, FL, FD, GD, GD, FL, GD, FL

SERIES II. 1-mile interval

(Recommended speed of mile interval—FRESH to GOOD. Leg action—DRIVE with 3 to 6 intervals of SWING within each mile.)

Table for determining GD pace for 1-mile Series

If best 2-mile time is:	Recommended 1-mile pace is:
9:00 —— 9:15	4:30 —— 4:35
9:16 —— 9:25	4:40 —— 4:45
9:26 —— 9:35	4:45 —— 4:50
9:36 —— 9:45	4:50 —— 4:55
9:46 —— 9:55	4:55 —— 4:58
9:56 —— 10:05	4:58 —— 5:05

Mile A 4 to 6 × mile at GD. Walk or jog 4 to 6 min. after each mile

Mile B 8 to 10 × $\frac{\text{mile}}{\text{8 min.}}$ at **FD** (FD is 3 to 5 seconds per 440 slower than GD)

Mile C 9 × $\frac{\text{mile}}{\text{8 min.}}$ at GD, FD, GD. . . . . .GD, FL, FL. . . . . .GD, GD, FL

Schedule II

(Recommended for P.M. workout when practices are scheduled twice daily.)

Week	Sunday	Monday	Tuesday	Wednesday	Thursday	Friday	Saturday
1. —	60–90 min. Speed Play	440-F	Mile-C	220-A	880-A	Mile-B	440-E
2. —	60–90 min. Speed Play	880-B	110-B	20 min. Jog 20 min. S.P.	220-C	440-C	880-A

3. —	60–90 min. Speed Play	Mile-C	660-C	220-D	Mile-A	20 min. Jog 20 min. S.P.	880-D
4. —	60–90 min. Speed Play	440-E	110-C	20 min. Jog 20 min. S.P.	220-B	110-A	660-D
*5. —	60–90 min. Speed Play	880-C	440-D	220-B	20 min. Jog 20 min. S.P.	110-D	440-A

* After 5th week adjust kind and amount of work to individual needs.

Typical Mid-Season Schedules for Distance Runners

(College level by geographical location)

Schedule "A"—Midwest

Precede each day's training with *Warm-up* and conclude with *Warm-down*. Modify for high school athlete according to age and experience.

MONDAY 8–10 miles of continuous running. (Vary course.)
8 × 150 yards, ⅞ speed. Jog interval, 150 yards.
TUESDAY 4 × 880 yards, ¾ to ⅞ speed. Jog interval, 440 yards.
2 × 660 yards, ⅞ speed. Jog interval, 330 yards.
WEDNESDAY Repeat Monday's schedule.
THURSDAY 4–6 miles of continuous running. (Vary course.)
Run ¾ of competitive distance at desired pace for week.
FRIDAY 4–6 miles of continuous running. (Vary course.)
SATURDAY Competition.
SUNDAY 10–15 miles of continuous running. (Vary course.)

Schedule "B"—Southwest

MONDAY 8–10 × 440 yards at 60 to 66 seconds. Jog interval 220 yards.
or
8–10 × 220 yards at 24 to 28 seconds. Jog interval 110 yards.
TUESDAY 4–6 × 880 yards at 2:04 to 2:15. Jog interval, 440 yards.
WEDNESDAY One-milers, 2 × ¾ mile at desired competitive pace for week.
Two-milers, 2 × 1½ miles at desired competitive pace for week, or 2–4 miles of continuous jogging.
THURSDAY 10–15 × 150 to 180 yards on track straightaway at ¾ speed. Jog interval, 150 yards.
FRIDAY Easy jogging.
SATURDAY Competition.

Even Track Pace Schedule

DISTANCE—	2 MILE	1¾	1½	1¼	MILE	¾	880	660	550	440	330	220	110
TIME—	10:40	9:20	8:00	6:40	5:20	4:00	2:40	2:00	1:40	:80	:60	:40	:20
	10:20	9:06	7:48	6:30	5:12	3:54	2:36	1:57	1:37+	:78	:58+	:39	:19+
	10:08	8:52	7:36	6:20	5:04	3:48	2:32	1:54	1:35	:76	:57	:38	:19
	9:52	8:38	7:24	6:10	4:56	3:42	2:28	1:61	1:32+	:74	:55+	:37	:18+
	9:36	8:24	7:12	6:00	4:48	3:36	2:24	1:48	1:30	:72	:54	:36	:18
	9:20	8:10	7:00	5:50	4:40	3:30	2:20	1:45	1:27+	:70	:52+	:35	:17+
	9:04	7:56	6:48	5:40	4:32	3:24	2:16	1:42	1:25	:68	:51	:34	:17
	8:48	7:42	6:36	5:30	4:24	3:18	2:12	1:39	1:22+	:66	:49+	:33	:16+
			6:24	5:20	4:16	3:12	2:08	1:36	1:20	:64	:48	:32	:16
			6:12	5:10	4:08	3:06	2:04	1:33	1:17+	:62	:46+	:31	:15+
					4:00	3:00	2:00	1:30	1:15	:60	:45	:30	:15
					3:52	2:54	1:56	1:27	1:12+	:58	:43+	:29	:14+
							1:52	1:24	1:10	:56	:42	:28	:14
							1:48	1:21	1:07+	:54	:40+	:27	:13+
							1:44	1:18	1:05	:52	:39	:26	:13
								1:15	:62+	:50	:37+	:25	:12+
									:60	:48	:36	:24	:12— :11.5
										:46	:34+	:23	:11+
										:44	:33	:22	:11
												:21	:10+

VERTICAL COLUMN Desired total time for distance indicated in column heading

HORIZONTAL COLUMN Desired cumulative time for this distance at that point in run

Table for Computing Total Distance Run When A Given Interval of Yardage Is Repeated a Specified Number of Times

(Numbers in parentheses represent miles; other numbers represent yardage)

NUMBER OF REPETITIONS

INTERVAL	2	3	4	6	8	9	10	12	14	15	16	18	20
110	220	330	440	660	880	990	1,100	1,320	1,540	1,650	(1) —	(1) 220	(1) 440
150	300	450	600	900	1,200	1,350	1,500	(1) 40	(1) 340	(1) 490	(1) 640	(1) 940	(1) 1,240
220	440	660	880	1,320	(1) —	(1) 220	(1) 440	(1) 880	(1) 1,320	(1) 1,540	(2) —	(2) 440	(2) 880
250	500	750	1,000	1,500	(1) 240	(1) 490	(1) 740	(1) 1,240	(1) 1,740	(2) 230	(2) 480	(2) 980	(2) 1,480
330	660	990	1,320	(1) 220	(1) 880	(1) 1,210	(1) 1,540	(2) 440	(2) 1,100	(2) 1,430	(3) —	(3) 660	(3) 1,320
440	880	1,320	(1) —	(1) 880	(2) —	(2) 440	(2) 880	(3) —	(3) 880	(3) 1,320	(4) —	(4) 880	(5) —
550	1,100	1,650	(1) 440	(1) 1,540	(2) 880	(2) 1,430	(3) 220	(3) 1,320	(4) 660	(4) 1,210	(5) —	(5) 1,100	(6) 440
660	1,320	(1) 220	(1) 880	(2) 440	(3) —	(3) 660	(3) 1,320	(4) 880	(5) 440	(5) 1,100	(6) —	(6) 1,320	(7) 880
880	(1) —	(1) 880	(2) —	(3) —	(4) —	(4) 880	(5) —	(6) —	(7) —	(7) 880	(8) —	(9) —	(10) —

8
Relay Racing

Relay racing has become an established part of the American track and field program. Few events have done as much to popularize the sport. Their speed, excitement, and suspense is interesting for both contestant and spectator. Team effort, in a sport otherwise characterized by individual performance, is at its finest. The responsibility of each member of the team frequently inspires an otherwise mediocre runner to achievement beyond his recognized capacity; in such a case, the runner profits by his sense of accomplishment as much as the team does by his performance.

An 880-yard and a one-mile relay are included in the standard high school dual meet schedule of events. The one-mile relay has traditionally climaxed the college program. In most college meets, a 440-yard relay is included.

Championship meets, consisting entirely of relay events, have become a popular feature of the early season high school and college track programs. Some include field events scored as relay performance. These meets have done much to attract large numbers of participants and serve as a medium for the discovery of individual talent.

CLASSIFICATION OF EVENTS

A variety of relay combinations have been developed. They may be classified as follows:

Sprint Relays

440-yard relay (4 × 110 yards)
880-yard relay (4 × 220 yards)

Sprint Medley Relays

110, 220, 440, and 880 yards
220, 110, 110, and 220 yards
440, 220, 220, and 880 yards

Distance Relays

Four-mile relay (4 × 1 mile)

Distance Medley Relays

440, 880, ¾-mile, and one mile

Middle Distance Relays

One-mile relay (4 × 440 yards)
Two-mile relay (4 × 880 yards)

Shuttle Hurdle Relays

4 × 120 yards, high hurdles
4 × 120 yards, low hurdles

Relay races are named according to the distance run by the four members of a team. When the laps are short it is called a "sprint" relay and when they are long a "distance" relay. When the laps are of intermediate length it is called a "middle-distance" relay. When each man runs a different distance it is called a "medley" relay. The combined distance run by the members of a team is also used in naming a relay. When each of the four men runs a quarter mile, the race is called a "one-mile" relay.

The ideal relay team is made up of four good members. Frequently, however, an "anchor" man, the last to run on a team, is so superior in ability that his performance alone is sufficient to win the race for an otherwise weak team. This is particularly true in the "distance-medley" and "four-mile" relays where an especially strong "anchor" man has more opportunity to come from behind and defeat a more equally balanced team.

High and low hurdle races are frequently run as "shuttle" relays. The distance run by each member is 120 yards, or a total of 480 yards by the combined team. The members, in shuttle formation, are lined up alternately at each end of a 120-yard straightaway. The race starts and finishes at the same line. Each member runs down or back over the hurdles set up in his assigned lane. Two adjacent lanes are used by each team so that hurdles can be set up safely in the right direction for each hurdler. An outgoing runner, who takes a crouch start position at his line, cannot start until his incoming team-mate enters a predetermined "break" zone. This is a difficult rule to enforce and competent officials must be assigned to each end of the straightaway to check on violations.

TECHNIQUES OF PASSING THE BATON

The baton exchange constitutes the major technique of relay racing. (It is not, however, a consideration in hurdle relays.) Split-second timing is involved. Guesswork is eliminated by the use of accurately measured checkmarks. Coaches and athletes must realize that successful relay racing is not possible unless the foursome has worked diligently on its baton-passing so that its execution is precise and speedy.

Track rules require that the baton be exchanged within a 22-yard passing zone. The baton, but not necessarily the runner, must be in this zone when it is exchanged.

An International Amateur Athletic Federation Rule that permits a runner in the 400-meter relay to start 10 meters in advance of this zone has been approved and adopted by the National Collegiate Athletic Association and the National Federation of State High School Athletic Associations. While he can start from this advanced point, the runner cannot pass the baton within the 10-meter restriction.

This rule is used in Olympic and other international competition and those supporting its adoption contend that it has strengthened our performance in these meets. The earlier start, they believe, increases a runner's momentum. Likewise, they feel that he will be more relaxed in a longer zone and consequently will execute a better exchange. Teams that use the longer zone have improved their times by five-tenths of a

Visual Exchange: Standard Technique. Left to right hand. Receiver faces away from pole.

second for the 440-yard relay; such an improvement appears to justify a use of the modified rule.

Regardless of the exchange rule followed, the pass must be well timed, executed smoothly and with continuing speed. To achieve this aim, two styles (determined by event) are used. Variations and combinations are possible.

THE VISUAL EXCHANGE

In the one-mile, two-mile, distance medley and four-mile relays, a *visual* exchange is used. The outgoing runner is primarily responsible for its timing and proper execution. For those running laps of 440 and 880 yards, a checkmark or "go-point" 17 feet before the back exchange limit line is established. For those running a mile, a 15-foot go-point is used.

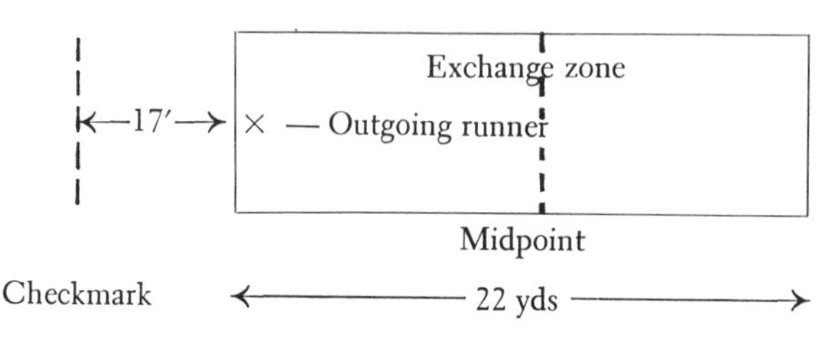

The *outgoing* runner positions himself at the back limit line of the exchange zone. He faces the *inside* of the track. His *left* foot is back. He watches his teammate approach.

When the incoming runner hits the 17-foot checkmark, the outgoing starts running. His speed is determined by that of his teammate's finish. His aim is to pull him out to a strong finish without running away from him. The receiver's eyes are forward as he starts. Arm action is normal. When he reaches the midpoint of the exchange zone he looks back. If necessary, his looking back may be prompted by a signal from the incoming man.

As he looks back the receiver extends his left hand (palm up) to a position just above the level of his waist. As the passer, who carries the baton in his *right hand*, takes his last stride before the exchange, he reaches out, and with a downward motion, places the baton firmly in the receiver's open left palm. The receiver grasps the baton securely to complete the exchange. He is never overtaken by his teammate.

On his first stride after the transfer, the outgoing runner changes the baton to his right hand. In this action the baton is turned as it comes in front of his body. The top half remains open for the next exchange.

Visual Exchange: Right to left hand technique. Receiver faces pole.

The outgoing runner sprints at *maximum* effort to the turn of the track.

Variations of this exchange are used. The advantages of the version just described (the *inside* version) are:

(1) The receiver has good visibility of the curb and incoming runners.

(2) He is protected from crowding during the exchange.

(3) His starting position is balanced and relaxed.

(4) There is little chance of the baton being knocked out of his hand.

Both runners should be familiar with the rule to be followed in positioning the outgoing runner. Various rules have been devised in an attempt to equalize the advantage of an inside position at the exchange line. Recently a rule popularly termed the "California" exchange has been adopted. It simply provides that the receivers take their lane position at the end of each lap of the race according to the order in which their incoming teammate *enters* the finishing straightaway. As each exchange is completed, the receiver whose passer is next to come in will move toward the pole.

The California exchange requires alertness by both runners. The receiver must move toward the curb as he awaits his incoming teammate. The passer must keep his eyes on this man and judge the angle of his finish so that he runs to the approximate point, presumably close to the pole, where the pass will be completed. This pass is not well executed by many teams, with confusion and loss of time resulting.

THE BLIND EXCHANGE

In the 440- and 880-yard relays, a blind (nonvisual) exchange is used. The primary responsibility is on the *incoming* runner. The first requirement for a successful execution of this exchange is the location of an accurate checkmark or go-point. It is measured backwards from

Blind Exchange: Right to left hand technique.

the back limit of the exchange zone and its location can be determined only by experimentation and practice. Its ultimate effectiveness is measured only by the test of competition.

If International Rules are used, the following chart may serve as a guide to determine checkmarks for the 440-yard relay:

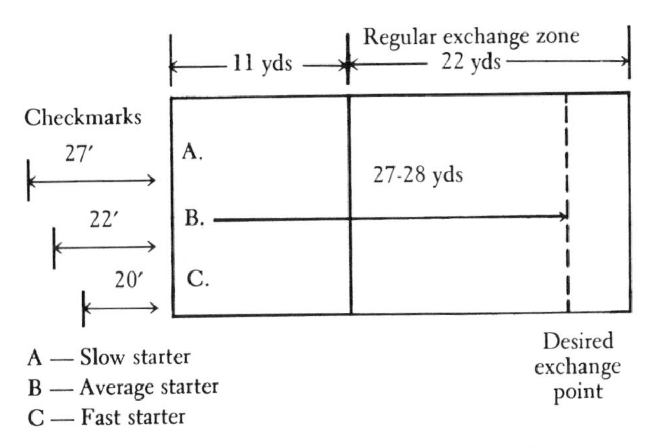

The above marks may be adjusted to the individual runner. In the 880-yard relay they should be reduced to 13–17 feet, depending upon the speed of the incoming and start of the outgoing runner.

The Extended-Arm Exchange

The extended-arm version of the nonvisual exchange is almost universally employed. There are variations of this baton passing technique usually referred to as left-to-right, right-to-left, left-to-left, and right-to-right hand exchanges. Most teams favor the more traditional left-to-right hand exchange. (Pass with left hand, receive with right hand.)

Other variations in the nonvisual exchange are determined by the manner in which the incoming runner places the baton in the extended hand of the outgoing receiver. Some coaches believe that the baton should be exchanged on the *upward* swing of the incoming runner's arm; others on the *downward* swing. Most teams employ an upward exchange in the sprint relays while a downward exchange is used in the middle and longer distance relays.

Factors which determine the style of exchange adopted include: (a) the distance of the race, (b) the adaptability of the exchange style to the individual members of the team, (c) the distance gained by the extended arm of the passer and receiver, (d) the point in the passing zone where the exchange takes place, and (e) the confidence of the team members in the style employed. Experimentation and results in competition usually determine the final choice.

Fundamentals of the left-to-right hand exchange

(1) The receiver assumes a standing position just inside the back line of the exchange zone, with his back to the curb of the track. His *right* foot is back. His eyes are on a previously established checkmark, usually 7 or 8 yards outside the passing zone.

(2) A verbal signal, frequently a "Go," is given by the incoming runner just prior to reaching the mark. As his teammate hits the mark, the receiver starts at maximum speed employing the same arm and leg drive as in a regular sprint start. *Both* arms are used vigorously.

(3) At a point predetermined by practice, usually 5 to 8 yards inside the passing zone, the receiver extends his right arm backwards. His outstretched hand is held just above his waist. The palm of his receiving hand is *down*, thumb out of the way, forming a wide cupped target for the passer.

(4) At this point the incoming runner places the baton in the receiver's right hand. The action is timed with the upswing of the passer's left arm. If the pass is well synchronized, the baton is exchanged when the two runners are running at an equal rate of speed. It is the responsibility of the incoming runner to place the baton in the receiver's hand, and his eyes should remain on the target until the pass is complete. The pass should be firm and the passer should make sure that his receiver has a secure grip on the baton. The action throughout is smooth and continuous. The receiver never slows down, nor is he ever overtaken by the passer.

(5) On the first stride after the pass is completed, the receiver changes the baton to his left hand using the same technique described in the visual exchange.

Variations of the extended-arm exchange

(1) There are teams that use a *downward* action of the passer's arm for both the sprint and distance relay exchanges. When this style is used for a sprint relay, the palm of the receiver's hand is up, heel of the hand parallel with the track—thumb out of the way. The passer places the baton in the receiver's hand on the *downward* swing of his passing arm, rather than on the upward. Other fundamentals, previously described, are the same. The advantage of this action is that it is similar for all relays and is believed by some coaches to be a safer method of passing.

(2) There are teams that use and get good results with a *right-to-right* hand sprint exchange. Those advocating its use contend that most athletes are right-handed and consequently this exchange is easier to master. Since there is no change of baton from one hand to the other, the chances of dropping it are reduced. Arm action is continuous. Time is not lost. (Frequently two strides are lost in other methods.) A substitute can readily replace an injured team member.

THE 440-YARD RELAY—SPECIAL CONSIDERATIONS

Under International Rules governing the 440-yard relay, runners 2, 3, and 4 on a team position themselves, facing the *outside* of the track, at the back limit of the 30-meter passing zone. Checkmarks are accurately established. *Right* foot is back.

While the exchange between runners 2 and 3 is executed on the straightaway, all four members of the team must either receive or pass the baton on a curve of the track. Certain modifications in running and baton passing technique are therefore necessary.

As he enters the exchange zone on the curve, the *incoming* runner, who attempts to stay in the center of the lane, straightens his body position slightly. The pull on his inside arm, which throws him somewhat to the outside of the lane, is slackened preparatory to the pass.

The *receiver*, as he starts his run, attempts to maintain a straight line from his starting position to a point midway in the exchange zone, aiming for the inside one-third of his lane.

The exchange is executed at a point 16 to 17 yards inside the passing zone. In a left-to-right hand exchange, the *outgoing* runner, as previously explained, extends his right hand directly behind his right hip. The *incoming* runner, who runs to the *outside* of his lane so that his *left* foot falls just behind his teammate's *right*, completes the pass as a left-to-right handshake is simulated.

THE STRATEGY OF RELAY RUNNING

The 22-yard passing zone is formed by lines drawn 11 yards on either side of the finish line. Within this zone, each runner must pass the baton to the teammate succeeding him. No member of a relay team may, in order to relieve his teammate, run outside these limits. However, some believe it is wise to take advantage of these zones to over-distance or under-distance the members of a team according to their ability. If the first runner on a team is a better all-round performer than the second, it might be well to have him sprint to the extreme end of the exchange zone to take full advantage of his speed. Similarly, if the second man is inferior to the third, it may be beneficial to have the latter receive the baton in the forepart of the passing zone. Both strategies should be employed with care.

Different strategies are utilized for placing team members in a running order. Traditionally, most coaches have placed their best starter, preferably a good competitor, in the leadoff position. This is obviously to get good position for the team at the start. In this plan, the weakest member of the team is positioned second; the strongest, but not necessarily the fastest man, runs third; the anchor man in this combination is, of course, the best all-round man and strongest finisher.

Some coaches break with tradition by running their weakest man in the leadoff position. The next three are placed according to relative ability, building up gradually to the strongest man running in the anchor position. Others have positioned their strongest runner in third position. Such a strategy aims to build up a substantial lead against those who run their weakest man in this position. The advantage gained, it is contended, may be sufficiently great to offset the ability of the usual strong anchor lap runner.

TRAINING

Training for relay running consists primarily of getting runners accustomed to carrying a baton and practicing the exchange.

During certain parts of the daily practice period, individual members of the team may carry a baton as they train for regular events. During his warm-up jog a runner may carry a baton and practice transferring it from one hand to the other. Or two-man exchanges, using the proper technique, can be practiced while the runners jog. Many coaches use baton practice, at competitive speed, as part of the warm-up procedure.

A more highly organized method consists of a regular run with team members stationed at approximately 40-yard intervals. Each attempts to approximate competitive finishing speed at the end of each exchange. Members of the team are placed in the exact order they will run in competition so that they will become better acquainted with each other's strengths and weaknesses and will develop teamwork and spirit.

In practicing for the relays, the regular exchange zone, or a similar one marked on the track, should be used. The squad can assemble at this location to hear the rules and tactics of relay running explained, then practice them. Sometimes teams may line up in different pole positions from which they can practice the break for the pole after the exchange. A maximum sprint-for-pole position on each exchange is stressed. Checks are made to be certain there is vigorous arm action throughout the exchange, with the reach of the baton coming only on the last stride of the transfer.

The sprint exchange requires diligent practice and repetition. Members of the team should practice in the order in which they will run in competition, with alternates filling in when necessary. Accurate checkmarks should be used. These should be established with warm-up clothes removed and under conditions closely approximating competition. Several teams may be lined up on the track with lane positions rotated so that team members gain the experience of passing and receiving, as well as running, with competitors on both sides of them. Exchanges should be practiced on a curve as training for competition.

The 440 relay (4 × 110), practiced with either the visual or blind exchange, is an excellent practice exercise for all the relays. It approximates competitive conditions for members of the sprint team. It constitutes a form of interval training for those running longer distances. And it provides experience in baton-passing for both types of runners.

Some coaches devote an entire practice session to relay running as a regular part of each week's practice schedule. Field event men as well as runners participate. All members of the squad enjoy such practices; the work is fun and breaks the monotony of regular practice. Intersquad competition is keen and stimulating, and the relay practice engenders team spirit. By utilizing medley relays, the right training distances may be provided runners in the various events.

In final preparation for relay running, a practice period should be conducted in which members of the team run through the exact distance they will be running in competition. Accurate lanes and staggers should be marked on the track for this important practice period and all rules of competition strictly adhered to.

COMPETITION

(1) General suggestions for individual running events apply.

(2) Make sure the team's leadoff man has a baton. His starting blocks (if used) and a mallet or tamp to set them should be readily available.

(3) In meets where it is required, make sure, when the team reports, that a card listing members is ready for presentation.

(4) Report well in advance of starting time. Make sure all members of the team know the exact location of all starts, finishes, and exchange zones.

(5) Checkmarks should be carefully measured and clearly marked as part of the team's warm-up procedure.

(6) Rules should be clearly understood by all members of the team.

(7) In races starting from scratch, the leadoff man should grasp the baton firmly to avoid its being knocked out of his hand.

(8) All runners should grasp the baton firmly, but without undue tension, throughout the entire race. Special caution, to avoid dropping, should be taken throughout the exchange.

(9) If the "California" exchange rule is used, the outgoing runner should move *continuously* toward the curb as his teammate approaches. The passer should have the receiver clearly identified and run *directly* to his location.

(10) In all races where a break for the curve is required, the receiver should sprint at full effort until it is reached. Many relay races are won or lost at this point.

(11) Regardless of how well a team has perfected its exchange in practice, all members should use judgment and be prepared to make split-second changes and adjustments as competition demands.

(12) If a baton is dropped, don't panic. Retrieve it quickly and continue with the race. A baton dropped inside the 22-yard exchange zone may be retrieved by either runner. If an incoming runner drops the baton before he reaches the zone, only he may retrieve it.

9
Hurdling

Hurdling is a variation of sprinting. The difference lies in the placement of obstacles in the path of the sprint or run. The adapted stride, necessary in clearing the barrier, constitutes the motor skill of the event.

The standard hurdle events on the American collegiate and scholastic track programs have traditionally been the 120-yard high and 220-yard low hurdles.

The Olympic and AAU Championships include a 400-meter and 440-yard hurdle event. Shorter races are scheduled for indoor competition. The high school low hurdle event has been standardized at a distance of 180 yards in which eight hurdles are to be cleared. The colleges, in an attempt to develop Olympic talent, have replaced the 220-yard low hurdles with the 440-yard intermediate hurdles. In each event all hurdles must be officially cleared; that is, the hurler must go over (not around) the hurdles, his trailing leg must also go over the hurdle, and he must not hinder or have contact with other hurdlers; a hurdler is not disqualified for upsetting a hurdle.

The present-day form of hurdling is of rather recent origin. Hurdlers in earlier days knew very little about modern hurdling technique, and most of them just ran at the hurdles and jumped them the best they could. A bent lead-leg position characterized this early form. The relatively straight lead leg, its sharp downward thrust, the well-timed arm action, the body "dip," the delayed action of the recovery leg—all are modern innovations.

SOMATOTYPE

Modern hurdling requires a man with speed. Most good collegiate and scholastic hurdlers are capable of running 100 yards in approximately ten seconds or better. Some coaches believe that an athlete who can run 100 yards in that time, and can high-jump or long-jump, can probably be taught to hurdle. Others think it is a good plan to make a hurdler out of a sprinter who is not quite fast enough to hold his own in a sprint race.

Height, accompanied by speed, is an asset. Most championship hurdlers have been at least 5′10″ tall. A hurdler's "leg split" (likely to be good if he is tall) is important, as are coordination, agility, and looseness of the hips.

Hurdling, perhaps more than any event, requires an athlete with the right temperament. To start with, training takes work and lots of it. One great hurdler used "100 hurdles a day" as his objective. Efficient hurdle clearance requires flexibility, especially in rotation of the hip

Hurdle Chart

Events	Number of Hurdles	Height of Hurdle	Distance to 1st Hurdle	Steps to 1st Hurdle	Distance Between Hurdles	Steps Between Hurdles	Distance to Finish
120-Yard High Hurdles (Collegiate)	10	3′6″	15 Yards	8 (7)	10 Yards	3	15 Yards
120-Yard High Hurdles (Scholastic)	10	3′3″	15 Yards	8 (7)	10 Yards	3	15 Yards
180-Yard Low Hurdles (Scholastic)	8	2′6″	20 Yards	10	20 Yards	7	20 Yards
440-Yard (400-Meter) Intermediate Hurdles (Collegiate)	10	3′	40 Yards	21–22–23	40 Yards	13–15	40 Yards

socket of the trailing leg. Just the exercises alone for this single element of training demand a self-discipline like that of a ballet dancer.

There are ten obstacles to be cleared. Bumps, bruises, and falls, particularly at the outset, are inevitable. An athlete who can not "take it" and come back for more will probably not be very successful as a hurdler. In their need for persistence, hurdlers have sometimes been compared with boxers.

STARTING THE BEGINNER

There are a number of ways to teach hurdling technique. For the beginner it is a new motor skill, and instruction must be basic and simple. The coach must establish the athlete's confidence and find a way to minimize the fear of falling. The start should be slow and training should follow a progressive sequence.

THE SIMULATED HURDLING ACTION

For those without previous experience, the basic motor skill of hurdling can be introduced effectively and safely without a hurdle. Two lines, approximately six feet apart, are established as takeoff and landing points. A mark to represent the hurdle is added approximately midway between. The beginner's first action is to *walk* up to the first line and *spring* over the mark to the second line. A forceful *push* from the takeoff foot is emphasized. The lead leg is extended in front and the trailing, or takeoff, leg follows through in a natural recovery action—at right angles to the body. The entire action is counted out, "Push! One! Two!" "Push" is the takeoff; "One," the landing; and "Two," the recovery. This step is repeated until the learner masters the coordination and timing of this basic movement. The distance and height of the travel is gradually increased, the importance of the "push" and followthrough action stressed. The walk-through is followed by a jog approach and then a slow run. Each time the simulated hurdling action, using the lines as a guide, is repeated.

THE SIDE STRADDLE

Following a reasonable mastery of the simulated hurdling action, the beginner is ready to try a "side straddle." The basic action is the same except that a hurdle is added for clearance. The teaching procedure is the same. At the high school level a low hurdle may be used. For the grade school or junior high pupil a modified barrier 1½ to 2 feet high is recommended. In performing a "side straddle," the beginner does not go squarely over the hurdle. He performs the same action as in step one, springing from one line to another, at the *side* of the hurdle, but close enough to it to require his clearing it with his *trailing leg only*. The distance between the takeoff and landing points (lines one and two) is gradually increased as the pupil gains confidence in his clearance action. As side-straddle practice continues, the fundamentals of correct hurdling technique are introduced and practiced one at a time until full-action hurdling is simulated.

FULL ACTION

Following his practice of the side straddle, the learner is ready to try full-action clearance going squarely over the hurdle. Use of a standing start continues. Stress is on correct running form and "bounce" in approaching the hurdle. If practice is outdoors, a grassy area should be used. Indoors, a thin rubber mat should be used as a landing area. Accurate steps to the first hurdle are not introduced until hurdle clearance is fairly well mastered. Common faults to be corrected at this time will be: (a) takeoff too close to the hurdle, (b) trailing leg under the hurdler instead of at right angles to body, (c) insufficient followthrough of trailing leg with knee not sufficiently raised, and (d) incorrect arm action. Corrections should be made one at a time as learning progresses.

THE 8-STRIDE APPROACH

The 8-stride approach is introduced following practice of the full layout. A standing start is used. One low hurdle is set up 15 yards from the starting line. A tentative takeoff mark is established approximately 5′6″ in front of the hurdle. This distance is gradually increased.

From his standing position, the hurdler steps on the starting line with his *takeoff* foot and runs full speed at the hurdle. Such an approach should bring him to his takeoff mark in eight strides. Since the standing start allows a full first stride, the average beginner masters this correct approach without difficulty. Some may require two or three attempts. Some may come too close to the hurdle rather than have difficulty reaching it. For those experiencing difficulty, a 14-yard approach may be used until the correct approach is mastered.

THE CROUCH START

A crouch start approach is next introduced. Starting blocks, spaced and positioned the same as for sprinting, are used and all fundamentals of a correct sprint start are employed. In order to reach the takeoff mark for the first hurdle in eight strides, the hurdler must place his takeoff foot in the front block. Arm action must be vigorous. The distance of the first step out of the blocks is gradually shortened or lengthened to bring the hurdler to his takeoff mark in good hurdling position.

STRIDES BETWEEN HURDLES

Following a mastery of the 8-stride approach, the hurdler is ready to try the 3-stride action between hurdles. Two hurdles only are used for this attempt. If the 8-stride approach to the first hurdle is correct, most beginners have no difficulty accomplishing the 3-stride action between hurdles. For those having difficulty, the following fundamentals should be checked: (a) cutting down too close coming off the first hurdle, (b) takeoff too far from first hurdle, (c) poor running form between hurdles. If difficulty still persists, the distance between hurdles may be reduced to nine yards until coordination and timing are developed.

RAISING THE HURDLES

The final step in teaching the beginner is gradually to raise the height of the hurdle to 3 feet and then to 3′3″ for the high school athlete (3′6″ for the college athlete). The number of hurdles is increased until a full flight is used.

THE HIGH HURDLES

Advanced hurdling technique is largely a matter of improved speed and hurdle clearance. A mechanically correct start is an important first step. All fundamentals previously discussed apply. Some unusually tall or fast hurdlers have to reduce their first stride out of the blocks to avoid coming too close to the first hurdle. An experienced hurdler, with the assistance of his coach, is capable of making this adjustment. While most hurdlers use 8 strides to the first hurdle, there are those especially tall athletes who can cover the distance in seven. This is an advantage if the hurdler's seven-stride approach brings him to the first hurdle in position for efficient clearance. A hurdler using a seven-stride approach must place his *takeoff* foot in the rear block at the start. A 14.0-second high hurdler should reach the top of the first hurdle in 2.1 to 2.3 seconds. If this time

a. The takeoff. Lead leg flexed. Low body angle. Body square with hurdle. Eyes on hurdle top.

b. The drive into the hurdle. Chest down over lead leg. Opposite arm and leg well co-ordinated. Takeoff foot on ground adds force to momentum.

is slower he should concentrate on improving his start. The *first* and *last* hurdles are the most important in running a successful high hurdle race.

THE TAKEOFF

Correct hurdle clearance is affected by a proper takeoff. Smaller and shorter men are inclined to use a "jump" style. Because of lack of height, such an athlete finds it necessary to leave the track in a fairly erect position. His first action is upward as in broad jumping. Then, he delays forward and downward recovery until he reaches sufficient height for proper clearance.

A tall hurdler usually gets his best results by taking off at a much lower angle (the "step" style). He uses a distinct body dip that drives his body *across* rather than over the hurdle. His longer legs and greater height enable him to land closer to the hurdle. Hurdlers of medium height combine the action of the "jump" and "step" styles.

Regardless of style used, a delayed trailing leg action is essential to mechanically correct layout position. It requires concentration, timing, and practice. The inclination of the beginner is to bring his trailing leg up to the side immediately upon takeoff. When combined with a takeoff that is too close to the hurdle, such a fault results in a "float" or "jump" action. It cuts down on forward drive and momentum. In correct delayed action the trailing leg stays in contact with the track as the drive across the hurdle starts; this adds force to the hurdler's momentum. However, as the shifting downward drive of the pelvic girdle forces it to do so it comes through *fast.* As it leaves the track there is a vigorous pull from the hip. The knee comes through higher than the foot. A revolving reach out of the bent trailing leg is employed. This is a critical point in successful high hurdling. There have been few, if any, 13.6-second high hurdlers with a slow pull-through of the trailing leg.

The optimum takeoff distance is the one that best permits the athlete to clear the hurdle with a balanced forward driving action. It may vary from 6′10″ to 7′6″ from the hurdle. The landing coming off the hurdle may vary from 3′10″ to 4′6″. Both vary with the hurdler's height. The common fault is to take off too close to the hurdle.

The hurdler's position at the time of the takeoff must be squarely in front of the hurdle. Eyes focus on its top. As the drive starts, the lead leg is flexed just as it would be in a normal stride. It should not be straightened. The bent lead leg permits the athlete to bring his chest down over his knee, thus assisting in the dip and layout. This leg must remain in proper alignment. No deviation in correct sprint form should result from this action. Once the drive across the hurdle starts, the athlete's eyes focus on the *top* of the next hurdle.

Arm action, as the layout starts, is similar to that employed in sprinting. Opposite arm and leg work together. This action helps preserve alignment and balance. Since the stride over the hurdle is harder and longer than normal, the compensating action is more extreme.

c. The layout. Upper body bent well forward. Trailing leg bent in right-angle position. Knee higher than foot. Arm action straight forward.

d. The recovery. Good lead snapdown. Knee of trailing leg well lifted. Delayed pull of balancing arm starts out and down.

e. Fast trailing leg brought around directly in front of hurdler. Note vigorous and well-coordinated arm action as stride for next hurdle starts. Body angle good.

THE LAYOUT

There are four factors which determine speed, coordination, and balance across the hurdle.

(1) Momentum or drive.

(2) Fast trailing leg pull-through.

(3) Pull of the balancing arm outward and downward toward the track.

(4) Fast front leg snap-down.

The hurdler's position over the hurdle is an elongated dip. The upper body bends well forward at the waist. The compensating arm is thrust forward and parallel to the lead leg. Its reaching action helps force the athlete's upper body down into its well-aligned layout posture.

The trailing leg deviates momentarily from normal sprinting form. In its bent position, at the peak of the layout, the knee is higher than the foot. However, the foot should be well lifted with toe pointing outward, at an approximate right angle to the lower leg, and parallel with the track. If the hurdler allows the ankle of the trailing leg to drop too far below the knee, he has failed to emphasize the foot lift or is prevented from making it because of inadequate body lean. If his form is correct, the level of his head in the layout position varies only slightly from its level during a regular sprint stride.

VELOCITY

Hurdling velocity is best defined as the time it takes an athlete to drive across a hurdle from point of takeoff to time of landing. With correct form this time is approximately $\frac{1}{5}$ second. For a full flight of high hurdles it would equal 2.0 seconds. Thus, an athlete who can run 120 yards in 12.0 seconds, and clear the hurdles correctly, should run the full flight in 14.0 seconds. Observation reveals that good hurdlers are slower in their clearance time than is generally believed.

The hurdler and his coach should not set up optimum clearance time without careful consideration of the individual. A hurdler who does not run well on the flat may run a good race because he drives well over the barriers and maintains a good average speed. A man who is not exceptionally fast between hurdles may run a fast flight because his clearance velocity is high. A man with slow clearance time may make it up by running faster between hurdles.

To ensure a fast clearance velocity, the hurdler must take off at a very low angle, drive the compensating arm vigorously forward, lead with his head, and dip sharply at the waist. He must never become so step-conscious that he does not drive off the ground and maintain a high velocity across the hurdle.

THE RECOVERY

In his recovery action, the hurdler's lead foot hits the track at a point about four feet from the hurdle. This cut down, along with the extreme body lean, permits him to quickly resume his normal running action. Failure to do so results in a braking action and unfavorable body angle.

The trailing leg, which comes through late but *fast* is brought around directly in front of the body. In principle, the timing of this action represents a sprint stride. As the lead leg cuts down, the trailing leg comes through for balance as in running. One leg is forward, the other back. If the trailing leg is hurried, both are forward at the same time. This is contrary to correct running mechanics and should be avoided. The first stride off the hurdle is not exaggerated.

The action of the compensating arm which was thrust forward vigorously with the lead leg in the layout, is of vital importance in recovery. As it comes into position to aid the athlete in his first stride off the hurdle, *it should be delayed as long as possible* and then cut *out* and *down* toward the track. A twisting action of the body however should be avoided. If timed correctly, this entire action is smooth and balanced. There is no wobbling or lost motion as the hurdler continues his approach to the next hurdle.

ACTION BETWEEN HURDLES

Three even strides are taken between the high hurdles. In mechanics, they should be as close to correct sprinting form as possible. All fundamentals are stressed. Arm action is vigorous. Eyes are forward and on the next hurdle. Gravitational line of weight falls through the supporting foot throughout. The hurdler must not allow his body to lean back lest he find himself in poor takeoff position at the next hurdle. Each hurdle must be approached squarely.

THE FINISH

The finish of a high hurdle race is largely a matter of balance and quick recovery off the last hurdle. Action is similar to that of the sprinter.

The distance from the last hurdle to the finish is short. Many races are won or lost at this point. There must be no letdown or wobbling. The hurdler's 3-stride tempo must be quickly accelerated into maximum sprinting effort. Body alignment and progression must be kept straight forward. Arm action is vigorous. The chest is thrust forward. Eyes are on the tape as the athlete drives through and beyond it. A finish technique for this part of the race can be developed. It should be included and practiced regularly as part of the hurdler's training.

THE LOW HURDLES

Low hurdling today is exclusively a high school event. The distance is 180 yards. Eight 2′6″ barriers, spaced at 20-yard intervals, must be cleared.

The technique of low hurdling is essentially a modification of an elongated sprinting stride. Clearance is not as exacting as in high hurdling. However, the start is the same, and all fundamentals apply. The 20-yard distance to the first hurdle is covered in ten running strides. Some smaller athletes use more. Others lead with alternating legs as each hurdle is cleared. Most coaches agree that an athlete who cannot take ten strides to the first hurdle, and seven between, should be changed to another event.

The hurdler's action out of the blocks and to the first hurdle must be at full sprinting effort. His stride must be consistent. He must concentrate his attention and effort on being first to reach the hurdle, rather than on the number of strides he takes. Action across the hurdle emphasizes efficiency of body alignment and balance. Very little, if any, deviation in timing or body elevation is required. An average takeoff of 7½ feet in front of the hurdle and a landing point of 4½ feet behind the hurdle are used. Body dip is not pronounced. A cut down of the lead leg is not emphasized. The horizontal position of the trailing leg and its elevation is not as essential as in high hurdling. Arm action between hurdles is vigorous. At the point of takeoff, the hurdler's shoulders are parallel with the top of the hurdle. In case of emergency, he should be prepared to lead with either his left or right foot.

The longer distance from the last hurdle to the finish makes this an important part of the low hurdle race. With added effort and sprinting ability, the hurdler who is behind can improve his position. Likewise, the one leading can be overtaken. It is therefore essential that recovery and balance off the last hurdle be prompt and efficient and that full sprinting effort be exerted in the drive for the tape.

THE INTERMEDIATE HURDLES

The intermediate hurdle races are exclusively collegiate, AAU, and Olympic events. The standard distance is 400 meters or 440 yards, and the height of the barriers is three feet.

The intermediate hurdle races, regardless of distance, favor a tall, strong athlete. A strong hurdler who has been trained for the "440" usually makes a better candidate than the quarter-miler without hurdling ability. The race is a demanding one. It requires endurance and strength. A knowledge of pace is essential. It should be practiced with the athlete running at his full, but relaxed, striding effort.

The number of strides taken to the first hurdle varies with the individual. Some take 21, others require 22 or 23. A stride can be added or cut by changing feet in the blocks. As a guide, it is well to adjust the number to the most efficient and consistent pace of the individual hurdler rather than to a set pattern.

The development of composition (artificial surface) tracks has had a significant effect upon the stride pattern in the intermediate hurdles. The "bounce" yielded by the consistently fast and uniform surface of such tracks has made it possible for some athletes to cover the distance between hurdles in as few as 13 strides.

Traditionally, most good intermediate hurdlers have attempted to establish an even stride pattern between hurdles, usually 15, and to continue it throughout the race. In establishing a world record, a recent Olympic champion covered the first six hurdles in 13 strides and the remaining four in 15. This pattern follows somewhat the timing of a flat 400-meter dash—a strong fast start, a full but relaxed sprint stride, and a hard drive at the finish.

Other than the slight variation required in adjusting to the added height, the basic technique of intermediate hurdling is essentially the same as that of low hurdling. Good body balance, as each hurdle is cleared, is essential.

Action of the lead leg starts with a knee lift. The knee is slightly bent as it crosses the hurdle. The opposite arm is swung straight forward, but it should not extend across the hurdler's chest since this results in a rotary motion of the shoulders. Body angle in the drive across the hurdle is approximately 45 degrees. The exaggerated dip employed in high hurdling is not used, and the form over the hurdle should approximate the powerful stride used between hurdles.

Trailing leg action in the intermediate hurdles is hurried more than in high hurdling. Balancing arm action is delayed longer and is smoother.

On the 7th, 8th, 9th, and 10th hurdles, the followthrough and reach of the trailing leg should be emphasized. It assists the hurdler in maintaining his stride as fatigue increases.

Ideally, action between the hurdles approximates that of the athlete running a flat 400-meter race. All fundamentals of body mechanics, relaxation, and smoothness of stride prevail. The ability to run the full distance without a break in even strides is a distinct advantage. Those who cannot do so must learn to make adjustment in the number from 15 to 17 without cutting down appreciably in speed. This is often necessary at the 7th, 8th, or 9th hurdle. In case of emergency the ability to lead reasonably well with either foot forward is a must.

The finish of the 400-meter hurdle race is similar to that of the 400-meter run. All fundamentals of relaxation and correct body mechanics apply. Sprinting ability is an asset as in all other races.

TRAINING

The hurdler's training aims to develop speed, endurance, flexibility, and efficient mechanical technique. The kind and amount is adjusted to the physical capacity and needs of the individual. The start is slow, the build-up gradual. An overload of work is necessary for the hurdler to be in maximum condition.

Each day's training is preceded by a warm-up jog and special exercises designed for hurdling. "Side straddling" precedes full-form hurdling. An exercise in which the athlete uses five quick steps between the hurdles is frequently used to develop quickness of action and body dip. Assuming his form is correct, the more times a hurdler goes over the hurdles, the better hurdler he becomes.

Daily training is divided between high and either intermediate or low hurdling. Since high hurdling requires a more refined skill, a majority of the day's practice is devoted to it. As in training for other events, the hurdler should aim to strengthen his weaknesses. Perfection of form is stressed throughout.

A full flight of hurdles, at each height to be run, should be repeated several times prior to the day of competition. The hurdler should be thoroughly acquainted with the demands of the event. The number of hurdles to be cleared increases as the season progresses until a full flight is mastered.

In practice exercises it is well to run two or three hurdlers side by side. A familiarity with competitive conditions is thus established.

All hurdle races are run in lanes. The 120-yard high hurdles are run on a straightaway. The 180-yard low hurdles (high school) may be

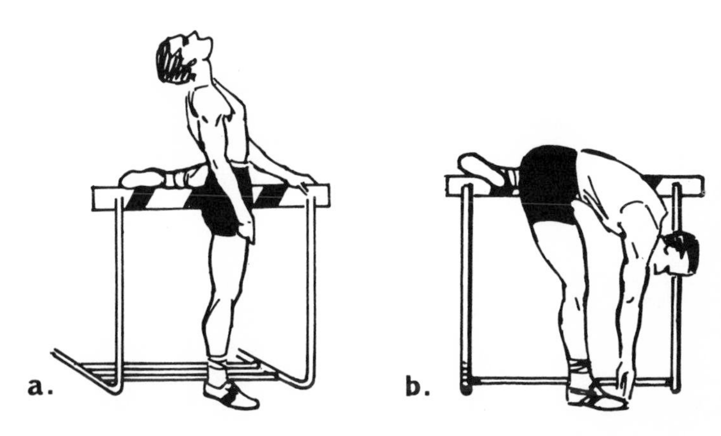

Rear Leg Exercise: From an upright position, (a) bend upper body forward and downward to position (b). Touch both hands on the ground. Alternate legs. Set hurdle at various heights.

run on a straightaway, or from a staggered start, coming off, or going around, one turn. The 400-meter and 440-yard hurdles are started from staggered lines and run around two turns of the track. In the 400-meter and 440-yard hurdle races, those starting in the inside lanes (1, 2, and 3) have an advantage since they can judge their pace by the hurdlers in front of them. Until the final straightaway is reached, those in the outside lanes must depend upon a judgment of pace gained largely through experience. For this reason all intermediate hurdlers should practice starting from both inside and outside lane positions and include pace work as part of their regular training.

Hurdlers are subject to bruised and cut knees, ankles, and heels from hitting hurdles during practice. Hurdlers who hit their knees on the hurdle are probably not employing correct technique. Heel bruises come from raising the body too soon coming off the hurdle. Floating over the hurdle or cutting the balance arm too soon, and/or fast, are other faults that cause this injury. The ankle of the trailing leg is bruised by (a) dropping the toe on the pull-through, (b) carrying the knee too high, and (c) not pulling correctly from the hip.

Until such faults can be corrected, bruised knees may be prevented by using a practice hurdle with sponge rubber taped neatly over the top of the cross piece. Sponge rubber may also be taped directly over an injured spot on the body. Pads and heel cups may be used in shoes as an early season preventive measure. When indoor training requires running on boards or other hard surfaces, sponge rubber, or other similar thin mats, may be used as a landing area. Hydrotherapy, and as a final

Lead Leg Exercise: The takeoff foot is on the ground. Lead foot is on hurdle. Dip upper body forward extending both arms. Return to upright position. Alternate legs.

resort, rest, may be necessary as a treatment for especially sensitive heel bruises.

All skin abrasions should be thoroughly cleaned, treated with appropriate medication, and covered with gauze. A hurdler who is not physically sound will not do his best in practice or competition and it is not advisable to force him into either. A physically sound alternate man will many times perform better than an injured champion.

The hurdler's daily and weekly training schedule is governed by principles previously considered. Adjusted to individual differences, it includes:

(a) Adequate amounts of stretching and bending exercises.
(b) Starting practice, driving over two and three hurdles.
(c) Practice of full technique over five and seven hurdles.
(d) Sprinting distances of 50 to 75 yards for speed.
(e) Interval running at distances of 150, 220, and 300 yards.
(f) Low and intermediate hurdle practice follows high hurdling. Practice over three, four, five, and six hurdles at full flight pace several times per week. Always limit this part of practice to not more than seven hurdles.
(g) In each daily practice session sustain effort until fatigue interferes with mechanical efficiency. Rest at least one day before competition and more if a sluggish condition at end of season warrants it.

COMPETITION

(1) All suggestions for sprinters apply.
(2) Warm up slowly and thoroughly. On cold days keep warm-up

clothes on until race starts. Take at least three to five high hurdles at full effort three times before race starts.

(3) Always try to beat opponent to first hurdle.

(4) Never look to the side during a race. Eyes are always ahead and on top of next hurdle.

(5) Never stop or give up in a race because of early position or hitting a hurdle.

(6) Use arms vigorously throughout the race.

(7) Drive hard off the last hurdle. Many races are won from this point to finish line.

(8) Do not let down in preliminary or semifinal heats, regardless of position.

(9) In running hurdles around a turn, start and run on inside of lane.

Back Leg Pull-Through Exercise: *Execute with balanced arm cut.*

10
The Shot Put

The shot put is probably the most standardized and popular weight event on the American track and field program. It is included in the official schedule of events at all levels of competition. It is thrown by men and women. In junior high school meets, an 8-pound shot is used. In high school competition the shot weighs 12 pounds. In collegiate and Olympic competition the weight is 16 pounds.

The Official Track and Field Rules require that the shot be delivered from a circle with a diameter of seven feet. Its circumference is marked with a metal, wood, or plastic band which rises not more than ¾-inch above the level of the circle. Today, most circles have a concrete or black-top surface. A concrete surface with $1/64$-inch roughness is recommended. On such a circle, a painted line two inches wide is substituted for the band.

A white toe-board in the shape of an arc, so the inner edge coincides with the inner edge of the circle, is fixed in the front of the circle. The arc is 4 feet long along the inside surface; it is 4 inches high and 4½ inches wide.

Radial lines 2 inches wide extend from the center of the circle through the extremities of the stop board. They continue out to form an area into which legal puts must be made. The inner edges of these lines bound the sector.

The rules are explicit in requiring that the shot be put from the shoulder and not thrown. The competitor may not allow it to pass behind or below his shoulder during an attempt. He may use only one hand and is not permitted to have any mechanical device or harness attached to the hand or arm.

The area in which the shot lands should be level. Its surface should be constructed with material that is easy to groom and shows sharply the mark at which the shot lights. It should be located in an area that is safe but still visible to seated spectators. The shot put is a spectacular event. It is unfortunate that traditionally it has not been staged in an area where it can be afforded more recognition. If properly supervised and planned, both indoor and outdoor track meets can provide such staging. A well-marked landing area and competent public address announcing will do much to inform interested spectators and to motivate those participating in the event.

The dramatic improvement in shot putting achievement in recent years has not been accidental. Improvement has resulted not only from the superior physical qualities of those few who have achieved greatness but also from mechanical analysis, motivation, and discipline. Modern shot putting is scientific. Through diligent study and practice the modern athlete can master the most mechanically efficient method of using his superior physique in applying force to a weight within a given space. Motivated by competition, further scientific study, and work, he will continue to break records.

SOMATOTYPE

The shot put is an event for big men. Investigation reveals that a height of 6′2″ to 6′5″ and weight of 220 to 245 pounds have characterized most national and Olympic champions. Also, most of them have been capable of running 100 yards in ten seconds or faster.

Bigness, in itself, does not ensure success in shot putting. It must be combined with *explosive* power. This unique attribute is easily detected by an experienced coach. In combination with the well-known "snap" of the putting shoulder, it is essential for the greatest mechanical efficiency in this event.

Strength is obviously necessary to control and project to more than seventy feet an object weighing 16 pounds. A large hand and strong fingers and wrist are recognized assets. The quickness of action necessary in moving the shot from its start across the ring until its final release requires fine coordination and kinesthetic sense.

The time and study necessary for a mastery of technique requires patience and diligent practice. Without a temperament conducive to such diligence, few have achieved success.

The abilities to concentrate on competitive performance and to motivate oneself for what Parry O'Brien describes as the "supreme effort" are mental qualities that have characterized the great.

STARTING THE BEGINNER

Shot putting can be started early. By applying "mimetics" (imitation), an instructor can teach fundamentals of the balanced crouch, the shift across the circle, and delivery action in the early grades, to individuals or as part of basic physical education. The amount of related rhythm and coordination that can be developed at this time is surprising and satisfying to pupil and teacher. Indoor and outdoor practice, using an 8-pound shot, can be started at the junior high school level.

One of the most important requirements for starting an athlete in this sport is a safe place for him to practice. It is also essential that there be a number of shots for him to try, so that he can find through experimentation what is the best shape for him to work with. These two essentials for starting beginners are, in many instances, overlooked by even the experienced coach. Limited supervision is required only to provide a safe area for throwing. The learner should be required to "put" the shot rather than throw it. There are those strong youngsters who, at the junior high school level, are capable of throwing an 8-pound shot. Throwing is not only contrary to the rules but is dangerous to the growing and developing anatomical structure; it should be promptly discouraged.

Early coaching instruction, at all levels, should be simple. Handling the shot by "flipping" it from one hand to the other will cause it to fall naturally into a correct holding position. Once he has the "feel" of the shot, the beginner is ready to practice a stationary put from the front of the circle. He takes a comfortable stance at right angles to the direction of the throw and assumes a natural and balanced crouch position. Then he is instructed simply to drive the shot *straight* forward and upward, making sure that the delivery is executed with both feet on the ground. Height should not be emphasized. The reverse should not be taught or mentioned until, as a part of the putter's driving delivery, it becomes necessary as a balancing action.

The tendency at this time will be to lean forward at the waist. This can be corrected by advising the learner to keep his *right* elbow *behind* his right foot at the start of the delivery effort. Staying *behind* and *under* the shot is a fundamental that should be stressed from the outset.

Numerous repetitions of the stationary throw are executed. With detailed instruction kept at a minimum, the beginner familiarizes himself with the basic delivery action. He is then ready to move to the step-and-put action.

THE STEP AND PUT

In the step-and-put phase of learning, the athlete assumes an erect, but balanced and relaxed, stance at the rear of the circle. He faces the direction of the put. By this time, he will have gathered much from experience about the most effective position of holding the shot in his hand. Fundamentals, covered later as part of the complete form, may be checked at this point in accordance with the needs of each pupil. Assuming the put is to be made with the right hand, the left arm, with bent elbow pointing outward, is held in a relaxed position at approximately shoulder height.

To start his delivery, the athlete steps forward placing the heel of his right foot approximately at the center of the circle with toes pointing diagonally to the rear. Simultaneously, he drops into his delivery position. He places his left foot naturally at the front of the circle close to the center of the toe board. This completes the putting stance. He then makes the delivery as part of a continuous step-and-put action. All fundamentals of a stationary put apply as the delivery is completed.

Added explosive force is stressed as each repetition is executed. The "reverse," described in a later section, is eventually taught as a necessary and natural balancing and followthrough action.

After a reasonable mastery of the step-and-put technique, the beginner is ready to move to the complete form employing the shift across the circle. Refinements in advanced putting technique, which follow, are then introduced.

ADVANCED TECHNIQUE

Although there are individual variations in technique, modern championship shot putting follows a rather consistent pattern. A handhold which reduces tension and still permits a maximum of power at the terminal or muzzle end of the delivery is a matter of individual choice. Some good putters hold the shot well up on the base of the first three fingers of the putting hand. The thumb is to the front to assist in holding the shot as high as the strength of the fingers and wrist will permit. Others prefer to utilize wrist and forearm strength by holding the shot relatively low in the hand and finishing with the whole hand and wrist rather than fingertips.

The position of the shot at the neck is governed largely by the length of the arm bones and size of the arm muscles. Normally, it is held resting against the neck and clavicle approximately under the ear. The elbow of the putting arm points outward and downward. If the shot can be controlled, a holding position farther out over the shoulder tip will add greater terminal velocity and distance to the put. The free left arm, with elbow bent, is pointed outward in a relaxed position at shoulder height. The left hand is about at eye level. The shot must be held firmly in position as the shift across the circle is executed. *Controlled relaxation* is stressed throughout.

STARTING POSITION

A consistent starting position is essential. It must be relaxed but balanced. The distance of the travel (seven feet) and the time interval required for its execution (approximately 3/5 of a second) are short. Movement once started is difficult, if not impossible, to change. A nerve pattern is established. After a certain sequence of adjusting movements, the put starts more or less automatically. In each instance it follows the same pattern.

Preparatory to the put, the shot is held in the left hand. The right hand and wrist, free of the shot, remain loose and relaxed. The shot is transferred as the starting position is assumed. The initial stance is to the extreme rear of the circle. The athlete, in an erect, relaxed, but steady position, faces backward (opposite the direction of the put). The right foot points straight to the back. The left leg is extended slightly toward the front of the circle. The toe of the left foot touches the ground to assist in establishing a balanced position. Balance and timing at this point is critical. *The shift must not be rushed.* The athlete must have his body and the shot in complete control. His undivided attention must be on preparing himself physically and psychologically for the start of the shift which follows. At this time, some good putters concentrate on an object just below eye level at the back of the circle. They feel this helps in holding the upper part of the body back, keeping the head up, back relatively straight, and shoulders square while shifting across the circle.

THE SHIFT ACROSS THE CIRCLE

Four mechanical principles must be understood and applied in executing the shift across the circle.

(1) The longer the distance through which power can be applied to the shot, the farther it is likely to travel.

(2) Assuming correct form and balance, the greater the momentum generated and applied to the shot, the farther it is likely to travel.

(3) The speed and momentum gathered in the travel must be combined with the power and speed of the putting action.

(4) The body must move in the direction of the put and in a single vertical plane (the body maintains vertical alignment *and* it moves in an unswerving line to the front of the circle).

When in a complete state of readiness, the athlete starts the shift by lowering his head and shoulders to a point where his back is approximately horizontal with the ground. His eyes focus on a spot on the ground directly behind the circle. As he assumes this position, he bends his right knee to the point of greatest lifting power and rocks back until his weight is well over the ball of his right foot. The shot in this position is approximately 2 feet *beyond* the rear of the circle. Thus, the distance through which power can be applied to it in the shift across the circle is increased by this amount. In this position, he remains balanced and is ready to move forward.

As the shift action starts, the putter allows the weight of his body to start falling toward the toe board, adding momentum to his throw. This action is accompanied by a powerful drive forward from his right leg and foot. Simultaneously, the left leg is kicking forward in a direction

Initial Stance: *Athlete faces opposite direction of put. Position is erect, relaxed and steady. Note alignment of feet.*

The Balanced Crouch: *Head and shoulders lowered. Back approximately parallel to the ground. Weight over ball of right foot.*

Start of Shift Action: *Athlete's weight starts falling toward toe board. Drive from right foot and leg is powerful, while left is simultaneously kicked forward.*

slightly to the left center of the toe board. This shift of weight, combined with the drive and kick, results in a low fast glide across the circle. It moves the athlete straight forward, in a single vertical plane, to a point where his right foot is near the center of the circle pointing back at approximately a 45-degree angle. The left foot lands in a position against the toe board slightly to the left of center. The body position is now approximately the same as when the bent leg shift from the back of the circle was started. The putter's back is horizontal. His weight is well back over the right foot. The left is against the toe board. To avoid a loss of momentum, it is essential at this point that no "settling" or "cocking" of the shoulder occur. The force generated by the shift must flow continuously as the delivery action is started.

THE DELIVERY

The delivery consists of a sequence of movements from the foot to the tips of the fingers. Simply stated it includes a LIFT, PIVOT, and explosive PUSH. It starts as soon as the right foot is planted in the center of the circle. There should be no rotation or "cocking" of the right shoulder and arm at the end of the action. Such a fault decreases the velocity developed. The faster the shot travels as it leaves the fingers, the greater will be the horizontal distance. Any action which tends to diminish the terminal or muzzle velocity is detrimental to such results.

Left leg continues forward rapidly, while right leg is completing powerful drive.

The Lift: Athlete's power is completely under the shot as powerful delivery action starts. Right foot (at 45-degree angle near center of circle) pushes against ground. Left foot is against toe board slightly left of center. Right elbow is directly behind shot.

The Pivot: Note extension of right leg and pivot of right foot. Weight is driven up and over semi-straightened left leg.

As the shift is completed, the right foot lands first. It consequently starts pushing against the ground before the left. This permits a rock up onto the left foot. An extension of the right leg, combined with a forward pivot of the right foot, produces a lifting action. It drives the entire weight of the body up and over a partially flexed left leg. The powerful back and trunk muscles add force to the leg drive. This lift and explosive drive passes to the chest, to the shoulder girdle, and finally to the muscles of the arm. It culminates with the shot being delivered *upward* and *out*. The arm thrust is delayed until the trunk rotation is nearly completed. As it is made, the weight of the body is well over the semi-straight leg which straightens forcibly. It provides added impetus as the right arm and shoulder move into complete extension.

The right elbow must be directly behind the shot as the throwing arm is extended. The left elbow is brought back and down rather forcibly. A wrist snap and finger flip at the end adds final velocity and distance to the put.

The Final Delivery: Explosive action is upward and out. Note trunk rotation, straight left leg, and final wrist flip.

The Reverse: Reverse of feet keeps athlete in balance as he follows shot out over toe board.

The delivery is executed with both feet on the ground. The right foot should not leave the ground before the shot leaves the fingertips. Otherwise maximum driving force will be lost.

THE REVERSE

To complete his delivery, the putter reverses his feet. The right replaces the left at the front of the circle as he reaches out over the toe board. The left leaves the ground a split second later than the right and swings backward and downward. This action results from the explosive force of the delivery. It is a balancing action which keeps the athlete from fouling after the shot in released. Distance is gained, not by reversing, but by following the shot over the toe board so far that it is necessary to reverse to remain in the circle.

Mechanical Principles Applied to the Release

(1) It is generally agreed that the shot should be released at an angle of approximately 40 to 45 degrees from the level ground.

(2) The optimum angle depends upon terminal velocity. The greater the terminal velocity, the nearer the angle of release should approach 41 degrees.

(3) The better putter should throw at a slightly greater angle than the one of average or lesser ability.

(4) Other factors being constant, experimental evidence indicates that the height of the release is directly proportional to the horizontal distance.

(5) A man 6 feet 6 inches tall who releases the shot at approximately 7 feet, will have a slight advantage over the shorter man who releases it at a height of 6 feet 6 inches.

The distance that a shot travels depends upon *both* its *horizontal speed* and the time it remains in flight ($Ht = R$).

From a purely mechanical standpoint, 45° is the optimum angle of launch. However, mechanically it is advantageous to launch it at a somewhat smaller angle since the value of the gain in velocity imparted outweighs the decrease in time of flight.

Greatest terminal velocity depends upon the angle of launch.

TRAINING

A shot putter learns to put the shot by putting it, and the danger of overwork is remote. Practice from the start emphasizes *correct* skill. Improvement does not result from a repetition of errors. Each practice period should be a learning experience in which the athlete continually analyzes his technique.

The shot putter's training program aims to develop those qualities necessary for the most efficient execution of the skill. Most good putters today train the year around. If not engaged in fall sports, they devote this season to running, sprinting, general body development, weight training, and a study and practice of technique. Similar training continues indoors throughout the winter months. If an indoor practice surface does not permit throwing a regular outdoor shot, an indoor one is used. The athlete's weight training program at this time is at its peak. In all instances it should include those exercises and methods designed specifically for shot put development.

If a year-round training program is not followed, the athlete's early spring practice should start slowly. Hard throwing should be delayed until such time as those muscles involved in putting have been strengthened and conditioned. In spite of how good he feels, the athlete should guard against "throwing his arm out" before it has been prepared for such maximum effort.

Practice during the regular season must be regular and intense. It should be well planned and purposeful. In addition to a practice of technique, it should include exercises for the development of strength

Olympic champion Ron Matson demonstrates the combined sequence of shot-putting technique.

As he prepares to start his shift across the circle, Matson focuses his eyes to the rear of the circle and tilts his right shoulder.

As he goes into a balanced crouch, his left arm, held fairly straight and relaxed, moves to a position across his chest to increase the range of movement in initiating his drive across the circle.

As he starts his shift, Matson pushes off the toes of his right foot, exerting a powerful forward drive from his bent right leg. At this time there is a wide spread between his right and left leg, which has been extended forward to add momentum to his shift. The line from his left shoulder to his left foot, through his hip, is nearly straight.

As Matson completes his shift, he lands in the center of the circle on his right foot which points back at an angle of 45 degrees. His left foot makes contact slightly to the left of the center of the circle immediately after his right. There is a straight line between his shoulders and the shot, which has traveled in a level plane throughout the shift and is directly over his right elbow.

In frame 10, Matson starts his powerful delivery with a pivot of his right foot and a pushing, lifting extension of his right leg and hip. His hips and shoulders are in an "open" position facing the toe board. His chin is up and his head and eyes are focusing on the desired release angle.

During his final drive, Matson has both feet on the ground and his left leg is extended giving added vertical lift to the shot. He releases the shot at an angle of approximately 41 degrees, with a combined medial rotation, extension, and pronation of his hand, giving the shot an inside-out action.

The power of his delivery forces Matson into his reverse which finds him in a fairly erect position with a straightened right leg. His left leg swings to the rear to help maintain balance.

and should continue some limited weight training. Running and sprinting will help to develop endurance and speed. Developmental exercises should be taken at the *end* of the practice period rather than before. Shot putting precedes discus throwing.

Most good putters work hard four days of the week. Training is usually the heaviest on Tuesday and Thursday. Most putters rest or take only light work on Friday.

The *daily* and *weekly* practice pattern should be established by the individual. From experience, he should determine the one which gives him the best personal results. The following daily sequence is suggested:

(1) *Warm-up.* Jogging. Stretching and bending exercises involving muscle groups used in putting. Wind-sprints.

(2) *Putting from front of circle.* This is an important part of each practice period. It is used to perfect the delivery. It can be practiced with and without the shot. With his feet spaced in the delivery position, the putter drops back to a low crouch. His stance is *long.* He executes the delivery without a reverse. The emphasis is on *lifting, pivoting* the right foot, and *pushing* the shot straight forward with the right foot on the ground. This exercise may be followed by the step-and-put. The putter should avoid *fouling* in the exercises. Once established, fouling is a habit difficult to control in competition.

(3) *Practice of the shift across the circle.* (Core of daily practice.) Emphasize balance and control in starting position at rear of circle. Gradually increase speed to maximum at end of delivery. Coordination, combined with speed across the circle, is difficult. Speed should be increased only as the putter is capable of keeping it under control. Too fast a start across the circle frequently ends in a poor put.

Since speed across the circle is one of the essential requirements of successful shot putting, the athlete should spend a great deal of time on this exercise. As long as technique is correct, maximum-effort putting should not be discouraged. This phase of practice may be continued until the putter feels that fatigue is interrupting reasonably efficient execution.

(4) *Conditioning.* Repeat sprints of 50 to 75 yards. Runs of 220 yards. Weight training (Monday and Wednesday only).

WEIGHT TRAINING APPLIED TO SHOT PUTTING

Weight training, including various forms of resistive exercises with and without the use of weights, has become an accepted part of conditioning for the modern shot putter. It should be noted, however, that such training is a means to developing strength for shot putting and not an end in itself. The objective is not to see how much weight can be lifted. *Fast power* is needed by a shot putter; therefore he uses lighter weights. Exercises aim not only to develop strength, but also to decrease the length of time necessary to apply a given force.

Power is the force that creates motion. The faster a given force can be applied, the greater will be the shot's acceleration and distance of travel. All exercises should be done with weights light enough to ensure quick and explosive action. As a guide for beginners, some recommend a weight one-third as heavy as the athlete. This, however, should be determined by the individual and the results he obtains.

PROCEDURE

General instructions:

(1) Be thoroughly warmed up before lifting.

(2) Know and use the correct grip for each exercise.

(3) Keep center of gravity and weight directly over both feet.

(4) Keep back straight for the greatest utilization of strength.

(5) Use a variety of exercises that develop arms, legs, fingers, and abdominal muscles.

(6) Rest between sets of exercises.

Equipment. Exercises are performed with two kinds of equipment:

(1) Barbell—Long bar (4 ft.) with metal plates of proper weight attached to each end by means of an adjustable collar.

(2) Dumbbell—Short bar (1 ft.) with small plates of proper weight attached to each end by means of an adjustable collar.

Amount of weight. Start with barbell approximately one-third of athlete's weight (i.e. athlete who weights 180 pounds would start with barbell weighing 60 pounds).

Number of repetitions. Start with "sets" of seven and increase as condition improves. A "set" consists of seven continuous repetitions of the same exercise.

Rest interval between "sets"—2 to 3 minutes.

Recommended number of "sets" per exercise—3.

Typical exercise pattern:

(1) Execute an Extension-press 7 times. (Set 1.)

(2) Rest 2 to 3 minutes.

(3) Repeat 7 Extension-presses. (Set 2.)

(4) Rest 2 to 3 minutes.

(5) Repeat 7 Extension-presses. (Set 3.)

Rest 2 to 3 minutes—select a new exercise and repeat 3-set procedure.

EXERCISES

(1) *For Arms:*

Extension press—Standing position.

Two-arm snatch.

Prone press—Use bench.

Barbell pull-over—Prone position.

With dumbbell (20–30–40 pounds).

One-arm military press.

One-arm dead lifts.

One-arm curls.

(2) *For Legs:*

Half knee bends.

Squat jumps—Barbell on shoulders.

Straddle jumps—Barbell on shoulders.

Heel raiser (calf muscles)—Barbell on shoulders. As alternate exercise, set a 2- by 4-inch plank on the floor on its wide side, and stand on it (weight on balls of feet and heels hanging off the back).

(3) *For Abdominal Muscles:*

Sit-ups with plate on chest.

Trunk bending—Barbell on shoulders.

(4) *For Fingers and Hands:*

Push-offs from wall.

Finger push-ups off floor.

Pulley weight roll-ups.

COMPETITION

(1) Check all equipment the day before. Do not depend upon others to transport shot to and from competition.

(2) Weigh shot regularly to make sure it meets approved regulations.

(3) Know material with which ring surface is constructed and wear appropriate shoes.

(4) Arrive well in advance of starting time of event. Be thoroughly familiar with environment of putting area and ring surface.

(5) Warm up slowly and thoroughly. Know warm-up capacity and needs. Aim to make each throw, including the first, the best.

(6) Conserve energy between throws, but be warmed up and ready to put when turn is called.

(7) Know rules of event and comply with them at all times. (See Official Track and Field Rules.)

(8) An athlete should throw better in competition than in practice. When it comes to competition, the mental approach is the key to success.

11
The Discus Throw

The historical significance of discus throwing is well known. The immortal posture of the discus thrower, glorified by artist and poet since the time of Homer, not only symbolizes an excellence of athletic prowess but also represents a classic prototype of throwing technique. As it has evolved, the object of the throw is to attain the greatest distance within the limits of an 8-foot 2½-inch circle. The weight of a college discus is 4 pounds 6½ ounces; its diameter, 8⅝ inches. A discus weighing 3 pounds 9 ounces with a diameter of 8¼ inches is used by the high school thrower. Present-day rules require that the discus be thrown within a 60-degree sector. Discus throwing has come a long way since the time of the Greeks with their throw from a stationary position. Today's well-coordinated one and three-quarter turn probably accounts for much of the improvement over Martin Sheridan's early world record of 133 feet 6 inches established in 1900. The world's record for this event of 224 feet 4¾ inches indicates that man's achievement in the discus throw event deserves as much praise as the achievements in other field events.

SOMATOTYPE

There are three types of discus throwers: (1) the *power* type, (2) the *speed* type, and (3) the combined *speed* and *power* type. Of the three types the advantage lies with the *power-speed* type.

The characteristics of successful discus throwers can be deceiving. The taller, stronger athlete usually makes the better performer. While few have been champions, however, some smaller men with strength, controlled speed, and a fine sense of timing have made excellent throwers.

Because of the size of the discus, large hands are an asset. As the arm serves as the radius of the arc through which the discus moves, long arms are also a decided advantage.

Time, patience, and practice are required to perfect the timing of the turn and throw. An athlete whose temperament is conducive to such diligence may, in the long run, surpass his stronger but less conscientious teammate. A big but lazy athlete, regardless of talent, does not generally make a good discus thrower. Discus throwing requires work and lots of it. Those who are willing to work, even though they lack the ideal physical qualifications, may be surprised at the extent of their achievement.

STARTING THE BEGINNER

There probably is no one best method of starting a beginning discus thrower. For safety and good footing, a level practice area, removed from the regular path of traffic, should be selected.

For most, the handling of a discus is an entirely new experience. Its size, shape, and weight make it a projectile that is not easily or naturally controlled. The first step then is to get the "feel" of the new implement. This is simply a matter of repeated handling and easy throwing.

Much can be learned about a discus by "rolling" it much as one would a wheel. Even experienced throwers find this an effective early season exercise. To get the most efficient roll, the discus must be released from the inside front of the hand. The index finger plays a prominent role. In rolling the discus, the feel of the release is similar to that of the more horizontal spinning release used in regular discus throwing. Two or more throwers can practice this skill by rolling the discus from one to the other. When longer throwing starts, a roll can be used as a means of retrieving the discus.

After mastering the roll, the beginner will soon be experimenting with the regular horizontal release. From trial and error, he will learn much about controlling the discus, and he will observe its action in flight. A good deal of unnecessary coaching effort is expended in instructing the beginner in the handhold and the theoretical advantage of one type over another. As in developing other skills, the athlete learns by *doing*. Individual variations are discovered and found effective as the thrower becomes more experienced. As Frank Ryan of Yale University puts it, "An effective handhold is more a result of orientation than of direct coaching."

THE GRIP

There are two styles of discus handholds: (1) Closed finger: index and middle fingers together with most of the pressure applied to these two fingers and (2) Talon: full finger spread with pressure evenly distributed on all fingers.

The thrower's hand is placed palm down and flat on the discus. The first joints of the first three fingers are hooked over the edge of the discus. The discus is gripped with the fingers slightly toward the rear half. The wrist is cocked toward the rear of the discus to permit good wrist snap when throwing. The thumb and small finger are held in a comfortable position. These fingers determine the plane of the discus in flight.

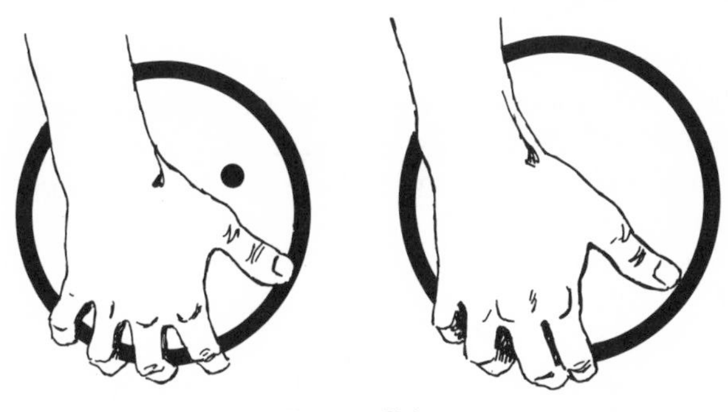

Discus Grips

The Talon Grip *The Closed Finger Grip*

Choice of handhold is an individual matter. The thrower should select the one which "feels" the best to him, gives him the best control, and brings the most effective results with his individual style.

THE STATIONARY THROW

After getting the "feel" of the discus, the beginner is ready to practice the delivery from a stationary stance. This represents the body's throwing position at the completion of the turn. It may be practiced from the front of, or outside, the circle. No discus is used at the start. A twisting, *torque* action is stressed.

In the stationary throw, the athlete assumes a balanced crouch, a position sometimes referred to as the "boxer's crouch." This analogy is significant. It suggests a stance from which the thrower can move quickly and rhythmically in any direction. His body is in complete balance and control, and his knees are slightly bent to assist in a maximum thrust of the hips. His feet, comfortably spread, are about 36 inches apart. The right points slightly backward, the left in the direction of the throw.

From this position the thrower first twists his hips from left to right in a full pivoting action. The upper body and arms swing loosely and freely. In the full swing to the right, the weight is shifted almost entirely to the right foot. The eyes at this point are to the rear. As the forward swing starts, the thrower straightens his left leg. He feels the "recoil" or "bounce" action resulting from the natural reaction of the antagonistic muscles of the hip and legs which have been stretched by the twisting of the body. Timed with the forward swing of the left shoulder, the "recoil" starts the "drag" action of the right arm. The action of the right hip and shoulder along with the dragging of the right arm adds momentum to the throw.

After practicing the twisting hip pivot, the beginner is ready to try the same action with the discus. At first, it will be awkward. Absence of centrifugal force will make the discus difficult to hold. For control, the thrower may have to steady it with his left hand. Delivery from the twisting position will be new and will probably be straight out from his shoulder. The discus in flight will wobble. These are natural problems for the beginner.

Lengthy explanations of the details of the complete form should be delayed until the thrower has familiarized himself with the action of throwing. The *reverse*, however, involves an important fundamental of weight throwing which should be understood at the outset by pupil and teacher. Mechanical analysis reveals that it is actually a *balancing* action. It unquestionably encourages and contributes to an effective follow-through. The problem is one of *timing*. If he starts it too soon, the thrower loses much of the force he should derive from contact with the ground. If he starts it too late, he is likely to stop or "settle" in his throwing stance, losing valuable momentum he had gained by his turn.

In essence, the discus is delivered from *both* feet. Actually, the momentum obtained from the body drive, which is estimated to result in approximately 100 to 150 feet of the thrower's distance, starts with the *right* foot. The left leg simultaneously braces against this drive. As the throwing action continues, the body weight shifts *up and over* the toes of the *left* foot. The momentum of the vigorous upward action and followthrough *forces* the thrower into a reversal of his feet to maintain balance.

Difference of opinion exists as to when the reverse should be taught. In opposition to traditional teaching, some coaches believe that it should be taught *early*. They contend that the reverse is a natural part of the throwing technique and serves to emphasize rotary action. Consequently they teach it with the stationary throw as an element of the follow-through.

Others contend that there should be no reverse in throwing from a stationary position. They maintain that the body momentum at this stage of learning is not great enough to make a reverse necessary. Further, they feel that if an athlete learns the reverse before he masters the other aspects of throwing he is likely to be throwing with one or both feet off the ground. Both points of view have merit.

Another question that will probably come up early in the process of learning is that of discus *height* and *trajectory*. Principles have been formulated and are included at the end of this chapter. Application of these principles can best be considered as refinements of advanced throwing. Rather than deliberately attempting to throw at a given angle, the beginner should concentrate on developing a delivery that is relatively parallel to the ground; he can expect that proper elevation will come from the drive of his legs and hips which provide the upward direction of force.

THE STEP AND THROW

The step-and-throw delivery is a variation of the stationary throw. It adds momentum to the delivery. It is an effective exercise in the transition from the stationary throw to the throw with the turn. If properly timed, it adds approximately 10 to 20 feet to the distance of a standing delivery.

In this delivery, the starting position is somewhat more erect. The stance is relaxed but balanced. The feet, pointed in the direction of the throw, are shoulder width apart. Two or three preliminary swings are taken. As the discus reaches its farthest point to the left, the athlete steps approximately fifteen inches forward with his right foot and assumes the delivery position. From here the delivery is completed as in the standing throw. This motion must be *smooth* and *continuous*. The "recoil" action of the hips and legs is utilized. The throwing arm, fully extended, is brought through after the right hip and shoulder, keeping the discus "on the drag." All fundamentals of the stationary throw apply.

THE TURN

After practicing the step-and-throw phase until he has reasonably well mastered it, the beginner is ready to add the *turn*. The learning of this transitional step need not be hurried. Added time spent in learning to control the discus may save time in learning to execute the turn.

If he has had the advantage of practicing with, and observing, a more experienced thrower, it is possible that the beginner will have done some experimenting on the turn by himself. If well coordinated, he may be executing it reasonably well by the time he comes to his coach for added instruction. This can be an advantage. Familiarity with the general nature of the turn may enhance his ability to master the details of its execution. He may be turning too fast or covering too much distance, but these faults can be corrected one at a time as practice starts within the confines of the official throwing circle. If the athlete has done no individualized practice, the coach of course will have to start from scratch on his explanation and instruction.

It is easier to explain and understand the purpose of the turn than it is to execute it. Actually, all the thrower is attempting to do is add *force* to his delivery. In shot putting he does this by shifting or gliding straight across the circle. In discus throwing, since the object to be thrown is lighter and has a different shape, he does it by turning. An extended arm provides the lever. The delivery is more of a whip. The method by which he executes the turn depends upon the individual. Traditionally, a *one and one-half* turn has been used. The direction of travel is more or less in a straight line across the circle. Today, most of our better throwers use a *one and three-quarter* turn. The left foot, from which the first pivot is made, is placed close to the rear of the circle; the result is a longer turn, which employs a hop and deviates somewhat from a straight line. It adds more momentum to the throw. This technique is more popularly known as the Fitch or Gordien style. The latter used it in establishing a world discus record. It was originally introduced by Phil Fox of Stanford University.

While the *one and three-quarter* turn has been widely adopted, there are those who find it difficult to master and others who use it incorrectly. Properly executed, it adds more momentum to the throw. Controlled speed is the thrower's objective. Too much speed, poorly timed, may actually cut down on throwing efficiency. When speed is too great for control, deterioration of form is extremely rapid.

In general, the beginner should learn the turn he plans to use permanently, rather than changing from one to the other. Regardless of the one decided upon, it is important that he (a) arrive at the front of the circle in correct throwing position and (b) have sufficient room in which to execute his delivery without fouling.

It is estimated that the final delivery, or power of the body drive, provides the major force of the throw. Nothing, then, should be sacrificed in the turn that would cut down on its mechanical efficiency. The delivery position has remained relatively constant over the years, so any improvement in the discus record has resulted from the added speed and momentum of the turn.

Various approaches are used in teaching the turn. In general, they are variations of the whole and part method. Some introduce the beginner to this phase of the form by showing motion pictures and strip films; this familiarizes him with the general nature of the turn and its relationship to the other parts of the form. Actual practice of the turn is usually started without the distraction of a discus. This kind of practice can be done indoors or out. The athlete simply "steps through" the foot work of the travel, emphasizing general coordination and timing. Little stress is laid on details at this time. The action is continuous but not fast. Numerous "dry runs" are executed until foot placement becomes accurate and natural. The reverse is then added and finally the discus is used.

When first used with the turn, the discus is awkward to control. Footwork is difficult to time. Some coaches ease this awkwardness by rigging the discus with a strap under which the thrower can slip his hand; this helps him keep the discus under control as he makes his turn. He can practice numerous turns without the distraction of dropping the discus, and he wastes no time in having to retrieve it either.

Another device used effectively is a throwing curtain. This is usually a piece of heavy canvas hung about 15 feet from a circle. Located under a stadium, or in some other suitable location, it serves as a backstop and saves time in the practice of the turn.

THE ONE AND ONE-HALF TURN

(1) A line is drawn through the center of the circle in the direction of the throw.

(2) A right-handed thrower assumes a balanced and relaxed stance at the extreme rear of the circle with his left side toward the direction of the throw.

(3) The feet are shoulder width apart. The *ball* of the *right* foot and the *heel* of the left (18 inches from the right) are placed on the center line. The hips and knees are slightly flexed.

(4) Several preliminary swings start the action. The bulk of the weight shifts smoothly from one foot to the other.

(5) When the discus, on the back swing, reaches its furthest point to the rear, the left foot turns in the direction of the throw. As the body begins a twisting turn to the left, the weight is transferred to the left foot by a *drive* off the right foot which should *remain in contact with the ground as long as possible.* The knee of the right leg stays close to the left as it is brought around. The throwing arm, fully extended, stays behind the right shoulder and hip, keeping the discus "on the drag" throughout the turning action.

(6) As the right foot lands, just beyond the center of the circle, the body's weight is again transferred over it as the final half turn is started. At this time the toes point more to the *rear* of the circle. The second part of the turn is executed like the first part, with the left knee close to the right, leading the body in its twisting action. The throwing arm stays behind the hip and shoulder.

(7) As the left foot comes around to complete the second turn, the thrower assumes his delivery stance. There need be no direct effort to place the left foot if the pivot over the right has been correctly balanced. It should naturally place itself in correct

alignment just inside the front of the circle, about 12 inches to the left of the center line. From here the delivery is executed as described in the stationary throw.

TEACHING CUES

Do not expect perfection at the outset in teaching the one and one-half turn. The presence of the discus in the thrower's hand is going to disturb the smoothness of the pattern. Numerous repetitions of the turn must be executed before the thrower's action will be smooth and natural. Emphasis throughout should be on perfecting the *whole* form. At the outset *control* and *timing* is more important than momentum. The athlete should be permitted considerable leeway in throwing naturally without being interrupted by excessive coaching and attention to minor details. However, "practice of the *right* skill makes perfect," and the following mechanical errors should be corrected, *one at a time*, as soon as they are detected and can be corrected without a decided interruption of the thrower's natural effort.

(1) Failure to grasp discus with joints of the fingers.

(2) Excessive "winding up" or "pumping" preparatory to throwing.

(3) Tightening up or bending over excessively in the preliminary stance in the back of the circle. This stance should be natural, easy, and relaxed. Eyes and head should be up and out.

(4) Failure to keep both feet on the ground until the last possible moment in starting the turn. The average thrower has a harmful tendency to raise the right foot almost immediately.

(5) Failure to execute the turn entirely with the legs, keeping the upper body completely relaxed and "wound up."

(6) Failure to keep the discus away from the hip and at shoulder height in making the throw. The discus should be lifted at the start of the throw rather than at the time of release.

(7) Failure to move horizontally rather than vertically in executing the turn. If the feet are off the ground too long, power and momentum are lost. The *push* from *both* feet drives the body *forward*.

(8) Throwing the left arm outward and to the left in an attempt to increase shoulder momentum. This fault pulls the body forward too soon and diminishes the drive of the right leg and hip.

(9) Reversing feet too quickly in the delivery thus losing power from the body drive.

(10) Failure to straighten the left leg in a bracing action at the time of delivery.

(11) Stopping or "settling" just prior to the throw rather than making it a continuation of the turn.

(12) Looking down, rather than up and out, at time of throw.

(13) Failure to keep the left foot straight forward and to come up on the toes of this foot in the followup at time of delivery. This results in "round-housing" or pulling across the body at the end of the throw.

THE ONE AND THREE-QUARTER TURN

(1) Starting position at the extreme rear of the circle is the same as for the one and one-half turn, except that thrower's back is to the direction of the throw.

(2) Three preliminary swings are taken. The "bounce" action is felt by the thrower, gaining in intensity with each twist.

(3) As the backward swing of the right arm is made, the left foot swings back to a point near the ring and about 15 to 20 inches from the right foot, to take advantage of a longer travel distance. (Observation indicates that the travel from this position is about 10 feet as against 8 for the regular turn.)

(4) The turn starts with a full "hop" or "off-balance whirl." The hop starts with a firm drive off of the right foot which stays in contact with the ground until the last moment. The thrower's back leads the action, shifting the drive off the right leg to the left. This is sometimes referred to as the "fall" around the circle. The travel is in more of an arc than a straight line. Both feet are off the ground momentarily, but this is a well-timed action. The right arm and shoulder keep the discus on the drag. There is an extreme *left* shoulder lead.

(5) As the turn is completed the right foot lands in its regular throwing position on the diameter line at about the center of the circle. The distance of the hop is about 54 inches. If this hop is well timed, the left foot falls naturally into its proper throwing position about 12 inches to the left of the center line. This timing requires constant and repeated practice. The important objective here is to land in good throwing position. To accomplish this, the drive of the turn may have to be cut down somewhat according to the needs of the individual thrower.

(6) In the final throwing position, the left leg is planted firmly and straightened. With the aid of the driving right leg it activates the lift. The chest, chin, and head are up.

(7) The reverse comes as a natural balancing action brought on by the extreme momentum of the whirl. The right hip at this time is well forward. The right foot points straight ahead. Several added turns usually are required to keep the thrower in the circle. The eyes then follow the discus.

Olympic champion Al Oerter demonstrates the one and three-quarter turn.

During the turn, ooth of the thrower's legs remain bent at almost identical angles.

Level of thrower's head and shoulders remains constant throughout. Action of head precedes body's movement.

Position of discus in thrower's hand is perpendicular to the circle until time of delivery. This carriage allows discus to trail farther behind shoulders, permits a greater arc in which to pull discus and increases speed of turn. Throwing arm is straight, never bent, *and is on a level plane with shoulders. Discus is always on the "drag."*

Left (free) arm is swung out and around to left as means of getting upper body around quickly in turn. It is "cocked" in front of the thrower's body as his right foot is planted for start of the delivery.

Thrower drives *into the turn and* drives *out of it (note the "off balance fall" and quick recovery).*

As the delivery starts, the thrower's weight is on his right foot. His straight left leg braces against the front of the circle.

The final delivery is a "flinging" action which combines a pivot of the right foot, an unbending of the thrower's right leg and a lift and shift of his hips in the direction of the throw. Both feet are on the ground at the time of delivery. The right hip leads the discus. The upper body is straight and not leaning into the throw. Head and chin are up; shoulders are spread.

The reverse is a balancing action and follow through. The thrower's right foot does not leave the circle until the discus leaves his hand.

TEACHING CUES

Errors in the execution of the one and three-quarter turn will be detected and corrected in the manner described for the one and one-half turn. Fundamentals of the Fox style, with variations more recently introduced by Fitch and Gordien, are included here because of their widespread application:

(1) Not only the hips but the entire upper body and shoulder lead in this style of throw. Momentum is increased but is difficult to control.

(2) An "off-balance fall" around the circle is emphasized. To maintain balance requires faster action of the feet.

(3) As a result of the fast whirling action, the right shoulder is driven through *fast* on the delivery, making this a part of the reverse.

(4) The extreme shoulder lead employed in the turn requires that the right foot be carried well to the left of the center line to allow sufficient room to execute the delivery without fouling. This phase of the turn must be practiced assiduously.

(5) The "hop" action is emphasized, but it should aim to drive the body *forward* rather than upward. The push occurs after the weight of the body has passed beyond the foot.

(6) Contrary to traditional teaching, the reverse is taught early.

(7) In teaching this style of throw, avoid squelching an athlete's unimportant idiosyncrasies of style. The beginner should not be held back in his early effort to execute the *whole* throwing pattern with as much momentum as he can control at the moment.

(8) Mastery of this style requires literally thousands of repetitions. Early progress may, at times, be discouraging, but those who are willing to work at it will get surprising results.

(9) Do not discourage individual variations and adaptations of this style. There is nothing sacred with this newer method of placing the left foot. Do not make it an end in itself and insist that all throwers use it. There is considerable evidence that its use by some individuals will decrease throwing efficiency. In such cases, the traditional straight-line style, which still permits a good turn may be advisable.

(10) In teaching the turn, it is well to keep the few basic criteria of correct execution clearly in mind. Two equally effective turns may vary in certain details.

(11) Use the term "sling" rather than throw in describing the delivery.

Motion pictures of the athlete are a valuable training aid. Each thrower should be filmed at least once during pre- or early season. Three consecutive shots from the following positions are recommended: (1)

directly behind the circle, (2) to the left or right side of the circle, and (3) a safe position in front of the circle. A speed of 24 frames per second will provide excellent pictures for a study of technique. For the advanced thrower, one slow motion shot from each position at a speed of 36 or 48 frames per second is recommended.

TRAINING

The pattern of training for the discus thrower is similar to that for the shot putter. General guidelines apply.

As in shot putting, the emphasis is on *throwing*. Year-round training is recommended. If not engaged in other sports, the thrower should do adequate amounts of running, sprinting, general conditioning, and throwing in his off-season, when there is not the pressure of competition. His training is more leisurely, but it should be purposeful. This is the time for him to study and analyze the event. He can experiment with variations in technique and take many practice throws for form and conditioning. An absence of ideal practice conditions should not deter his practice. The foot work of the turn and other fundamentals can be executed in a very limited space.

During the indoor season, if field house facilities are not available, the athlete may practice fundamentals in an easily improvised indoor throwing site. A space 12 feet in width and in length, with a 10-foot ceiling is all that is needed. In this space a piece of heavy canvas is hung from the ceiling, with several feet extending onto the floor. A rubber discus is used, and the athlete throws from a simulated discus ring a distance of 3 feet into the canvas curtain. His objective in this limited space is conditioning and technique, not distance.

Weight training is an important part of the thrower's off-season conditioning program. It is to be remembered that weight training is a conditioning aid and not an end in itself. The kind and amount of exercises should be carefully selected and adjusted to the weight and strength of the individual athlete.

During the off-season many good discus throwers lift weights four days weekly. On these days, two to four of the following exercises are repeated seven times:

Monday and Thursday

Two-arm presses

Two-arm curls

A tricep exercise

Reverse curls

Rowing exercises
Sit-ups on an incline board
Chinning with resistance
Presses behind the head

Tuesday and Friday

Three quarter knee bends
Heavy pull-overs
Front squats
Bench presses
Dead lifts
Shoulder shrugs
Dumbbell rises
(bench and 45-degree incline board)

A *variety* of sport activity during the winter months is recommended. Handball is an excellent and stimulating game for the big man. It develops much of the speed, agility, and balance related to his more specialized event. For the big and heavier athlete, it is an excellent means of weight control.

Once the competitive season arrives, the practice schedule is regular and intense. The amount of practice is limited only by the amount of time available and willingness of the individual athlete to work. Many practice, at full effort, five days weekly with competition on the sixth. Fatigue during a given practice session should be considered. When it results in poor timing or coordination, the thrower should move to another phase or conclude practice.

DAILY PRACTICE PLAN

Daily practice should be well planned and purposeful. It should be *sequential* in nature with each phase leading to the next, up to the full throwing effort. Throwing for distance should be controlled only to the extent that it has an adverse effect on form. Shot putting should precede discus throwing. Weight training should be limited to Monday and Wednesday and come at the *end* of practice. Each thrower should determine *by experience*, and follow, the daily and weekly practice patterns which give him the best personal results. The following *sequence* is suggested:

(1) *Warm-up*. Jogging. Stretching and bending exercises. Wind sprints.
(2) Throwing from a *stationary stance* followed by *step and throw*. Emphasis on correct delivery position. Experiment with angle of flight and plane of discus against varying wind conditions.

(3) *Practice of the turn* (with and without the discus). Emphasis on smooth, well-timed glide or hop. Throwing curtain and strapped discus may be used as time-savers during part of this phase.

(4) *Whole-action throwing* (core of daily practice). Emphasis on speed and momentum *consistent with correct form.* Check all fundamentals of *combined turn and delivery.* Continue until thrower feels fatigue is interrupting reasonably efficient execution.

(5) *Conditioning.* Repeat sprints of 50 to 75 yards. Runs of 220 yards. Weight training—Monday and Wednesday *only.*

MECHANICAL PRINCIPLES APPLICABLE TO DISCUS THROWING

(1) Gravity is a constant force acting on all objects.

(2) Momentum of one object may be transferred to another object.

(3) The momentum of a projected object depends upon its mass and velocity.

(4) The effectiveness with which the body moves other objects depends upon the amount, direction, and speed of the force applied. (Torque and centrifugal force.)

(5) Any object which is projected into space is subject to at least two forces during its flight—gravity and air resistance.

(6) If an object has linear motion, the air resistance is constant over all the surface presented for contact with the air.

(7) The discus offers minimum resistance if it presents its outer edge to the line of flight.

(8) If the palm of the hand holding the discus faces the direction of the throw, the discus presents a flat surface to the line of flight and is held back.

(9) A vibrating or weaving discus gives almost as poor results as a broadside flight because of actual resistance to forward motion and the downward resistance on the upturning edge.

(10) When there is no wind, *if the initial velocity could be maintained,* the greatest distance would be expected when the angle of delivery approached 45 degrees. Successful throwers get a good deal of height in their throws.

(11) When the angle of delivery is greater than 30 to 35 degrees, the ability of the thrower to impart a high initial velocity is reduced and performance suffers. The generally accepted angle is 30 degrees.

(12) When throwing *with* the wind, greater range can be achieved if the angle of delivery is slightly increased.

(13) When throwing *into* the wind, the best range can be achieved if the angle of delivery is reduced (flat) because the edge of the discus presents a smaller surface for wind resistance.

COMPETITION

(1) Check all equipment the day before. Do not depend on others to transport your implements to and from competition.

(2) Weigh your discus regularly to make sure it meets approved regulations.

(3) Make sure you have the correct kind of shoes for the ring surface from which you will be throwing. This is particularly important for meets away from home.

(4) Arrive well in advance of the starting time for your event. Be thoroughly familiar with the environment and the condition of the throwing surface.

(5) Warm up slowly and thoroughly. Know your warm-up capacity and needs. Your aim is to make each throw, *including your first,* the best.

(6) Determine wind conditions with each throw and adjust trajectory and plane of discus accordingly. (See Mechanical Principles.)

(7) On rainy days, carry a towel to keep the discus dry. A wet discus weighs more than a dry one. One ounce of added weight is equivalent to a loss of approximately 2 feet in distance.

(8) Conserve energy between throws, but be thoroughly warmed up and ready to throw when your turn is called.

(9) Know the rules of your event and comply with them at all times. (See Official Track and Field Rules.)

12
The Javelin Throw

The javelin throw, when properly executed and supervised, is a spectacular and thrilling event. However, it has not been widely accepted or developed by American athletes and coaches. In most instances, it has been barred from inclusion in high school track meets. Not all college conferences include it as an event in their programs. Where adequate facilities are not available, and supervision poor, it can be an extremely dangerous event. When improperly executed, the javelin throw can also be injurious to the thrower's elbow.

A dramatic improvement in the world javelin record has occurred in recent years. This sudden improvement is usually considered to be the result of a superior throwing technique that has only recently evolved. Studies by Ganslen and Jarvinen[1] do not support this contention. They find no evidence to suggest that modern javelin throwers have developed a better way of throwing. The original Finnish javelin style has dominated this event for many years. Ganslen[2] hypothesized that the improvement is due to major changes in javelin design, most notable of which was a marked increase in surface area. The various wind tunnel investigations gave support to this conclusion. The lift/drag ratio is the most important relationship in aerodynamics. The difference between the lift/drag ratio of the new Western or "Held" javelin and that of other javelins delivered at a comparable angle of inclination is very great. "It is apparent," contends Ganslen,[2] "that the great increase in the total surface of the javelin has materially contributed, without question, to the exceptional performance being made by modern javelin throwers."

SOMATOTYPE

Size is not a factor in javelin throwing. We have had champions of varying stature and weights (135 to 200 pounds). Track coaches have agreed that a good long throwing arm, with a large hand, is a decided advantage. Some look for good football passers and baseball players. Others have discovered and developed athletes who couldn't throw a football or baseball any great distance but who adapted themselves very well to the javelin. Natural ability and coordination are very valuable assets, but the average athlete, by careful study and with proper coaching, may develop good form and ability.

[1] R. V. Ganslen and M. Jarvinen, "Finnish Javelin Throwing," *The Scholastic Coach*, 19:8, February 1950.

[2] R. V. Ganslen, "Javelin Changes Needed," *Track and Field News*, 8:9, October 1955.

THE GRIP

There are three methods of gripping the javelin: the American, Finnish, and Hungarian. The Finnish style is most commonly used today. In this style, the javelin is grasped with the thumb and second finger, not the forefinger. The tip of the finger is placed against the binding where the end of the cord is tucked under the last loop. The first and second joints are curled around the shaft. The thumb also grips behind the binding. Its tip touches the tip of the second finger or lies straight along the shaft if the hand of the individual thrower finds this position more comfortable. The forefinger (flexed, not straight) is stretched back along the shaft and is curled around it. The third and little fingers, spread apart, grasp the binding. The shaft of the javelin should rest in the hollow of the hand against the base of the thumb. The grip is firm but the shaft, resting lightly in the palm, must not be squeezed tightly. There are many advantages of this grip: the second finger is larger and stronger than the forefinger, thus aiding more in the throw; the forefinger acts to steady the shaft, keeping it from leaving at a tangent and from whipping; it is possible to give some spin to the shaft as it leaves the hand. A wrist snap provides final impetus to the throw.

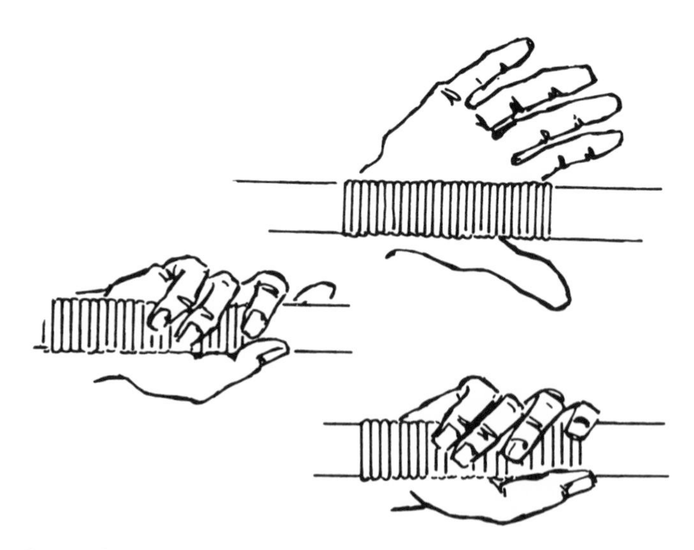

The Grip: The javelin must be held so it lies diagonally across the hand. Either the index or the middle finger is placed around the shaft next to the cord. If the middle finger is so positioned, the index finger is placed either along or around the shaft.

The main difference between the American and Finnish styles of gripping the javelin is that the pressure is on the second finger in the Finnish style and on the first in the American. The Hungarian grip, used very little by the Americans, places the thumb and second finger in the same position as the Finnish style, but the forefinger is straight back on the shaft. Tremendous pressure is placed on both the forefinger and second finger. This style eliminates any tendency of the competitor to pull down on the javelin at the instant of release and gives the javelin great height immediately.

THE CARRIAGE

There are three accepted methods of carrying the javelin. Most coaches recommend the Finnish style. In this method, the javelin is carried above the right shoulder, point down, with the hand at a level just above the ear.

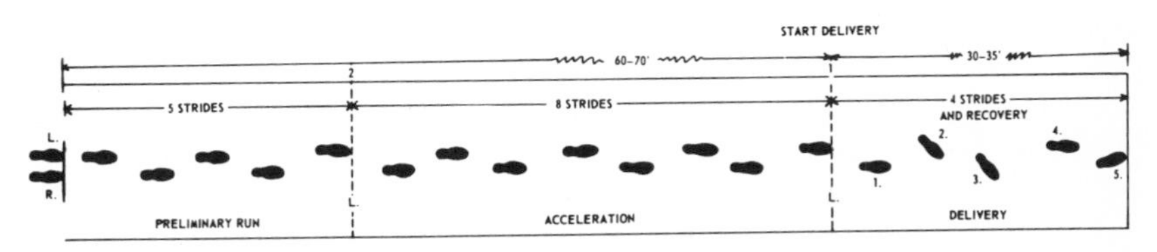

The Approach Run

The American carriage is over the shoulder, with the point of the javelin slightly higher than horizontal. In the third carriage, also American, the arm is down and extended back, the tip of the javelin is even higher. The palm of the hand is away from the body so that there is no rotation of the wrist. The first two methods of carriage are preferable to the latter. When the javelin is carried with the arm extended behind, it tends to turn the body sideways and to slow up the run. Likewise, it is extremely difficult to keep the spear straight in line of flight, since the point is liable to swing out. When he carries the javelin in this manner, the thrower has his mind on the javelin. When he carries it above the shoulder, the thrower can forget the javelin and can concentrate on his run and checkmarks.

THE APPROACH

The approach run is determined by the type of footwork used. There are four types: (1) the hop-step style, (2) the rear cross-step style,

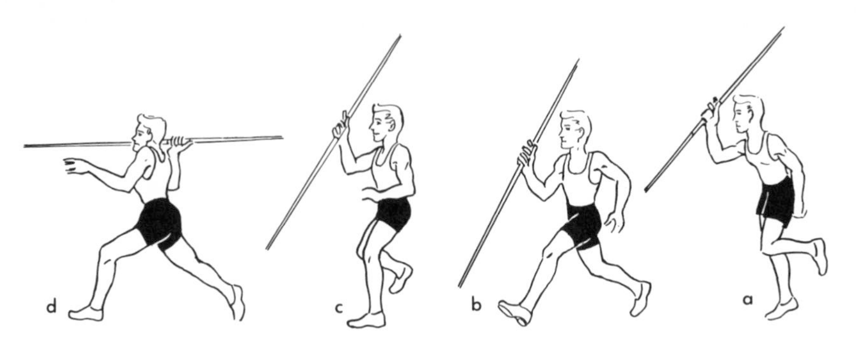

The Carry (Finnish Style)

a, b—The carry is above the shoulder, point down. Hand is at level just above ear.
c—Point is down as left foot strikes ground.
d—Arm starts to move back from carry position preparatory to throw.

(3) the front cross-step style, and (4) the combination hop and front cross-step. The first two are American, the last two Finnish. The first two do not require a long run, usually 50 to 60 feet. They are easier to learn but do not get as good results in performance as the Finnish styles. Their principal disadvantage is that the thrower slows down too much for the gather. Some authorities say that any style of footwork is *good* if it allows the thrower to get into the throwing stance in complete control of himself and without diminishing the momentum acquired by the approach run.

Since the recommended approach used by practically all of the world's best javelin throwers is the Finnish cross-over style, it will be used in the description which follows.

In the simpler of the Finnish approaches, culminating with the front cross-step footwork and throw, the run is much faster and longer than for the American method but is not at full speed. The total run is approximately 105 feet. Two checkmarks are used. One is 90 feet from the takeoff board; the second is 30 feet from it. All these distances vary slightly with the individual.

The preliminary run is to gain speed. The left foot strikes the first checkmark and the thrower runs at top speed for eight strides where his left foot strikes the second mark. This part of the approach is much faster than in the American method but is not at full speed.

From the second checkmark (struck with the left foot) the thrower will take five steps to complete his throw. He counts them to himself: "*one*," as the right foot strikes the ground, "*two*" as the left foot comes down—continuing to "four," when the throw is made. Until the count of "two," it is important to keep the body and the feet straight to the front. At "two," the left foot is turned slightly inward.

On the third count, the thrower executes a front cross-over step with his right foot (crosses his right leg in front of his left). The right foot, as it hits the ground, is turned out, almost parallel with the toe board. On the count of "four," the left foot comes through into a long stride, which places the thrower's body in position for the delivery, and the throw is made (see drawing). The fifth count and step are a semi-reverse, with the right foot coming down just behind the toe board. The line of the right foot at this point is at right angles to the board, body square to the front.

The faster a javelin thrower runs, and the quicker he can stop, the greater upper-body velocity he will develop. Those employing the Finnish style contend that it is easier to maintain a fast rate of speed going through the last four steps because the feet are pointing straight forward, the crossover is smooth, and the hips are in proper throwing position.

THE THROW

In executing the throw the action of the throwing arm is timed with the five-count footwork just described. At the count of "one," the right arm is raised slightly and the point of the javelin is brought up to the level of the shoulder. Here care should be taken to keep the javelin aimed directly in the line of flight. The arm is then drawn back of the shoulder for the throw, reaching its extreme backward limit at the count of "three." Here the body turns automatically to the right during the cross-over step. The arm starts forward at "four." The throw is made from a wide stance with both feet planted firmly on the ground. This stance is much wider than the one that climaxes the American style of approach run. The leg spread is just as wide as the thrower can comfortably make it. To check his forward progress and still maintain speed at this time, the thrower lands on the heel of his right foot and leans his body backward at an angle of approximately 30 degrees.

When the throwing stance is taken there is no longer a 90-degree turn of the right hip as previously used. The right hip is already parallel with the throwing line, the javelin stays in the thrower's hand only a fraction of a second, and there is a quick extension of the right leg which drives the right hip forward and upward. Concentration at this time is on the movement of the shoulders and chest. As the arm is brought back for the throw, the body must be erect and the stomach must not be thrust out or bowed. The right shoulder is drawn back so that the back end of the javelin almost touches the ground. The right arm comes

The Throw

a. The cross-over (right in front of left). Heel leads. Right hip stays parallel with throwing line. Shoulder moves back with full drop of javelin.
b. Full draw back. Left foot advanced in long stride. Righ foot almost parallel with toe board.

c. Long body spread. Feet firmly on ground and point straight forward. Chest is up, and head is slightly to left.
d. Erect body position. Left foot is in direction of throw. Note vertical plane of elbow carried high ahead of hand grip.

forward with the hand carried well above the head rather than past the ear. If the body were erect at this point, the hand would pass almost directly above the center of the head, but it actually goes to the right of it because the body is bending forward and to the left. The head must not tilt too far nor turn too much to the left, nor should the body break at the waist.

The throw consists of applying to the javelin a multiple force that starts with the right hip, which swings forward sharply. The movement of the hip is followed by the back muscles below the right shoulder, then by the elbow, *last by the hand.* A followthrough of the body (into the reverse) and a final wrist flip complete the throw. It is important to remember that the javelin is *whipped* rather than thrown like a baseball. The entire effort is to put as much of the weight of the body into the throw as possible, rather than to depend primarily on the arm.

The reverse completes the throwing technique. The thrower may hop once or twice on his right foot to retain balance, but with this throwing style he should seldom foul if his checkmark is properly established.

COMMON FAULTS

(1) Gripping javelin too tightly.
Correction: Grip javelin only tight enough to ensure control.

(2) Failure of elbow to *precede* forearm in throw.
Correction: Keep forearm in *vertical* plane when throwing. This automatically results in elbow *leading* throw.

(3) Throwing with point of javelin *too high* in its vertical plane.
Correction: (a) Stress low javelin point. (b) In drawback, on count of "one" bring point of javelin across *chest.* (c) Prior to delivery, keep point of javelin from rising above head. (d) For maximum flight, release javelin at 45-degree angle.

(4) Point of javelin *drifting* out of line in horizontal position—usually to *right* of direction of throw.
Correction: Use observer to detect error. Concentrate on aiming at a *set* point directly in front of thrower in practice.

(5) Inconsistent count pattern or change in number of steps.
Correction: Establish a pattern thrower can use effectively and stay with it.

The Followthrough and Reverse

a. The throw is completed and the reverse ensures the check.

b. Thrower hops once or twice to retain balance.

(6) Poor execution of cross-step on count of "three."
Cause: Step too short. Upper body tension. Failure to carry body weight sufficiently low. Execution of steps while high on toes.
Correction: Work on lowering center of gravity. Raise knees. Execute series of *continuous* cross-steps for distance of 40–50 yards.

TRAINING

Preseason training is of great importance in javelin throwing. Prescribed weight and isometric exercises, which develop the specific back and arm muscle groups used in performing the event, can be a valuable year-round and early season form of practice. Popular early season weight training exercises include: pull-overs (from bench), military press, curls, and sit-ups. In these exercises, the weight training procedure included in Chapter 10 may be used. Pulley weights may be used for developmental purposes, particularly of the arm and shoulder muscle groups. The Finns suggest that the best exercise to develop the muscles used in their style of throw is wood chopping. Almost the same motion is involved throughout.

Many good exercises can be done in the gymnastics room—doing kips on the bar, hanging on rings, and swinging the body. All such activity involves "pulling" on the back muscles used in throwing. Walking on the hands is good. Most tumbling activities are helpful.

Learning to grip the javelin correctly is one of the most important first steps in training and should be practiced assiduously. Practice of the throwing stance—the rear leg bend, the leading hip action, the proper position of the elbow, the proper height and position of the javelin over the head—are all exercises that can be practiced from a stationary position. Practice of the stance and grip can be done indoors as well as on the field.

Once the regular season starts, sprinting and starting are highly recommended training exercises since the thrower must not only run at near maximum speed, but also turn while running and stop. This activity calls for extreme exertion of the leg muscles. Shot putting is often considered to be helpful as training for javelin throwing, mainly because it provides practice in getting the hip into the throw. The bent knee action is also helpful.

Walking with the javelin to develop a timing of the swing, so that its point is always down on the left step, is a highly recommended practice exercise. The speed of this exercise may gradually increase from a walk to a jog, followed by a full run. The timing of this phase of the run should be natural and not forced.

Walking through the five count steps, with and without the javelin, can be practiced to develop a smooth front cross-over glide. Form throwing is done at three-quarter speed with an emphasis on smooth execution of the steps, cross-over and final delivery action. The approach run is practiced at full speed into the 5-step action with the final throw made at one-half effort. Once the thrower's footwork becomes consistent, checkmarks to avoid fouling in competition are established by determining the distance needed for the 5-step delivery and allowing an additional margin for necessary adjustments.

An athlete learns to throw the javelin by repeated practice of the correct throwing technique. Today there is less concern than formerly about the danger of injury to his throwing arm from overwork, as long as the javelin is in proper alignment and the large muscles of the trunk and legs are used correctly. Safety is an important consideration in javelin throwing and the throwing area should be roped and marked off with colored flags during practice and competition.

THE WEEKLY AND DAILY PRACTICE PATTERN

(1) The individual performer, with the advice of his coach, should develop and follow the practice schedule that meets his individual needs and gives him the best results in competition.

(2) Many good throwers limit their heaviest training to the first three days of the week. Most also participate in the shot put and discus events. Practice of these constitutes additional training activity.

(3) Each day's practice should aim to strengthen that phase of the event in which the thrower is the weakest. This need not involve full-effort throwing. The athlete may throw the javelin into the ground at a distance of 40 to 60 feet in front of him emphasizing quick hip rotation, maximum rearward arm extension, followthrough, and release.

(4) A slow and thorough warm-up, particularly of the arm, shoulder, and back muscles, is the first step in daily training during the early and active competitive season. It should be preceded by easy running and a few accelerating sprints. Developmental exercises included as part of the general warm-up are: trunk and shoulder rotation, trunk bending, sit-ups, push-ups and exercises that stretch the groin and large leg muscles.

(5) An important part of each day's preliminary warm-up consists of short, easy throws of 20 to 30 feet into the ground. In this part of his warm-up the thrower makes sure he grips the javelin correctly, throws with his elbow leading his forearm, and throws the javelin straight in front of him.

(6) Practice runs and work on checkmarks are included in each day's practice. The swing of the javelin during this phase of the

practice, making sure that the point of the javelin is down on the left step, is stressed.

(7) Many good throwers have found by experience that it is advisable to take no more than six hard throws during the week, if competition is to come on Saturday. Such hard throwing should be limited to one day weekly. In early season, this may be Wednesday. During the late season, some recommend hard throwing only on the day of competition.

(8) Weight training, if continued at all during the active competitive season, should be performed at the conclusion of the daily practice and limited to the first three days of the week.

(9) Throwing into net (canvas curtain) with weighted balls: the Jorma Kinnunen (Finnish) technique. Based on development of throwing power and speed. *This is preseason training.*

Procedure: Start from a position 10–12 feet from net. Take two or three steps and release ball 3–5 feet from net. *Use correct javelin throwing technique.* Start slowly and build up gradually.

Number of throws: Finnish throwers start with 20–30 times per training session and work up to 150–200 throws. (This should be adjusted to the age and experience of the thrower.)

Weight of balls: Start with 5 pounds. After a 2-month period reduce to a 4-pound ball. *At start of regular season (April) discontinue ball throwing.* Work only with javelin.

Number of days weekly: Three. Alternate every other day with short sprints. Include exercises on pulley weights.

13
The Running High Jump

Jumping for height has been a challenge to man since early times. Contests have been either from a standing position or with a running approach. The running high jump has been adopted as a standard event on the American track and field program.

The fine neuromuscular control necessary to execute the sequence of the approach, leg swing, takeoff, leg lift, layout over the bar, and turn for landing make it a truly artistic event. Such control requires great patience and careful attention to detail. A world's record jump of 7 feet 6¼ inches is undoubtedly one of the remarkable athletic achievements of our time.

There are two basic considerations in high jumping: (a) *lift* and (b) *efficient clearance.* Of the two the most important is lift; it determines how high the jumper is capable of raising his body off the ground. "Styles" of jumping have developed. They refer to the method by which the jumper attempts to effect the most efficient clearance of the bar. Lift takes place on the ground—style in the air. Much attention over the years has been directed to a study of style, but today greater attention is being correctly directed to the development of an efficient lift.

Those speculating on future records for the event predict that when man develops the ability to utilize fast horizontal speed, and is able to project himself at a high (80-degree) angle of takeoff, he may be able to jump as high as eight feet.

SOMATOTYPE

Most of today's great high jumpers are tall men (six feet and over). Height, however, should more properly be considered an advantage rather than an absolute necessity. Nevertheless, other conditions being equal, a tall man, because his center of gravity is high, has an advantage over a short one.

Cureton observes, "The relatively greater length of the bones has always been obvious among high jumpers. Longer bones require longer muscles. In addition the center of gravity is higher to begin with, which is a fact of great importance in high jumping."[1]

Studies[2] of the highest jumpers among animals have been made in an attempt to discover common characteristics that might apply to man. These revealed that animals with an arched lumbar region and hind legs

[1] T. K. Cureton, "Mechanics of the High Jump," *The Scholastic Coach* (April 1935), p. 404.

[2] A. Brazier Howell, *Speed of Animals* (Chicago: University of Chicago Press, 1944), p. 172.

tucked under the body were better fitted for leaping than those with straighter limbs. Such research further suggests that body posture as a whole appears to have an effect on successful high jumping. Cooper suggests that a man whose body is long-limbed and lean and has limberness and flexibility and potential strength—as have the bodies of animals that are good jumpers—will, himself, be capable of becoming a good jumper. However, he adds that there are other factors to be considered and it appears that present day great high jumpers do not depend as much upon spring from the takeoff leg as upon lift from the free leg.[3]

Some research, not recent, has been done on anthropometric measurements in relation to success in jumping. Krakower[4] found that long legs were advantageous. Track athletes were found to be long legged and short trunked compared to an unselected group.

Della[5] conducted an experiment to test Campbell's hypothesis that a relatively long heel-to-ankle construction of the foot is advantageous; the experiment also tested a different hypothesis (a development of a theory by Howell), that a relatively long ankle-to-toe measurement is best suited for jumping. Della concluded that, while there is some evidence to indicate that these individual differences in skeletal structure of the foot affect jumping, the relationship between total foot length and jumping ability is not significant.

Cureton[6] found that expert jumpers were above average in height, with long legs and a somewhat shorter trunk than would be expected. He attaches importance to their long thigh and calf muscles (which he believes are capable of greater range of action and more work) and to their broader and stronger feet.

JUMPING STYLES

There are basically three styles of high jumping. All others are modifications. Jumping style has been evolutionary in development. The "scissors" style was used before 1892. In this form, the athlete kicks up with the leg closest to the bar, clearing it in a sitting position.

[3] J. M. Cooper, "Some Comments on High Jumping" in *Track and Field Journal*, ed. Tom Rosandich (Djakarta, Indonesia: The Organizing Committee for the IVth Asian Games, 1962), p. 302.

[4] H. Krakower, "Skeletal Characteristics of the High Jumper," *The Research Quarterly*, 6:2 (1935), p. 75.

[5] D. G. Della, "Individual Differences in Foot Leverage in Relation to Jumping Performance," *The Research Quarterly*, 21:1 (1950), p. 8.

[6] T. K. Cureton, "Mechanics of the High Jump," *The Scholastic Coach* (April 1935), p. 9.

In 1892 Michael Sweeny revolutionized the event. He introduced a style (later known as the "Eastern" style) in which the body's position as it cleared the bar was changed from vertical to horizontal. In its original form the jumper appeared to be clearing the bar on his back with both legs extended in front of him. A "cutoff" modification was later added. In this variation the clearance was more on the side. The trailing leg was cut sharply backward and downward, turning the jumper so that he landed on his takeoff foot, facing the bar.

In 1912 George Horine added a further innovation. He took off from his inside foot. Employing a "rolling" turn, he cleared the bar in a layout on his side. He set a world record of 6 feet 7 inches using this style. It came to be known as the "Western" style and is sometimes referred to as the "Western roll."

In 1933 the rules in the high jump were changed so that a jumper might clear the bar in any position so long as he took off on one foot. Prior to that time it was illegal if the jumper's head went over the bar first or if his hips were higher than his head. This change permitted the dive. It led to the development of the "straddle" style which has been adopted by most championship performers. In this style the jumper clears the bar facing downward. Charles Dumas, Valeri Brumel, and John Thomas, all using this style, have cleared the bar at seven feet.

During the mid-1960's a new jumping style evolved. It was a radical departure from the traditional styles. It had only one proponent, Richard Fosbury. The jump, early referred to as the "Fosbury Flop," has since been more appropriately termed the Fosbury "back-layout" technique.

Fosbury was not the first jumper to clear the bar on his back. He was, however, the first high jumper to clear the bar on his back with the head leading.

Fosbury developed his style by trial and error. In the ninth grade, he jumped 5 feet 4 inches using the scissors jumping style. In the tenth grade, he used a layout scissors style and jumped 5 feet 10 inches. In the eleventh grade, he turned his back to the bar more and more and jumped 6 feet 3¼ inches. In his senior year, in the Oregon State High School Championships, he won the event with a jump of 6 feet 3 inches, but earlier in the year he had a jump of 6 feet 6 inches.

In his freshman year at Oregon State University, Fosbury experimented temporarily with the straddle roll. He practiced it for 9 months and his highest jump during this time was 5 feet 11 inches. The following summer, going back to his own back-layout style, he jumped 6 feet 7½ inches. At the beginning of his sophomore year at Oregon State, Fosbury abandoned his experiment with the straddle form and concentrated on his back-layout variation. Using this style he jumped 6 feet 10 inches on six occasions. In his junior year in college, Fosbury jumped over 7 feet in six meets. That year he won both the NCAA indoor and outdoor championships, setting new records with jumps of 7 feet 1¼ inches and 7 feet 2¼ inches. He climaxed his junior year of competition by qualifying for the United States Olympic team. In the 1968 Olympic Games at Mexico City he astonished the sports world by winning a gold medal with a record jump of 7 feet 4 inches.

The reaction of coaches to Fosbury's style varies. Some feel that it is definitely a milestone in the evolution of high jumping. Others are not sure. Numerous athletes have adopted the style and are experimenting with it, some with great success. Bill Elliot of Texas, jumping 7 feet 3¼ inches, with a variation of the Fosbury style, leads an impressive list of young world-class high jumpers employing the back-to-the-bar approach. Hungarian Istvan Major has cleared 7 feet 2⅝ inches using this technique. A 16-year-old South African, Emile Rossouw, has twice gone 7 feet for national and African continental records. A 16-year-old girl, Debbie Brill of Canada, has "backed over" at 6 feet ¼ inch.

Members of the medical profession are cautious in their reactions to the Fosbury innovation. Some feel that its use should be restricted because it can result in serious neck injuries, including cervical fractures and transection of the spinal cord. Critics base their concern on the fact that many aspiring high jumpers will attempt to emulate Fosbury's style without understanding the mechanics of the jump. Others risk injury by jumping into landing pits not suited to this kind of jumping.

While the number of jumpers and coaches turning to the back lay-out style of high jumping grows each time an athlete reaches the limelight, all should be cautioned about imitating any particular athlete's form. They must realize that the champion athlete usually evolves his style in light of his particular capabilities; what is good for one might not be suitable for another. Pat Matsdorf of the University of Wisconsin, utilizing a bent-leg straddle style, surpassed Fosbury's record and that of Russia's Valeri Brumel, with a world record jump of 7 feet 6¼ inches.

In the 100 years of competitive high jumping in the United States, jumping techniques, particularly the layout over the bar, have undergone drastic changes. The next 100 are likely to see many more.

STARTING THE BEGINNER

It is suggested that beginners start by learning the "scissors" form. Most of them will be familiar with it. This style, in which the jumper clears the bar in a sitting position, is the simplest, the easiest to teach, and the most fundamental. Natural jumping ability can be discovered and then other modifications in form developed later. When beginners are started with a "roll" form of jump, many develop the habit of turning into the bar on their take-off rather than getting the initial *upward* lift, essential to all correct jumping styles.

Running with a "light touch" or "spring" should be stressed. Practice of a springing run may well precede the first attempts at jumping. The lead leg "kick," and proper timing of the arms and inside shoulder lift which accompany it, may also be practiced before actual jumping starts. "Foot preference" (left or right) to determine which will be the free, or lead, leg can be discovered by having the learner step through a few simulated "football" kicks to discover which feels the more natural for kicking.

While form and technique are important, it is well at the outset to allow the beginner considerable latitude in discovering his own ability without interruption by the coach. Corrections in form, *one at a time*, can then be made as he becomes ready for advice.

Both the beginner and advanced jumper should use a regular aluminum heel plate or plastic cup inside the shoe of the takeoff foot to protect the heel from bruising. Thin sponge rubber may also be used for this purpose. A new type of jumping shoe with a "lifter" in the heel has been developed and approved for jumping. It is being used with great success by some of today's better jumpers.

During the indoor season, when a jumping pit is not available, some coaches use a trampoline as an aid in teaching. Simple jumps and turns familiarize the beginner with rotation and control of his body in the air. Correct landing technique (backdrop) can be practiced by those using the back-layout style of jumping. Various exercises can be performed on a mat to illustrate and practice correct layout form and body rotation used in straddle form jumping.

MECHANICAL PRINCIPLES OF HIGH JUMPING

The science of high jumping depends upon three major groups of mechanical elements: takeoff velocity, angle of takeoff, and layout over the bar. They apply regardless of the style of jump employed. An understanding of them, by coach and athlete, is an important first step in a mastery of form.

TAKEOFF VELOCITY

Takeoff velocity depends upon:

(1) The elastic rebound from the *foot stamp* and the force of muscular action in extending the angle, knee, and hip joints which immediately follow.

(2) The inertia of the free leg and the lift of arms acts upward in the direction of flight. This inertia at first strengthens the force of the foot stamp and then lifts the body in the direction of the movements.

ANGLE OF TAKEOFF

There is a definite relationship between angle of takeoff, vertical height, horizontal distance covered, and the amount of projection force or takeoff velocity.

(1) It is economical of energy to take off as close to the bar as possible.

(2) The time of the body off the ground is governed only by the height of the jump.

(3) The takeoff angle varies from 50 to 75 degrees, with the larger angle being ideal.

(4) For a given amount of energy in the spring, the higher jump will be made with the takeoff as close to the bar as will permit clearance—closer to 2 feet than 5. The distance covered horizontally will be nearer to 3 feet than 8.

(5) The height of the jump depends upon velocity of takeoff and the takeoff angle.

(6) The energy of the jump depends upon the velocity of the takeoff for a jumper of a given weight.

(7) A jump of 7 feet requires a takeoff velocity of 22 to 25 ft./sec. and a takeoff angle near 78 degrees; it will cover approximately 3.76 feet, horizontal distance.

LAYOUT OVER BAR

The object of the layout is to clear the bar with the center of gravity being raised the least possible vertical distance. It is possible for an object, such as a rope, to pass over a bar with the center of gravity always below the bar. This requires the least energy of all. When a jumper takes a jackknife position, the center of gravity lies outside the body. With a dive and roll over the bar, a jumper may actually pass over the bar while the center of gravity passes below it.

All modifications of style after the body is in the air are for the purpose of executing a better layout over the bar and keeping the center of gravity lower.

Takeoff velocity and proper angle account for more than 90 percent (approximately) of the height of the jump among better jumpers. In spite of the value of these two factors, it is important to develop good layout "technique" because the 10 percent difference it makes in total execution is enough to determine the winner in close competition.

APPLICATION OF PRINCIPLES TO PRACTICE—THE "STRADDLE" STYLE

The "straddle" style, so named because of the jumper's position while clearing the bar, has been almost universally adopted as the most efficient and scientific form of high jumping. Most coaches agree that it is the most efficient technique yet discovered. Its advantages are its simplicity and its close approach to mechanical perfection. This style will be used in the following discussion of mechanical principles applied to advanced technique. Unless otherwise indicated it will be assumed that the jumper will *take off* on his *left* foot.

THE APPROACH

The approach and takeoff are important essentials of successful high jumping. They determine, to a very large degree, the jumper's speed, rhythm, and most important, the ultimate correct position of his body for its vertical lift-off.

The jumper should have a definite starting point and angle of run. Both should be accurately measured so they are the same each time he jumps.

There is no arbitrary rule on the distance of the run. It may vary from 7 to 9 strides, depending on the individual jumper. Angles of approach vary from 26 to 35 degrees. Check marks are used by most good jumpers because they assure a consistent run. One is usually the jumper's starting point and the other his fourth or sixth stride. He should be so familiar with the second mark that watching it does not make his approach mechanical or detract from concentration on his more important take-off.

The run should be relaxed, springy, and as a general rule, *straight*. Richard Fosbury, who employs the back lay-out technique, approaches with a slight arc. This, however, is an individual variation and not recommended for all jumpers regardless of style.

A relaxed run that accelerates to almost full speed at takeoff is used by most good jumpers. There is a trend today among better jumpers to use a faster and longer run. The speed of the run, however, must be *controlled*; how much a jumper can use depends on the strength of his legs and his ability to convert horizontal velocity to vertical momentum at the time of takeoff.

The jumper's eyes focus on the takeoff mark until his last two strides. At this point he raises them to look at the bar. His last two approach strides are lenghened and hips lowered as he gathers for the lift-off. On his next-to-the-last step, his arms drop behind him. On his last step they swing forward and upward vigorously to assist in the take-off. Timing here is very important.

ANGLE OF APPROACH

The angle of approach is important from the point of view of the length of time that the body is over the bar. The shorter the duration of this time, the slighter the possibility of dropping on the bar. The time is shorter when the run is made from directly (90 degrees) in front of it. It is intermediate at 45 degrees and greater from smaller angles. However, the side approach permits leaving the ground closer to the bar, which is an advantage. Practical observation shows that most jumpers adopt a 45-degree approach.

POINT OF TAKEOFF

The point of takeoff for jumpers, even when they are using the same jumping style, is not uniform. It varies because of the difference in the length of leg, the direction of the run, and the speed with which the jumper approaches.

There is an apparent advantage in the jumper taking off close to the standard on the side from which he approaches. The surface here, because it is not used as much as that closer to the center of the bar, is usually smoother. In a takeoff from this location he will clear the bar at its lowest point and have more room in the pit for a safe landing. The takeoff point must be far enough from the bar to permit the lead leg to swing forward freely without hitting the bar. Most good jumpers take off at a point approximately 24 inches from the bar. Others use an arm's length to measure the optimum distance. It is important that this point be adjusted during competition as height increases. It may need to be moved farther back because of the increased force of the drive. The approach is completed by a fully accented last step and a slight crouch of the takeoff leg.

GATHER AND FOOT PLANT

In preparation for the explosive spring, a settling down is necessary to aid in the upward swing and lift. The knee and hip should be slightly bent in the crouch just before the takeoff. This flexion permits a more forceful action of the muscles across these joints. A definite stamp of the foot should take place at this point. The foot stamp increases the force of reaction against the collision between foot and ground and also stretches the muscles and joint ligaments across the arch of the foot. The elastic rebound is more forceful in proportion to the force of the stamp. The foot push should start with the heel all the way down as this permits a longer range of action of the calf muscles and a more forceful push.

KICK AND LIFT

The well-timed and forceful kick of the lead (right) leg, which accompanies the takeoff, is one of the most important techniques of correct high jumping.

Essentially, it is the force that establishes the jumper's height. The direction of his momentum must be straight up before the jumper can shift his body into its horizontal layout position.

As the jumper springs from the left foot, he kicks the right foot upward as if to clear the bar at a continuation of the angle of ap-

The Kick and Lift

a. Stamp of left (take-off) foot is hard. Push off starts from heel. Note marked backward lean. Eyes on bar. Arms gather for upward swing.

b. Body rocks over to vertical position. Straight left leg directly over center of gravity. Lift of arms and left shoulder assist in up-ward drive.

c. Right arm straight out from shoulder. Left leg stays behind. Leg spread starts. Left foot points upward. Lift is not rushed.

proach. The lead foot is pointed *straight up*, aimed at a point 6 inches above the bar. This kick must be high and vigorous. The takeoff (left) leg should be directly under the pelvis (center of gravity) as this upwark kick is made. It is important at this point that the jumper avoid *leaning* or *turning into* the bar before the lift is completed. A lift of the left shoulder with a bent arm will assist in this upward drive. Most straddle jumpers use a marked backward lean at the time of the foot plant. As the lift takes place and the takeoff foot leaves the ground, the body then rocks over to its vertical position.

As the kick of the lead (right) foot takes place, the jumper's right arm is swung upward; in a bent position, it is completely over his head at the top of his kick. As the body turns over the bar this arm is first straightened and lifted and then swung downward toward the pit to assist in raising the left hip over the bar.

LAYOUT

The layout or "straddle" of the bar occurs at the height of the kick. It should not be started until the jumper feels that he is *above* the bar. The pelvis is the key. It is shifted from a vertical to a horizontal position as the jumper's lead (right) leg starts down. The legs, well spread, straddle the bar as the jumper assumes his face down position. The left leg, in a bent position, is raised following the upward shift of the left side of the pelvis. Contrary to popular misconception, the left leg is not straightened as a result of this action. It should be pointed out in

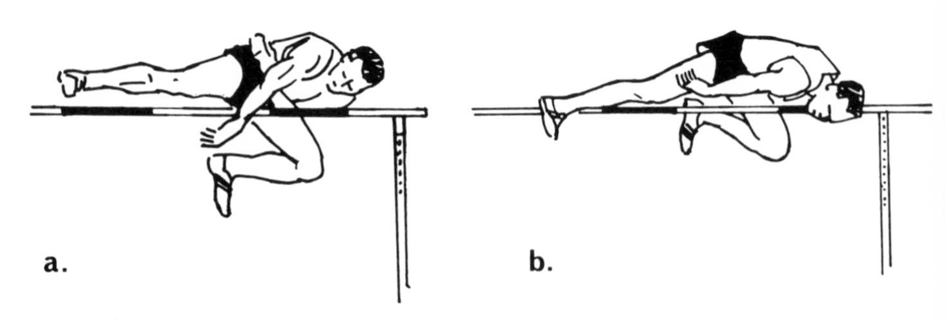

The Layout

a. Body in horizontal position parallel with bar. Alignment from right shoulder to heel is straight. Bent left arm is tucked close to stomach. Note inward rotation of right foot.

b. Start of head and right shoulder drop. This action precedes hip shift. Straight right arm is parallel with body. Right shoulder is lifted.

this connection that *a jumper cannot increase his upward velocity by flinging the arms or legs upward during flight.* For every action there is an equal and opposite reaction. For every part of the body jerked upward, there is another part lowered. The body can be rotated or twisted about the center of gravity by these movements, but its mass as a whole cannot be raised. The projection energy comes from the ground-push and upward inertia of the limbs.

Many jumpers have difficulty in getting the left leg over the bar. To effect clearance, most jumpers turn the left foot upward, pointing the toes toward the sky. Looking back in the direction of the takeoff, with a roll of the head, further assists in raising the left hip.

The position of the trailing (left) arm varies in the layout. Some press it, in a bent position, tightly against the stomach and chest. Fingers extend to a point under the chin. Others straighten and lift it upward and backward to help raise the left shoulder over the bar. Some carry it under the hip. The best position is the one that each jumper finds from experience is most effective for him.

The jumper's descent, following the hip shift and layout, is a matter of completing the roll. Landing is usually on the right side or back.

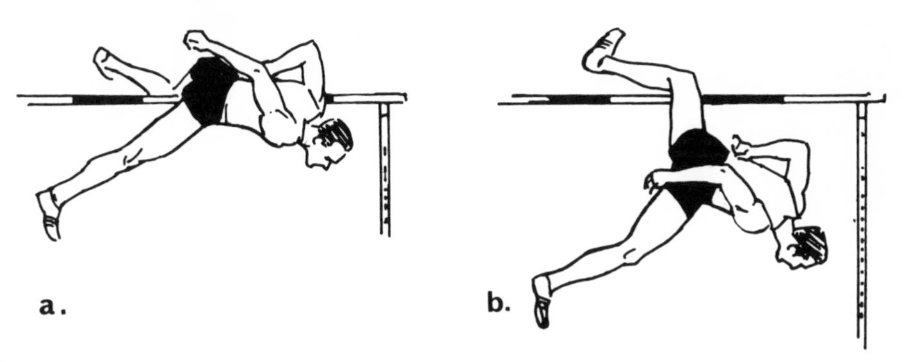

The Head Drop and Dive for Pit

a. Hip shift is fast as jumper dives for pit. Right leg is straight, left is bent. Bent left arm pulls left shoulder away from bar. Head and shoulders are lower than hips.

b. Head drop and dive for pit continues. Leg spread is wide. Bent left leg follows shift of left hip. Rotated left foot points upward.

THE BACK-LAYOUT (FOSBURY) TECHNIQUE

Mechanical principles previously covered apply to this style of jumping. The principal difference in execution is the layout position. The landing is also different. To avoid injury, the jumper should understand and master it well. A safe landing pit is essential. A jumper who decides to use this form should start early and make sure he can adapt to the peculiar variations its proper execution demands.

THE APPROACH

As in other styles of jumping, the jumper must have a definite starting mark and angle of run. His run should be smooth and springy. He should have a method of measuring both the angle and distance of his run so that it will be consistent wherever he is jumping.

The angle, speed, and distance of the run vary with the individual. The run used in the back-to-the-bar style of jumping is much faster than in other styles. It may be that one of the advantages of the back lay-out over other styles is the fact that it does not employ as much action of the free arm and leg. This enables the jumper to use a faster and longer run adding velocity to his jump.

Fosbury utilizes a wide-angle approach of eight steps. He faces the bar almost perpendicular to it and runs in a slight arc. This seems to help him convert forward speed into upward force.

Bill Elliott of Texas, one of the younger world-class jumpers using the back-layout (7′3¼″), employs a 15-step run which is much straighter and faster than Fosbury's.

Generally speaking, the jumper's eyes are on his takeoff mark until the last two strides. As he gathers for his takeoff, his focus is raised and he looks up over the bar.

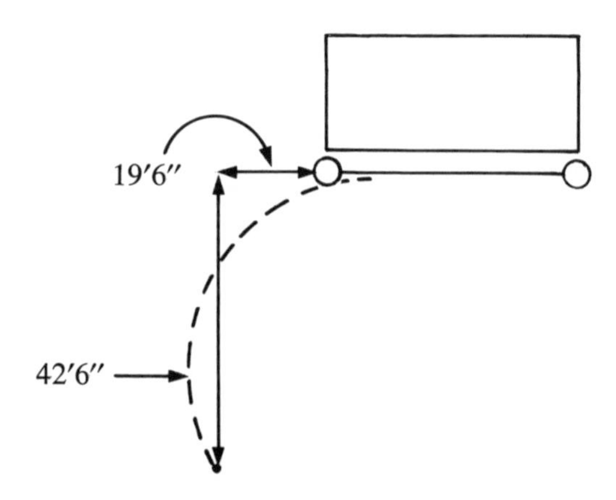

The Fosbury Approach

THE TAKE-OFF

A jumper who approaches from his left takes off on his *right* foot, which points at an angle of approximately 15 degrees.

Just prior to lifting off, the jumper drops his hips and bends his right knee. This action provides greater leg flexion and adds force to the push off. It may be noted that one of the advantages of the back-to-the-bar technique is at take-off where the jumper need not lie back as in straddle-style jumping. In the last three strides, the hips do not have to pass under and ahead of the shoulders. Rather, the hips drop slightly allowing the takeoff leg to extend forward providing greater leg flexion and velocity in the lift-off.

As the upward push-off starts, the jumper straightens his right leg and drives his left knee forward and upward. Simultaneously, his right hand and arm, bent at the elbow, swing up in unison with the left knee. The left arm drops to the side. A lift of the right shoulder accompanies this action.

At takeoff it is vital that the jumper's action be *straight up, not into the bar*. His take-off foot is not twisted to assist with the turn which occurs as he leaves the ground and *follows* the lift-off. As he starts his turn, the jumper looks at the bar over his *left* shoulder preparatory to the layout. He completes his turn during the upward lift of his body and is in his back-layout position as he starts across and over the bar.

THE LAYOUT

The layout over the bar is a simple one. It involves, primarily, a *slight* arch of the jumper's back to clear his hips. The jumper's shoulders at this point must be kept *parallel* with the cross bar. His arms remain at his sides; open hands are close to the body. Arms must *not* be raised, left shoulder must *not* be dropped. Such action will force him *downward* on the bar. Over the bar, the jumper rotates backward on an axis through his hips. During the layout, he looks at the bar over his *left* shoulder, chin tucked down to his chest. Over the bar his back is flat, hips tilted slightly forward.

As he clears the bar the jumper is in a *flat* position without too much arch of the back. His back and thighs are parallel with the ground. His lower legs, bent at the knee, hang at a 90-degree angle.

THE LANDING

Leg clearance is finally accomplished by simultaneously extending the legs and flexing the thighs. This lifts the jumper's legs over the bar,

Olympic champion Richard Fosbury demonstrates the back-layout technique.

At the end of his arched approach, the jumper's takeoff (right) leg is extended. His opposite (left) leg, bent at the knee is tucked. There is a slight drop of the hips. Takeoff is at the extreme end of the pit opposite the left bar standard.

At takeoff the jumper's body is in a vertical position. His right leg straightens and his left knee drives upward. The takeoff foot is not twisted and he

does not *turn toward the bar. His bent right arm drives forward and upward in a balancing action with his raised left knee, and his right shoulder is lifted. His eyes are on the cross-bar.*

After he leaves the ground, *the jumper initiates his turn. His action is still* upward. *His left shoulder, which is lower than his right, turns away from the bar and his raised left knee starts across in front of his hips. His left arm remains at his side.*

Following his lift off, the jumper looks at the bar over his left shoulder and continues his turn. His momentum continues upward but is now in the direction of the bar. His shoulders and hips are almost parallel. His arms drop to his sides and his bent left knee comes down opposite his right one.

As he starts his back-layout, the jumper's hips, which are now parallel with the bar, are elevated. His legs bent at the knees are in a hanging position. His arms, fully extended, are held close to his hips.

In his back-layout position the jumper's shoulders, which have already started downward, are slightly lower than his hips. This forms a slight arch in his back under which the bar passes. His arms are at his sides. The jumper's center of gravity is now outside *his body.*

As he clears the bar the jumper simultaneously flexes his thighs and extends his legs. As he prepares for a back-drop landing in the pit, the jumper's straight legs are parallel with the bar standards and his arms are over his head.

and pulls his head and chest toward the legs at the same time, preventing an over extension of the neck. The landing takes place on the shoulders, similar to a "back-drop" in trampolining.

TRAINING

Successful high jumping requires good all-round physical condition. Training, in all instances, should be adjusted to the individual. Jumping power depends upon the physiological behavior of the individual muscle fibers. Not all muscle tissue is alike in quality. It varies among individuals and also among the different muscles in a single body.

There are several theories that attempt to explain why shortening accompanies stimulation and combustion within the individual fibers. There is an optimum speed of shortening for each muscle to produce the greatest power in a given time. Cureton observes:

> It is important to realize that the mechanism which limits the speed of contraction of muscles in men is inherent in the fibers and depends upon nutrition and conditioning and is not under immediate control of the will. While pale fibers are thought to contract faster, the principal physical condition which limits the speed of any type of muscle contraction is the viscosity and relative fluidity of the muscle. Careful training is essential as a means of favoring this condition.[7]

A jumper's daily practice schedule should be regular and purposeful and should be part of a well-planned general practice pattern. If a minimum of fitness has been maintained throughout the year, the training schedule may be accelerated. The athlete who competes during the indoor season must time his training and reach his peak of condition accordingly.

For those who limit their jumping to the outdoor season, the start should be gradual. Four to six weeks of preliminary training, similar in most respects to that prescribed for other track and field athletes, is recommended prior to starting training on strenuous jumping. Included in such training would be:

(1) Easy jogging and running.

(2) Stretching and bending exercises with special emphasis on muscles of the back and hips; execute as part of the warm-up run.

[7] T. K. Cureton, *ibid.*, p. 35.

(3) High kicking and "jump-ups."

(4) Rope skipping.

(5) Weight training.

(6) Running and sprinting with an emphasis upon a "light touch" and high knee lift; include distance running up to 3 miles.

(7) Hurdling. (There are coaches who believe that hurdling is a good event to combine with high jumping and that conditioning in one contributes favorably to the other.)

(8) Long jumping.

Work on form should be started gradually and in accordance with the jumper's general condition. Assuming he has understanding and mastery of basic technique, form work during early season includes a "timing up" and refinement of the various parts of the complete technique, all undertaken at low heights. The jumper simply "swings through" six to eight jumps to loosen up and get the "feel" of his jumping coordination. Little emphasis at this time need be placed on an accurately measured approach or takeoff mark. His objective is to clear the bar in an easy, relaxed, and natural manner. Running with a light touch and high knee lift should be encouraged. Little coaching at this time should be necessary.

During this period of preliminary training, the jumper and his coach observe the key parts of the complete jump. By raising the bar 3 inches at a time, common faults will gradually be indicated. Motion pictures of the jumper may also be taken. Video tape and high-speed cameras are available in many schools and may also be used. These pictures provide an excellent aid in pointing out errors and making corrections in technique. Motion pictures are a valuable aid at all stages of the jumper's training, but are probably most effective during the early season when a correction of errors is more critical and effective. Pictures of championship jumpers are also available and may be used at this time to illustrate correct technique for both beginner and advanced jumper. Common faults which may be observed and corrected, one at a time, include:

(1) Takeoff mark too close or too far from the bar.

(2) Incorrect angle of approach.

(3) Run not smooth. Uneven stride. Not relaxed. Insufficient knee lift.

(4) Run too long or too short. Too fast or too slow.

(5) Insufficient kick-up of lead leg in takeoff. Incorrect angle of kick.

(6) Insufficient foot stamp.

(7) Leaning toward or turning into bar—just before, or at time of, takeoff.

(8) Insufficient lift—not straight upward.

(9) Faulty layout position. Bunching of body over bar.

(10) Unnecessary or incorrect arm and leg action in layout position.

(11) Pulling head up away from bar.

After jumping form has been perfected, very little strenuous work is needed. Too much practice jumping should be avoided. A spring will quickly lose its elasticity (force of rebound) if it is hammered or jarred too much. All good high jumpers seem to report the same reaction. Too much jumping inhibits their best performance. Almost without exception, they state that the best results are obtained by jumping no more than two or three times weekly and not at maximum height. This is in accordance with the mechanical principles of elasticity. Muscles, ligaments, tendons, and even bones, are elastic structures. They lose their elasticity if hammered too much by pounding on hard surfaces. High jumping requires explosive force, keen timing, and suppleness. These factors are enhanced by sufficient rest prior to competition. Some coaches recommend a rest of a week or ten days during midseason before competitive jumping. The amount of rest, as well as other factors of training, will be indicated by the muscular and nervous makeup of the individual jumper.

COMPETITION

(1) Report for competition well in advance of starting time and become thoroughly familiar with the environment of the pit and approach area.

(2) Warm up slowly and thoroughly.

(3) Measure and mark the approach and the takeoff points accurately. Make necessary adjustments according to weather conditions and texture of approach area.

(4) Know the maximum height you can jump with confidence and do not waste energy jumping at lower heights.

(5) Do not wear warm-up suit during official jumps.

(6) Concentrate on clearing the bar on your first attempt at each height.

(7) Stay off your feet between jumps. Save energy for jumping.

(8) Precede each jump with a short run to loosen up and relax.

(9) Once your turn is called, do not delay your jump too long. A good jumper must believe in his ability and approach each jump with a "positive" attitude.

(10) Avoid repeated balks or "jump-ups." This exhausts you mentally and physically.

(11) Loosen shoes after your turn and immediately put on warm-up suit.

(12) Know the rules of your event.

14
The Running Long Jump

The running long jump is probably the simplest of the jumping events. Analysis of its mechanics, however, reveals that it requires explosive force, fine timing, and suppleness. The position of the jumper's body is vertical throughout, a less demanding position than that used in either the high jump or pole vault.

Basically, the problem of the long jumper is to gain as much distance as possible in a horizontal direction. In order to do this, he must reach his point of takeoff at nearly maximum speed and, with his final lift, propel his body violently forward and upward. Performance of today's world-class long jumpers indicates that they have achieved a high degree of mechanical perfection in the mastery of this skill.

In 1935 Jesse Owens established a world long jump record of 26 feet 8¼ inches, and it lasted for 25 years. Ralph Boston later surpassed this record with a jump of 27 feet 5 inches.

The current world record in the long jump of 29 feet 2½ inches was established by Bob Beamon in the 1968 Olympic Games at Mexico City. "By taking advantage of the extremely favorable atmospheric conditions in Mexico," states the *1968 Olympic Book*, "Beamon leaped with technical perfection into the 21st century. . . ." His jump happened so incredibly fast that few of those gathered in the stadium or press box realized that they were viewing what perhaps will go down as one of the greatest athletic achievements of all times.

SOMATOTYPE

It is difficult to identify a typical somatotype for long jumping. Athletes with various body builds have been successful. High velocity at the time of takeoff is essential. Sprinting ability therefore is of primary importance. Most of today's champions are capable of running 100 yards in 9.7 or better. There is also a relationship between high jumping and long jumping abilities. Today's record holder has high-jumped 6 feet 9 inches. Most champions have been capable of high-jumping 6 feet or better.

More research has been conducted on the characteristics of high jumpers than on those of long jumpers, but findings suggest a significant relationship. Long legs are an asset since they give the jumper a mechanical advantage of a higher takeoff position and longer leg extension. Strong abdominal muscles which fix the pelvis and draw the trunk forward play an important part in the jumper's action. All forms of jumping require strong feet; statistics indicate that those of jumpers are usually broader and larger. Powerful arms play a prominent part in jumping technique. Along with well-developed shoulders, they are a common characteristic of the better jumpers.

STARTING THE BEGINNER

It is not difficult to introduce the beginner to the technique of long jumping. The skill is a familiar one. There is a natural attraction for boys and girls at an early age to see how far they can jump, and most have, at one time or other, included it as part of their play activity. Others have participated in jumping contests of one kind or other. A modified form of long jump, the triple jump, is included today in various fitness tests.

Precaution should be taken to make sure that the landing pit is safe. It should be soft, level, and adequate in length and width. Where a frame enclosure or curb is used, sharp or protruding edges should be padded. The area should be free of obstructions so that athletes can make free and uninhibited run-throughs.

The runway should be smooth. If not permanently surfaced, it should be well groomed. It should be a minimum of 120 feet in length. The takeoff board should be solid, set flush with the runway, and kept well marked. The area between the takeoff board and the pit should be smooth and level. A well-maintained jumping area motivates both the beginning and the advanced jumper.

The first step in starting the beginner is an easy, relaxed run-through. A distance of approximately eight running strides may be used. No jump is taken. From his starting point on the runway, the jumper simply runs through the pit. The emphasis is on an even stride and light touch. The jumper repeats the run-through several times.

As the run-throughs are performed, the jumper and his coach observe a point within easy jumping distance from the pit where a natural stride of the takeoff foot consistently hits. This is then marked as a tentative takeoff point. The board is not used at this stage of learning.

The second step is a "pop-up." This is simply a shortened jump emphasizing height rather than distance. Using his previously established starting and takeoff points as a guide, the jumper makes his approach run and jumps into the pit. Little emphasis is placed on an accurate takeoff mark. The important thing is that the takeoff is executed from a natural stride regardless of where it is in relation to the pit. In this exercise the athlete is getting the "feel" of jumping *naturally*, while the coach is observing whether the candidate is a "natural" jumper. Emphasis is on height as well as distance.

The run-through and pop-up exercises may be conducted individually or with a larger group. Each jumper adjusts his starting and takeoff points according to individual stride. It is recommended that in discovering potential long jumpers, the coach include all members of the squad. The event is interesting, and it is a good conditioning exercise; and the only sure way of determining jumping ability is by performance.

After the beginner becomes familiar with the above fundamentals, his jumps for distance may be measured from his "point of takeoff." Thus, he can discover whether he has any natural jumping ability without being distracted by having to hit the takeoff board accurately. Those beginners who show promise can develop this refinement as they continue with advanced technique.

MECHANICAL PRINCIPLES OF LONG JUMPING

Effective attempts at long jumping depend upon an understanding and application of four sets of mechanical principles:

(a) Velocity
(b) Angle of Takeoff and Flight
(c) Center of Gravity
(d) Action and Reaction

VELOCITY

Velocity, applied to long jumping, is the amount of force generated by the athlete both in the running approach and in the vertical lift at the time of takeoff. To exert this force, the jumper must maintain contact with the ground. Rosandich[1] estimates that "Ninety-five percent of peak velocity is reached at a distance of 22 yards." This estimate has implications in determining the length of the run.

ANGLE OF TAKEOFF AND FLIGHT

With any projectile, the angle of departure that gives the greatest range, where the resistance is not a major factor, is 45 degrees.

Stone observes,

[1] Tom Rosandich, "The Broad Jump—Mechanical and Physical Considerations," in *Track and Field Journal*, ed. Tom Rosandich (Djakarta, Indonesia: The Organizing Committee for the IVth Asian Games, 1962), p. 249.

This might lead us to believe that the broad jumper should project himself from the take-off board at this angle if he is to get the greatest distance for his effort. This does not happen to be the case, because the horizontal component of the greatest force which he can exert at this high angle will not be sufficient to add to his already high forward velocity. The result is that he must lower the angle of departure to the point where the horizontal component of the final drive from the take-off will enhance his horizontal velocity. This, of course, is done at the expense of the vertical component of force. He must, therefore, search for the optimum angle of departure to achieve his greatest distance. Experience indicates that this angle is about 25 degrees. If the magnitude of the horizontal component of force could be maintained, and the angle of departure elevated to 45 degrees, much greater distance would be reached.[2]

CENTER OF GRAVITY

In long jumping, gravity causes the human body to trace an arc from takeoff to landing; this is referred to as the "parabola flight." The body's path of flight is established at the time of takeoff; after the takeoff, nothing can be done to alter it. The flight is most efficient when there is no rotation. A forward rotation, or "somersaulting" as it is sometimes called, is caused when the jumper's takeoff foot is ahead of his center of gravity at the time of takeoff. An erect body position at the time of takeoff will assist the jumper in preventing this fault.

ACTION AND REACTION

For every action there is an equal and opposite reaction. This principle applies in long jumping as it does in high jumping. The trajectory of the body cannot be altered by raising the arms or legs during the jump, and the center of gravity remains the same. The jumper's action in the air is important only as it assists him in maintaining the most advantageous position for landing.

THE RUN

The run, combined with the lift at takeoff, provides velocity for the jump. Its length varies according to the individual jumper, as some require a longer run than others. Many do not run far enough.

[2] W. P. Bowen, *Applied Anatomy and Kinesiology*, 1953 rev. by H. A. Stone (Philadelphia: Lea and Febiger, 1953), p. 357.

In long jumping it is important that peak velocity be reached as quickly as possible. Relaxation at the time of takeoff is a distinct advantage, so momentum gained early in the run enables the jumper to maintain proper speed at this important point in his jump without undue tension. For this reason, some jumpers start their run from a crouch position.

It is estimated that a sprinter, regardless of speed, reaches 95 percent of his peak velocity at a distance of 66 feet. This would indicate that a run of from 120 to 130 feet would allow sufficient time for a jumper to reach a peak of momentum and still have time to gather for his jump. Some run as far as 150 feet. Repeated runs at this distance require good physical condition. Relaxed sprinting ability and a smooth even stride are essential to the jumper. In the performance of the running approach, all the mechanics of correct sprinting apply.

CHECKMARKS

When the distance of the run is decided, one checkmark is established about 50 feet from the board. If properly reached with the takeoff foot, this checkmark should assure the runner that he will arrive at the board in good position for his jump. Once a smooth, consistent run is perfected, many good jumpers eliminate the use of checkmarks. Concentration on the checkmark, or "jockeying" to reach it, should never distract the jumper from making a natural run.

Some jumpers experience difficulty in establishing checkmarks. Others waste a great deal of time perfecting this phase of the jump. For the jumper with an even stride the use of a checkmark should not present a problem. It is well to remember that the checkmark is adjusted to the jumper's stride and not his stride to the marks. But until an even grouping of strides can be consistently maintained, repetition of the run is fatiguing; eventually, the uneven run becomes frustrating and discouraging. For those experiencing this difficulty, added work on sprinting and hurdling is suggested.

It is recommended that checkmarks be established and practiced on the track away from the distraction of the board and pit. The jumper should be thoroughly warmed up and should remove his warm-up suit before attempting to perfect his marks. A distance similar to the jumper's approach run is first measured. Two observers assist the jumper. One is positioned at the end of the run, which represents the takeoff board. The other is located 50 feet from it. At these locations, each observer checks the point at which the jumper's takeoff foot consistently hits in his run-through. Adjustments are made as run-throughs are repeated. When perfected, these points are marked. They are then measured and easily transferred to the regular jumping runway. This run-through should be a part of the jumper's weekly practice schedule because his stride may lengthen as his condition improves. Marks must then be further adjusted. Weather conditions and texture of the runway surface are other factors which must be considered in this procedure.

THE TAKEOFF

Preparation for the takeoff starts approximately four strides from the board. Confidence in hitting the board should enable the jumper to look up and out at the proposed angle of his flight at this time. His momentum should be at the greatest possible level that allows for a relaxed performance.

Difference of opinion exists as to the length of the takeoff stride. Traditionally, a shortened stride has been made at this point and was usually recommended. Observation and study of the body mechanics of better jumpers reveals that actually the last stride is longer. Our knowledge of the relationship between momentum and the center of gravity supports this conclusion; recall the fact that a shortening of the last step at the board places the jumper's center of gravity ahead of his body causing forward rotation. Velocity increases stride length. It is difficult, if not impossible, to keep the center of gravity over the takeoff foot with a shortened last stride. Force, which provides momentum for the jumper's lift, can be applied only from the ground, and a long last stride permits a longer application of force and time for a more powerful lift of the free leg. In addition, the jumper has time to fully extend his takeoff leg, an action which adds power to his lift. A deliberate over-stride at the time of takeoff would not be consistent with correct body mechanics. A stride that is natural and provides the smoothest transfer of the jumper's momentum from his horizontal run to upward flight would appear to be a better compromise.

The emphasis at the time of the takeoff is on height. The takeoff foot is planted firmly in a position directly under the body. It must be pointed straight forward at all times. Most of today's good jumpers use a heel-toe roll-up action. Others stay with the more traditional flat-foot "stamp" or "beat." The roll-up action lets the jumper start the takeoff with his ankle fully flexed and makes possible a strong action of the ankle extensors over a longer range. There is a little give in the knee which reduces the jarring of the runner's body and results in stronger action from the knee extensors. As the lift starts, the knee and ankle extend violently. At the same time the free leg swings vigorously forward and upward. The jumper's arms swing upward to assist in the lift. The eyes focus upward on the angle of flight. The head, chest, and hips must be up.

THE FLIGHT

Once his body is in flight, the jumper must prepare to land. To do it most efficiently and still allow for the greatest distance is the single objective of technique at this stage of the jump. The angle of flight is approximately 25 degrees from horizontal. The highest position is about midway in the jump and the angle of descent is the same as that of the rise.

THE "TUCK" TECHNIQUE

Two types of action are used in the air. The most common and easiest is the "tuck." In this style the knees are simply drawn up and then straightened. The arms, swung forward to assist in the lift, are extended to maintain balance. The trunk is bent slightly forward. The jumper appears to be sitting in the air.

As the descent is started, the jumper extends his hips and knees; he swings his arms backward. These actions incline the upper part of the body forward a little. The center of gravity is slightly above the trajectory of the feet.

The "tuck" is not the most efficient style of broad jumping. Its continued use is probably due to its simplicity; it is easy to learn. However, close observation reveals that when the legs are immediately brought up in the tuck style the jumper is *opposing the force of gravity* almost throughout the jump. The extended knee and leg position is difficult to maintain. As a result the landing is frequently made with the feet under the body, instead of being extended forward, resulting in a loss of distance.

THE "HITCH-KICK" TECHNIQUE

The second style of jump is called the "hitch kick" or "stride in air." It is more difficult to learn, and requires patience and practice. Coordination and a sense of timing are necessary for its mastery.

The term "stride in air" is probably not an accurate one. When used loosely, and without clarification, it can be confusing. As previously observed, the jumper's velocity cannot be increased once he is off the

Olympic champion Bob Beamon demonstrates the hitch-kick technique of long jumping.

As he takes off, the jumper's chin is lifted and his eyes look up and out. His takeoff (right foot) is under his center of gravity and there is a slight bend in his takeoff leg.

At lift-off there is a powerful upward drive of the jumper's left knee and a full extension of his takeoff (right) leg and ankle. His takeoff foot remains in contact with the board as long as possible to add momentum to his jump.

At the peak of his trajectory, the jumper's body is erect; *his extended right leg and bent left knee are directly under his center of gravity.*

As he reaches the top of his jump, the jumper's arms are swung behind, and then forward and upward in a "windmill" action, which along with his arched back, slows down the forward rotation of his body.

As he starts his descent, the jumper reaches with his right leg and assumes a hurdler's semi-layout position. His left knee is then brought forward even with his right in a recovery action, as he goes into an extreme body dip. At this time the knees of his extended legs are nearly even with his shoulders and his extended arms and hands are swung under his hips.

As he prepares for his landing, the jumper's fully extended legs come together and his arms are raised.

As he lands in the pit, the jumper bends his legs and swings his arms backward. Along with an elevation of his hips, this action keeps the momentum of his body forward and in balance as he completes his jump.

ground. There is no base from which to apply added force. To merely "stride in the air," therefore, adds nothing to the jump.

The term "hitch kick" is probably more descriptive of correct technique. If this style of jump is used, it should be carefully analyzed and understood by performer and coach. When improperly executed, it may interfere with landing and actually shorten the jumper's distance.

The first requirement for successful execution of the hitch kick is *height*, achieved by an erect body position and vigorous vertical lift. It involves a planting of the takeoff foot in a position directly *under the body*. The chest is thrust forward and upward and the shoulders are thrust back. Arms are bent in their forward and upward lift. The head and chin are up. The eyes look out. The free leg is well tucked, with the heel almost touching the back of the thigh. This vertical lift is not easy to time. It requires patience. It may be practiced by using short runs with pop-ups, emphasizing height and lift rather than distance.

Assuming a takeoff from the left foot, the jumper's free (right) leg swings vigorously forward and upward to start his flight. It should be stressed that at this point the takeoff (left) foot "stays behind," applying force from the board for as long as possible. If he brings it through too fast, the jumper loses force, and his timing, especially at the top of the jump, is affected.

At the peak of the trajectory, the right leg will be extended forward, *and then* down and back. This allows ample time for the left leg to complete its full extension before it follows through with action similar to that of the right. With the knee and foot lifted well up, the left leg, as it passes the right, moves forward to full extension. The right leg will then complete its cycle as it is brought forward and upward to join the left. Both are high and fully extended as the jumper starts his descent. At the crest of the trajectory, the jumper's arms are fully raised and then swing forward and downward on descent to assist in landing. The trunk is in an erect position throughout. It may lean slightly back at the peak of the jump. Just before landing, the jumper leans forward with the head and trunk. The hips are relaxed. The arms are forced forward and downward as the jumper prepares for his landing.

THE LANDING

Correct position in landing is one of the refinements of the great long jumper. It involves a definite technique that requires practice and timing. The legs are fully extended and parallel. Feet are 6 to 12 inchs apart. At the instant of landing the knees relax. The hips are lifted. The resulting momentum carries the jumper forward.

In landing the jumper aims for maximum distance and balance. As he lands in the pit, he must not fall backward. Neither should he fall forward on his hands. Either conclusion of the jump would indicate that his legs have not been fully extended and that forward body rotation has occurred during the jump. As the jumper hits the pit he swings his arms upward, enabling him to land in complete control with his body in good balance over his feet.

In a variation of the straight forward landing the jumper stiffens one leg fully and relaxes the other. This causes the body to fall to the side. Another style is to pivot completely out of the pit. Both of these landings require extremely fine timing. When poorly executed they cut down on maximum mechanical efficiency. Neither is recommended.

TRAINING

The training of a long jumper has much in common with that of the sprinter and high jumper. General principles covered for each apply. His practice must be regular. It follows the general daily schedule previously outlined in Chapter 3.

The jumper needs speed, endurance, and elasticity of the muscle group involved. His run must be accurate and consistent, and the various parts of his form must be perfected and well timed. His training exercises should develop these requirements. Frequently the long jumper participates in other events. In such cases, much of his conditioning is provided by the training he does for them.

Opinion differs as to the amount of rest needed between practice and competition. Some, with good results, train hard four days a week with only one day's rest before competition. Others find they get the best results from resting two days or more. This can best be determined by the experience of the individual jumper. Exercises characteristic of the long jumper's midseason training schedule are:

(1) Jogging and easy running for warm-up.
(2) Stretching and bending exercises for muscle groups involved in jumping.
(3) Weight training (half squats and leg presses).
(4) Repeat sprints of 50 and 60 yards. Practice each distance with both crouch start and jog rest interval. Adjust number to age and needs of jumper.
(5) Runs of 220 and 300 yards.
(6) Low hurdling.
(7) "Pop-ups" using 8-stride approach or shorter. Emphasize *takeoff* form and *lift*. Variation of this exercise includes long jump over cross bar at approximately 4 to 4½ feet. Use same approach emphasizing *landing technique*.
(8) Full approach runs to perfect checkmarks. Emphasize *fast start* and even strides. If jumper has difficulty adjusting checkmarks

after continued attempts, discontinue practice on runway and move to track. Practice for even strides at 150 to 220 yards.

(9) Full-scale jumping. Perfect all parts of form at maximum effort. Allow two days rest between full-scale jumping and competition.

COMPETITION

(1) If competition is away from home, determine surface of runway and make sure proper shoes are included as part of equipment, i.e., short spikes for all-weather surface.

(2) Accurately measure and record checkmarks the *day before* competition. Checkmarks should be so accurately established and practiced that little or no attention need be given to them on the day of competition. The emphasis and attention at this time is on *jumping*.

(3) Report for competition well in advance of starting time. Become thoroughly familiar with the environment of the landing pit and runway.

(4) Warm up slowly and thoroughly. Know your capacity and prepare to make your best effort on your *first* jump.

(5) Measure and adjust checkmarks *after* warming up. Take only enough run-throughs to determine condition of runway. Adjust marks according to weather, wind and runway conditions.

(6) If in another event, make every effort to perform your best jump before it starts.

(7) Make every jump count. Avoid balks or run-throughs without jumping.

(8) Do not delay your jump once your turn is called.

(9) Conserve energy between jumps, but make sure you are loose and relaxed before jumping.

(10) React confidently to "fouls." Determine the cause, make necessary adjustments, and concentrate on the *next jump*. It takes only one to win the event or set a record.

15
The Triple Jump

The triple jump, until recently better known as the hop, step and jump, is an established Olympic event. It has not, however, been a popular one in this country. Although E. B. Bloss established an American record of 48 feet 6 inches as early as 1893, athletes from other countries have dominated the event. Early records were established by jumpers from Ireland and the Scandinavian countries, and more recent ones by those from Australia, Japan, Brazil, and Russia. The current world's record of 57 feet ¾ inches is held by Victor Saneyev of the Soviet Union.

While high schools in the Southern states included the event on their schedules as early as 1930, it has only recently been added to the National Collegiate program. Its inclusion should strengthen America's Olympic stature.

Athletes from this country have adapted readily to triple jumping. Greater opportunity for competition has resulted in marked improvement in technique and achievement. Very few triple jumpers can long-jump more than 24 feet. It is predicted that a new world record in the triple jump is inevitable if a long jumper who can jump 25 feet will devote equal time to mastery of the triple jump.

SOMATOTYPE

Successful triple jumpers are not readily characterized by body type. The Japanese, although slight in build but quick in temperament and well coordinated, have traditionally been good jumpers. Iimuro, who could jump 51 feet, was 5 feet 4 inches tall. Talented jumpers from other countries, including the Irish, have been somewhat taller, ranging from 5 feet 8 inches to 5 feet 10 inches.

Most successful triple jumpers have been good sprinters; some have been good hurdlers. And long jumping ability is obviously an asset. Not all good long jumpers, however, have been good triple jumpers. This is probably due to the fact that they have not practiced sufficiently on technique to take advantage of their superior long jumping strength.

The event requires perfect timing. Efficient arm-leg coordination, combined with proper knee bend, figures prominently in good form. Good jumpers have the ability to control the body's center of gravity throughout the three phases of the jump. Apart from speed and natural spring, the ability to divide the triple effort into its proper proportions is a noteworthy attribute of those who are most successful. Generally speaking, a good long jumper who has the patience and the will to achieve a mastery of the added hop and step should potentially develop into a good triple jumper.

STARTING THE BEGINNER

Triple jumping may be introduced to beginners at an early age. It is not, however, as easy to teach and learn as the long jump. At the outset, some athletes have difficulty mastering the rhythm of the three-part timing, others with the change of feet involved. Some find that the transfer of momentum from the run to the takeoff is a problem.

A simple demonstration is an important first step in teaching. When followed by a slow, step-by-step whole-part approach, it usually brings effective results. The following sequence, adaptable to group as well as individual instruction, is suggested:

(1) From a standing position, balance on one foot. Bend the opposite leg, raising the knee so the thigh is parallel with the ground. Jump upward bending the jumping leg. Jump only high enough for a good knee bend. Reverse jumping foot to determine which feels the more natural.

(2) From the same starting position, hop a short distance. Bring the bent knee up as high as possible. Repeat until jumper gets the feel of the hop, and is in good balance on his recovery. Use both left and right foot for takeoff.

(3) Hop, landing on the *same* foot; and step, landing on the *opposite*. Keep knee of jumping leg bent and weight forward. Make the step long so that the jumper gets the feel of *moving forward*. Repeat until learner familiarizes himself with the coordination of this phase.

(4) Add the jump, combined with the hop and step. Practice three-part coordination from a standing position. For timing and rhythm, this action may be counted aloud—"One, Two, Three"—as in teaching a dance step. The complete action should be continuous and smooth in execution. There should be no stopping or slowing down between parts. The body should be kept *upright* throughout.

(5) Move to the jumping pit and runway. Add an approach run of 5 to 10 yards. Continue practice of three-phase action. Make the hop *low*, the step and jump *high*. Emphasize a bent knee following takeoff.

(6) Increase distance of running approach to 10 yards. Limit hop to distance of 10 feet. Increase hop to 13 feet as distance of run is increased. Gradually increase distance of both as jumping ability improves.

(7) Practice hop and step separately. Demonstrate the advantage of short hop resulting in a more efficient and longer step. Practice step and jump separately. Practice long jumping using the weakest leg for takeoff.

As regular exercises are started at the jumping pit, the coach or instructor should make sure that all safety precautions covered under the long jump are checked. The hop limit should be limited and marked. The takeoff for the jump should be established at a point where all jumpers can reach the pit with ease.

An exact takeoff during preliminary practice need not be stressed. If the distance of a jump is to be recorded, it may be measured from the point where the jumper can take off naturally without the distraction of having to hit the board. This will vary with each jumper. In selecting potential jumpers for competitive training, the most natural or best qualified may be identified in this manner. Checkmarks can be added later for those selected.

TECHNIQUE

Mechanical principles covered under the long jump apply to the triple jump. They should be reviewed and understood by both the teacher and pupil as advanced training continues.

Since the jumper's foot touches the ground twice after his takeoff, the principle of *eccentric thrust* is especially to be noted. Simply stated, it means thrust in an off-center direction. As applied to the triple jump, it means that each time the jumper's foot touches the ground, it should be directly under the center line of his body. Otherwise, because of eccentric thrust, he will be moving in a lateral direction rather than straight forward when he takes off for the next phase of the triple jump.

THE APPROACH RUN

Fundamentals of the run are the same as in the long jump. The run provides momentum for the jump. The faster the jumper can run in his approach, *and still maintain correct vertical body position* at the time of takeoff, the more horizontal velocity he will transfer to his jump.

The length of the run is determined by the strength and speed of the individual jumper. It must not be too long. If the runner is fatigued, and has to reach for the board, he may lean back at the time of his takeoff—thus causing the hop to be too high. The jumper's eyes should be forward and his head up throughout the run. He should look *up* at the time of takeoff. At this point, he should feel that he is moving *forward.*

THE HOP

The hop starts the three-phase action. To preserve momentum, it should be as low as possible. The stronger leg is used. Some good jumpers, with adequate training, have effectively taken off on the weak leg, but this is not recommended as a general practice. The foot plant varies with the jumper. Some find landing on the ball of the foot preferable because less momentum is lost. Others land on the heel or employ a flat foot.

As the hop takeoff starts, the drive of the free leg, flexed at the knee, is forward. The opposite arm drives forward and up to balance the powerful leg drive. The jumper's aim throughout is to keep his body in an upright position. This is a special attribute of the skilled jumper. The hopping leg, in bent position, is brought forward and through. The free leg is relaxed. Slightly flexed, it comes through automatically to counter-balance the action of the takeoff leg.

The bent hopping leg, thigh parallel to ground, lower leg relaxed, is *slow* to make contact with the ground. If a landing is anticipated, or the hopping leg moves down too soon, the jumper's body weight will be forward. This results in a short and hurried step, and loss of balance. The following step will therefore be low rather than high.

Proper arm action during the hop is important. As in running, the arms provide balance. They should travel in the same plane as the legs.

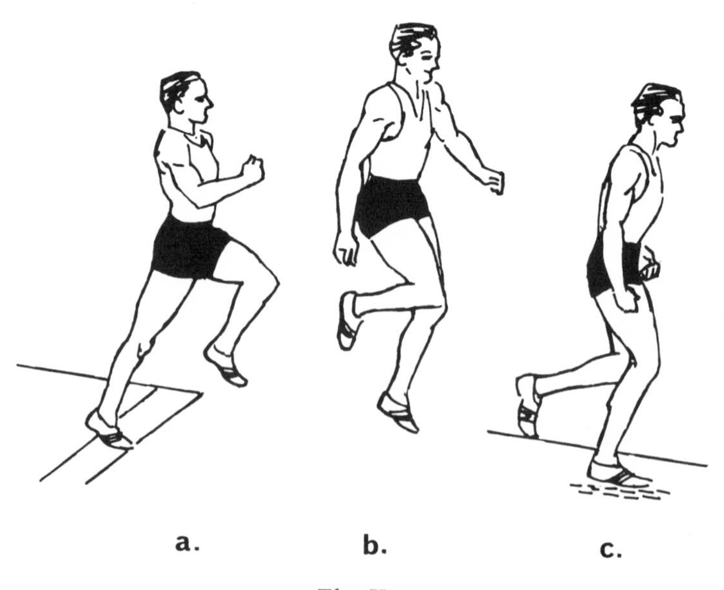

The Hop

Note upright position of body throughout. (a) Coordination of free leg and opposite arm is good. (b) At the height of the hop, the bent hopping leg is tucked for slow descent. (c) Body weight stays behind hopping leg in landing.

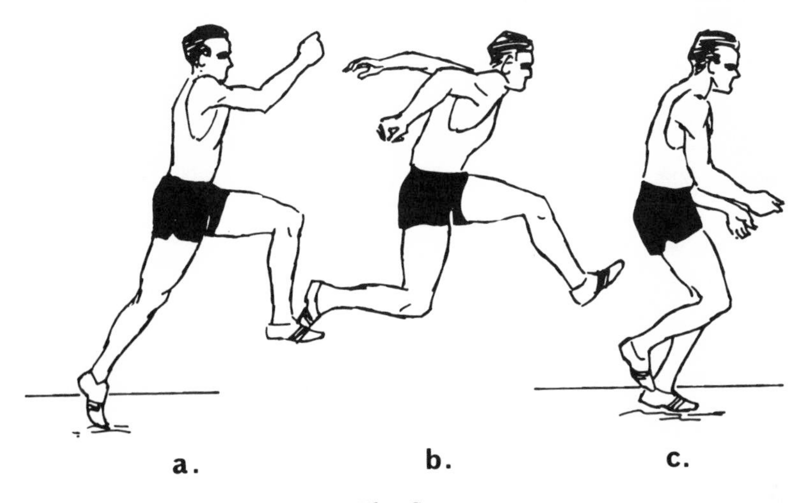

The Step

(a) Lift is good. (b) Trunk remains upright. Thigh of lead leg is parallel to ground. (c) Jumper lands in vertical position for final takeoff. Weight is behind jumping foot.

Action should be straight forward. If one arm swings too far to the rear at the time of landing, it will tend to pull the shoulder on the same side to the rear and will unbalance the jumper.

In landing following the hop, the jumper aims to land with his body weight *behind* his hopping leg. This ensures a greater angle of projection. The distance of the travel is thus increased.

THE STEP

The step, which follows the hop, is frequently the weakest part of the jumper's form. It is often shorter than it should be. The cause can usually be attributed to a hop landing that is inefficient for one of the reasons previously described.

In executing the step, the body weight should be kept behind the takeoff foot. The body's angle of projection should be closer to 45 than 25 degrees. The trunk is upright.

Immediately following the takeoff, the jumper flexes and draws his takeoff leg up under his body. The opposite (lead) leg is bent, with the thigh parallel to the ground. Arm action continues stright forward. From this position the jumper is in good balance and prepared, at ground landing, to execute a strong thrust which accompanies his final jump.

There are jumpers who bring both arms to the rear in the middle of the step flight. Those using this technique contend they are in better position to effect an upward lift in the jump takeoff. Others maintain that it enables them to keep their weight behind the jumping foot, a position that results in a more vertical takeoff. This technique must be well timed; if faulty, it results in a forward body rotation.

THE JUMP

If the step has been executed correctly, the athlete lands in position for a jump takeoff, for which the angle should be approximately 45 degrees. This is the last phase of the action. Fundamentals are the same as for the long jump. The athlete aims for maximum height. At takeoff he drives his arms and trailing leg vigorously forward and upward. The trailing leg, bent at the knee, is swung through as high as possible in order to elevate the hips. The emphasis here is on a "push-off" action.

Once he has left the ground the jumper attempts to maintain good body balance in the air as long as possible. He counteracts the tendency of his body to rotate forward and downward by maintaining his upper body (trunk) in an upright position. To maintain this position and prepare for the most efficient landing, jumpers employ several techniques similar to those used in long jumping.

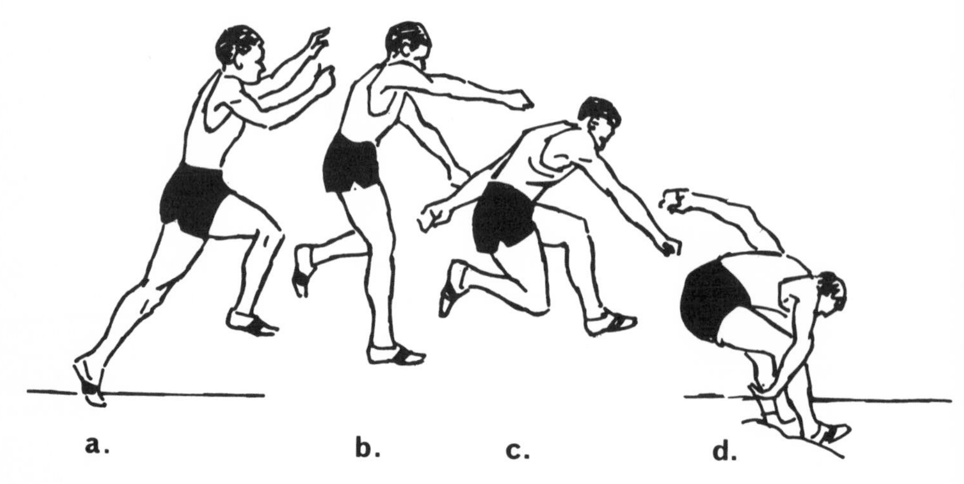

The Jump

(a) Jump takeoff, at 45-degree body angle. (b) Vertical position of trunk at height of jump. (c) Hitch kick during jump flight. (d) Flexed legs whipped forward in landing.

While the "hitch kick" is superior for long jumping, it is not recommended for this phase of the triple jump. The athlete at this stage of his jump is usually fatigued, which cuts down on his coordination, and his loss of momentum gives him too little time for efficient execution.

Most jumpers use a "hang" or "sail" technique in flight. In the "sail" style the jumper brings his left leg through, leading with his knee just as in a long jump takeoff. The right arm is simultaneously swung forward and upward. The right leg then moves upward and forward to join the left leg. The flexed left arm, which was first swung behind the body, then moves forward while the right arm moves down. The jumper is now in a position with his body leaning slightly forward, legs extended in front, knees bent and arms in front of his shoulders. Landing is made in this position with the flexed legs coming through at the last moment.

In the "hang" style the jumper simply flexes his legs and lets them "drag" behind throughout the jump. The upper-body (trunk) remains upright. The arms are swung forward and upward for lift and balance. The Japanese employ an effective variation of this arm action. Instead of swinging the arms forward and upward, they swing them from behind in a manner similar to jumping a rope. This is considered to be an advantage to the jumper because it helps keep him in an upright position. In this style the jumper looks toward the sky, maintaining his "hang" position as long as possible. Here again, as in long-jumping, the athlete's legs come through as late as possible in his final landing.

TRIPLE JUMP RATIOS

To achieve his best total effort the jumper must consider each phase of his jump in its relation to the other. He must *proportion* a certain amount of his total effort to each part so that he will not sacrifice distance in one to gain it in another. This is called his triple jump "ratio."

To ensure this balance some coaches attempt to assign an arbitrary percentage or distance to each part. Because of individual differences, this kind of fixed ratio is difficult, if not impossible, to establish. Even a championship jumper is not consistent in this respect. In comparing his jumps of equal distance, observation shows that in one his hop may be long, and in another, short. All of our better triple jumpers, however, employ a *long step*, and its proper proportion in relation to the other two phases (hop and jump) appears to be the key to triple jumping efficiency. Because of this relatively long step, which actually makes the three phases of his effort nearly equal, the modern term Triple Jump is probably more descriptive of the event than the traditional "Hop-Step-and-Jump."

In addition to distance ratio, the comparative height of the three phases of the action is significant. Mechanical analysis reveals that the hop should never be too high. In terms of flight path and control of the body's center of gravity, the hop is the lowest. The step is slightly higher with the jump the highest of the three. In other words, the jumper is gaining height each time he jumps.

TRAINING

The training patterns of triple and long jumpers have much in common. All-round conditioning is similar. Each requires training that develops strength, speed, and endurance. Exercises that develop the legs, including those for the knees and ankle joints, and exercises for the abdomen and back are important for jumpers in both events. Sprinting, hurdling, and prescribed endurance running are recommended for both. Training for the approach run in order to develop evenness and consistency of stride, is similar.

The individual differences and needs of each jumper must be considered. Often an athlete may be training for both events. However, once he reaches the takeoff board, his technique changes. The technique used in the triple jump is more complex, and requires greater training than that for long jumping.

Exercises different from those for long jump training are suggested especially for the training of the triple jumper:

(1) Repeat hops and steps from a standing position. Indoors and out. Good early season training. If indoors, use rubber mats to reduce the shock of landing on hard surfaces. Outdoors, use a grassy area. Stress a *high* knee lift on each hop and a flexing of the leg in landing.

(2) Hops for distance of 100 yards. Use both legs, one at a time. Weak leg twice as much as strong.

(3) Continuous long hops, and big steps for distance of 50 to 100 yards. Alternate legs. Gradually increase speed of hop and step with decrease of distance covered.

(4) Hop and step into pit using approach from *seven* to *eleven* strides. Emphasis on holding step as long as possible. Exaggerate distance of step.

(5) Step and jump into pit. Use short approach as above. Stress smoothness and *continuity in execution.*

(6) Hop, hop and jump. Flex knee on each landing. Stress triple rhythm.

(7) Repeat steps. This is the weakest phase for most jumpers, so devote added time to it. The exercise is simple. It involves the continuous execution of *long,* bounding steps for a distance of 100 yards. Alternate legs for each takeoff. Knee of flexed lead leg is brought up *high.* Vigorous arm and leg action is straight forward.

(8) Long jumps into pit. Take off on alternate feet. Use approach run of 7 feet.

(9) Ratio training. Numbers represent changing distances (in feet) of hop, step and jump. Execute exercise, increasing distances proportionately as follows:

10 — 10 — 10
12 — 12 — 12
12 — 14 — 13
13 — 15 — 13

TRAINING INNOVATIONS AND VARIATIONS

(1) Use of weighted belts during practice as added resistance and overload on muscles.

(2) Hopping over low hurdles spaced 8 yards apart.

(3) Hopping from low platform or box (6″–12″ high) to develop leg flexion and strength in landing.

(4) Placement of low hurdles between step takeoff and pit to develop height and increased forward momentum in this phase of action.

COMPETITION

See Long Jump (page 192).

16
Pole Vaulting

Pole vaulting is a fascinating and highly artistic athletic skill. Some believe it to be the most complicated of the field events. In no event can so many different things go wrong. For some this makes it a difficult event to coach. Rarely do we find a vaulter, even among the great ones, who is not committing some technical error. The secret of good coaching is to recognize and correct these deviations.

Pole vaulting is a highly scientific event. Much of it is mechanical and capable of theoretical analysis. Early research by A. C. Gilbert of Yale University contributed substantially to a discovery of many of these principles. The superiority of Yale pole vaulters, for a number of years, reflected this knowledge. Later, moving pictures provided a medium for investigation which resulted in a more accurate analysis of vaulting mechanics.

Better poles have been a significant factor in the improvement of pole-vaulting technique. Pole vaulting was added to the American track and field program in 1850. At this time a solid pole, with a spike in the end, was used. Early vaulters climbed the pole hand over hand and flipped over the bar. In 1880 official track rules were changed making it illegal to raise the lower hand over the upper while vaulting. This rule still stands.

Since that time various materials have been used for poles. Bamboo, steel, and light metal have had their day. Today, fiber glass poles are universally used. Fiber glass poles are made with plastic fiber. The fiber glass pole is a tube rolled out of nonalkaline spun-glass tissue bonded with a synthetic resin. This material has outstanding elastic qualities. Its multilayered structure provides the strength to withstand the extreme mechanical stress of bending.

There are significant advantages in using a fiber glass pole. It has been found that a vaulter can grip the pole 6 inches to a foot higher without taking the shock he would get from poles made of other materials. The second advantage is that a fiber glass pole is able to store energy in larger quantities than a rigid one and to return it in greater amounts to the vaulter. Further, fiber glass helps the vaulter make a smoother change in the pole's position from horizontal to vertical as he executes his swing up. Because of these advantages, fiber glass has become the choice of all world-class vaulters.

Bob Mathias, in 1948, was the first vaulter to use a fiber glass pole. Its popular use, however, did not come until 1962, when John Uelses, using such a pole, vaulted 16 feet for a new world's record. Progress since that time has been consistent and rapid, with a record of over 18 feet being established in 1970. Vaulters are fascinated by the energy stored in a fiber glass pole and the potential it offers for even greater achievement. Recent research reveals that a vaulter should be able to develop a "mechanically perfect" vault by carefully controlling and increasing his initial takeoff velocity so as to bend the pole to the extent that it would give him the greatest upward thrust. Study of technical flaws that prevent the full exploitation of the theoretically possible improvement in the push-up, and possible increase in the height of the handhold, continues. Coaching techniques are also being revised and improved. With continued investigation and experimentation, new records are imminent.

SOMATOTYPE

Pole vaulting has a peculiar attraction for athletes of all ages. However, not all have the natural strength, coordination, and courage to perform the event successfully. An early start is important. Much more could be done in starting beginners at an early age if proper equipment were made available for interested aspirants.

Ideal qualifications for vaulting are well known and have been described many times. Pole vaulting is one of the most demanding of physical skills, and it requires height, agility, speed, and coordination. Courage also helps, but it comes with practice as vaulting skill is developed. While the height of a vaulter is important, it should not be considered essential in identifying the prospective candidate. Like courage, it will probably come with maturity.

Most mature vaulters range in height from 5 feet 10 inches to 6 feet 3 inches. It may be assumed that, all other qualifications being equal, the taller man should vault higher than the short one. Quite obviously, he can hold the pole higher and his longer arms should enable him to push his body higher. Good upper-body strength is a must. There are, however, those who believe that the fiber glass pole has brought a new streamlined breed of vaulters into the track world. The powerful and bulky frames of Don Bragg and Cornelius Warmerdam, they contend, have given way to the more dynamic and compact body types of contemporary record holders. Strength alone is not carrying the "world class" vaulters over this new height. With the fiber glass pole, the main things now are speed and timing, though undoubtedly well-developed arms and shoulders continue to be an asset for one who aspires to clear 18 feet. Small, as well as large men, continue to make good vaulters. A coach would do well not to discourage because of body type an enthusiastic beginner who really wants to learn the event. Regardless of build, championship vaulting technique at any level takes a good deal of ability and many hours of hard work.

STARTING THE BEGINNER

A variety of devices and methods, both indoors and outdoors, are used by coaches in teaching the basic skill of pole vaulting. They group themselves into two broad categories, (a) developmental and simulated exercises and (b) instruction in basic fundamentals.

DEVELOPMENTAL AND SIMULATED EXERCISES

Simple rope climbing is an excellent means of developing arm and shoulder strength, an essential first step in the mastery of vaulting competency. Specific rope climbing exercises include climbing with: (a) hands and feet; (b) hands only, from a standing position; (c) hands only, extending the legs at 90 degrees; (d) hands only, from a seated position; and (e) repeated climbs. The performer may execute all of the above while wearing a weighted jacket or belt if he wishes to develop his strength further.

At least as valuable as rope climbing is the practice of rope vaulting. By this means, a beginner can practice on a rope almost every vaulting fundamental that can be executed on a pole. Rope vaulting is especially valuable where actual vaulting is not feasible during winter months. With a swinging rope, even the run can be simulated. Rope vaulting not only enables the beginner to master the whole concept of vaulting with little risk of injury, but also allows him to concentrate on and practice the individual components. He can repeat fundamentals many times without tiring. Once outdoor vaulting starts, warm-up exercises and review of fundamentals using a rope can be continued as a part of daily practice.

In rope vaulting a regular climbing rope, suspended overhead, is used. The beginner grasps the rope with both hands as high over his head as he can reach. If he is right-handed, his right hand will be on top; otherwise the left. From this position he can practice and perfect such important parts of the vaulting technique as: getting the head back and the eyes up; lifting the chest; keeping the arms flexed; pushing down on the pole; placing the plant foot directly behind the pole; leading with the takeoff knee; getting the timing of the delayed swing or hang; getting the knees into the chest; keeping the head rolled back during the ride; and riding so that the hips are higher than the shoulders. A demonstration of these aspects of vaulting by the coach or an experienced vaulter is an excellent teaching approach. Most beginners can execute most of them the first time they try. Others will need practice.

Exercises on a swinging rope follow those executed from a stationary position. The vaulter's momentum is provided either by a strong forward push off the floor, or by timing his approach so that he catches a moving rope on its back swing and then rides forward with it.

After developing the ride the next step is to extend both feet up along the rope. When his momentum has been almost fully expended, the vaulter pulls straight up the rope so that his shoulders come as far above his hands as possible. From this position he executes a turn and kick. This phase requires patience and practice. A right-handed vaulter is instructed to kick his right leg high and across his body, aiming at some specific object above. This facilitates the turn. A push down and release from the rope completes the action. The athlete should repeat this phase until he can perform it smoothly. As he progresses, he aims to time the pull along with the turn-kick, just as he would on a pole. A beginner with good coordination will execute this exercise well on the first day.

After he has developed the above fundamentals, the beginner may be introduced to rope vaulting over high jump standards. The bar is set low (4′ to 4′6″) and close to the rope. As confidence and ability develop the bar is moved up and the standards, set on boxes if necessary, are moved gradually back so that the vaulter can practice the complete swing-through, kick, and turn over the bar. By jumping and grasping the rope higher, the beginner gets a rough impression of the actual feel of vaulting. As he advances, a vaulter can gain further experience from exercises on a moving rope. Mats, properly placed for safe landing, should be provided in all instances.

Some coaches suggest that an effective method of starting a beginner is to have him vault up onto, and down from, a low box or platform. By this means, the athlete can learn fundamentals without fear of falling. He uses a strong, short pole; first he practices the swing-up, with a landing on the platform, then he works on the swing-down, or dismount. On the dismount, a turn around the pole can be added. In both instances, the beginner is instructed to stay close to, or "ride," the pole. This exercise is used indoors and out. As in gymnastics, "spotting" by the coach or an assistant should be provided.

FOUR FUNDAMENTALS

The beginner is introduced to the skill of vaulting with a pole when he moves to the vaulting pit. Here four fundamentals are stressed: (a) holding the pole, (b) the lead knee lift, (c) the hang from a straight top arm, and (d) hip elevation. No cross bar is used in practicing these fundamentals.

A beginning vaulter should not be rushed in his learning of these skills. He should concentrate on them one at a time and understand the relation of each to the well-timed complete vaulting technique. There

Holding the Pole

The Lead Knee Lift

are good vaulting coaches who believe that before ever attempting to clear a cross bar a young aspirant learning to vault for the first time should spend as long as 6 months to a year practicing nothing but these fundamentals. There is much merit and validity to this point of view.

HOLDING THE POLE

The beginning vaulter can be taught from a stationary position how to hold the pole. At this stage, an exact hold is not necessary and lengthy instruction should not delay his more active practice. It is more important that he get the "feel" of the pole, and he will learn much from trial and error. A few basic instructions at this time will suffice.

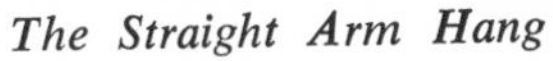

The Straight Arm Hang

Hip Elevation

For the beginner, a short pole, 8 to 10 feet long, is used. This may be a fiber glass pole, sawed off to proper length, preserving the plugged end. To insure a firm grip, the top 3 feet of the pole are taped. A fiber glass pole of this length will be light but rigid. This is an advantage since the beginner can handle it with ease and will have a firm base to swing from. Regardless of its length and quality, a vaulter's pole should be tested each time it is used. This is done by placing the point of the pole on the ground and pressing down forcibly in the middle to see if it will break. Confidence in the safety of his pole is essential to the progress of the young vaulter. One mishap at this stage of his learning may prove an insurmountable handicap to his interest and otherwise successful development.

If he is right-handed and using an 8-foot pole, the beginner will grip it with his top (right) hand (palm up) fairly close to the top. The greatest pressure in the carry will be on his thumb and index finger. With his left hand (palm down) he will grip the pole about 3 feet below his right hand. His left forearm, parallel with the ground, will cross in front of his body at about the height of his hips. In this position the vaulter should face squarely forward, with the point of the pole, at eye level, pointing straight ahead. Since it is important later in his pole plant, he should be reminded to carry the pole close to his right hip.

THE LEAD KNEE LIFT

Next the beginner is moved to a position in front of the plant box where he is taught the lead knee lift. The lead knee is so named because it is the knee that *initiates* the vaulter's swing up action.

Holding the pole in the box, with his extended right arm high over his head, the vaulter lifts his right knee forward and upward toward his chest. In this position his top (right) hand is directly over his left foot. There is a slight lean of his hips into the pole which results in a pulling action on his top arm.

The lead knee lift, since it teaches the beginner the importance of keeping his knee close to his body, is an important fundamental. It also starts his swing up and "rock-back" action which he learns later. Two essentials are stressed at this time: (1) keep the top arm fully extended, and (2) keep the entire action of the body, including the knee lift, straight forward.

THE STRAIGHT ARM HANG

The straight arm hang is taught basically the same as the lead knee lift. The vaulter's position is the same. The emphasis, however, is on the *fully extended* position of the vaulter's top (right) arm and the hang of his body from it. To get the feel of this action, the vaulter can push himself off the runway with his left foot and, hanging on the pole, swing into the pit. The essentials here are similar to the knee lift: stay close to the pole and keep the action straight forward.

HIP ELEVATION

Hip elevation is an important fundamental of fiber glass pole vaulting. It is imperative for the beginner to understand that in his swing up, not only are his legs extended upward toward the top of the pole, but his hips must also be lifted. In the swing up, beginners have a tendency to kick their legs forward, rather than upward, without elevating their hips. As a result they kick into, rather than up past, the bar.

The principle of hip elevation can be illustrated and practiced on a rope. If he has had the advantage of preliminary practice on a climbing rope, the beginner will be familiar with the action. Here he can hang, rock back with his head and shoulders, and swing up to an inverted position with hips and legs extended upward along the rope. On a rope, the beginner has a secure base to hang from, and if necessary, his coach can help him attain the desired position. This also gives him the "feel" of raising his hips and their relationship to the upward extension of his legs.

The practice of hip elevation on a pole is basically the same as on a rope. The inverted hang position is the same except the vaulter does not have a stationary base to hang from. He must execute it on a moving pole, cannot maintain his upside-down position for long, and must swing on into the pit for a landing. To gain momentum for his swing up, the vaulter, with his pole planted in the box, pushes off his left foot. Combined with his vigorous knee lift and straight arm hang, this starts his swing up action. Eventually, he executes this same action with an easy approach run which automatically leads into his learning and practice of the "pop-up."

THE POP-UP

The "pop-up" is an intermediate training exercise used to develop the all important rock-back phase of plexiglass pole vaulting. As soon as he can swing up reasonably well, using the four fundamentals previously covered, the beginner should start practicing this skill. No crossbar is used in this exercise. So that he will have a firm pole to swing from, the vaulter uses a low handhold. His run is short and relaxed so that his body is under control at all times.

The "pop-up" starts with a regular pole plant and take off. As he swings up, the vaulter drops his head and shoulders back and extends his feet toward the top of the pole. As his pole straightens, he concentrates on rocking back and lifting his feet high over his head. At the top of his swing up he hangs from a straight top arm. His shoulders are parallel with the runway; his feet are high and back over his head. (See page 223.) Hanging in this "upside-down" position, the vaulter completes the "pop-up" by simply riding the pole into the pit. There is no pull up or turn over.

All pole vaulters should learn to execute the "pop-up." It is an important step in the development of the beginner and a valuable warm-up exercise and continuing review of basic technique for the advanced vaulter.

THE COMBINED ACTION

After learning the four fundamentals, and practicing them in combination with the "pop-up," the young vaulter is ready to try the combined action of vaulting with an easy run. For this early training a safe landing pit must be provided. Since they are designed for modern pole vaulting, a portable one is recommended. If not available, one filled with properly encased sponge rubber trimmings should be used. The placement and safety of the landing pit should be checked before each practice by coach and vaulter.

If the vaulter is going to learn to vault correctly, he must approach the planting box in a straight line. There should be no side-stepping, turning to the side, leaning, or other deviation. In planting the pole, his top (right) arm must be raised high over head and the pole kept squarely in front of his body.

For this kind of practice a crossbar is not used and the beginner need not try to perfect his stride—just his direction. A bit of stride-chopping will bring his left foot down at the right spot for the takeoff. A beginner's first swings will be awkward. He will probably forget temporarily some of his instructions. This is a critical point in his early learning effort. Encouragement and patient instruction are essential. He should be constantly reminded not to jab the pole in, or jump at, the box and to lift his hips and feet towards the top end of the pole. With continued practice, the beginner will get the feel of the takeoff and rock-back and derive satisfaction from mastering it.

As soon as he gets the feel of a good swing, the vaulter may run a bit faster. From this point on his aim is to perfect the four fundamentals with a run and to blend them together into a smooth and continuous action. Regular observation by the coach provides needed encouragement and assures a practice of correct technique. As skill improves, the vaulter's run is lengthened in accordance with his age, strength, and development. For the beginning high school vaulter, it is gradually lengthened to a distance of at least 100 feet. Eventually, a longer pole is used and the vaulter's hold is raised to the highest point at which he can get a smooth takeoff and swing up. The taller the vaulter, the higher the hold. It is a mistake for the vaulter to hold the pole in such a way that he jerks against it on the takeoff. It should be remembered that when the hold goes up, the takeoff mark goes back.

As the young vaulter progresses, a longer run is used and check marks (see advanced vaulting technique) are established. Eventually, a crossbar is added to the standards and the beginner is ready to move forward to continued refinement of technique. The speed of his run is increased, providing it does not interfere with smooth execution. Beginners fail to take into account that when the hold is higher, the vault takes more time. Movement must be delayed and be more deliberate. This is an important refinement of correct fiber glass pole vaulting. It is a basic teaching point as the beginner continues his work on perfecting his technique.

ADVANCED TECHNIQUES

Advanced pole vaulting is a highly sophisticated skill. Fundamentals are few but important. There are variations in style but most world class vaulters follow certain basic mechanics. A vaulter should not expect to master them all at once; they take time, patience, and practice. Timing, smoothness, and perfection in execution come with experience.

POLE SELECTION AND CARE

The use of fiber glass has made the selection of a pole an important consideration. Many good vaulters fail to reach their greatest potential because they never quite find the pole best-suited to their individual needs. Considerable research has been done on fiber glass poles, and their selection is becoming more scientific.

Fiber glass poles are classified and selected according to critical load (P_c). Critical load is the amount of force, applied to the center of a pole from one end, necessary to cause it to bend. This force, or load, is determined by (a) the vaulter's body weight, (b) the height of his handhold, and (c) his takeoff (kinetic) speed. The vaulter's combined weight and speed bend the pole; his weight alone unbends it. The many possible handholds, along with the difficulty of measuring the amount of speed at takeoff, explain why there is considerable guesswork in pole selection.

In terms of strength, fiber glass vaulting poles are classified according to tensile strength, which is designated in terms of pounds. Theoretically, a vaulter weighing 150 pounds would use a 150-pound test pole. In practice, such is not the case. Most good vaulters use a pole 20 pounds stronger than the weight specified by the manufacturer. A recent Olympic champion weighing 165 pounds used a 180–185 pound test pole; another collegiate champion used one classified in the 165–170 pound test range. Because of the stress placed on poles, especially by inexperienced athletes, it is recommended that vaulters select poles 15 to 20 pounds above manufacturers' suggested weights. They should also take care not to cause structural fatigue in one pole by overusing it.

Some manufacturers classify poles exclusively according to the weight of the vaulter. This is not enough. The height from the top of the vaulter's upper handhold to the bottom end of the pole must also be considered. Formulas which combine the vaulter's body weight and the height of his upper handhold are available. Until a more scientific method is developed, their use is probably the best basis for pole selection. For purposes of pole selection, the location of a vaulter's top hand is usually determined by the point on the pole where it touches the crossbar when the bar is at the vaulter's maximum vaulting height.

The length of the pole is also a factor in its selection. This is usually determined by selecting a pole that allows the vaulter approximately 8 to 24 inches from his upper hand to the top of the pole. Thus, an athlete with a 12 foot 3 inch upper handhold would select a 14-foot pole, rather than one 15–16 feet in length. The extent to which the vaulter could bend the last pole used is a factor in selecting a new one. A pole should also "feel good" to the vaulter.

Because a light pole bends easily, many coaches make the mistake of starting a beginner on a pole that is too light. Most beginners can learn correct technique better on a heavier pole. After fundamentals are mastered, the vaulter can change to a lighter pole, selected according to his individual specifications, which he can bend correctly and use more efficiently.

Most experienced vaulters tape about 2 feet of the pole at the area of the hand grip. This keeps the hands from slipping when the pole is planted and throughout other parts of the vault. Various nonslip aids, such as "Tuf-skin" and other sprays, are also used to insure a secure grip on the pole.

Good vaulters take great care in protecting their poles from damage. Poles are stored carefully after each day's use and never left lying around where they may be damaged by careless handling, weather conditions, or use by other less experienced vaulters. Covers are used while transporting poles. Damage to the pole from falling to the ground is prevented by having another vaulter, or assistant, catch it after each vault.

The breaking of fiber glass vaulting poles is of concern to coach and athlete. Causes vary, but among those most often mentioned are: (1) use of pole too light for vaulter's height and weight, (2) use of pole too long for vaulter and higher than normal handhold, (3) "structural fatigue" caused by continuous use of pole, and (4) use of an excessively wide hand-spread.

Guidelines for Pole Selection

The selection of the proper pole is one of the most important factors in good vaulting.

(1) A vaulter should not select a pole rated less than his body weight.

(2) A pole that is too long for the vaulter should not be selected.

(3) A vaulter should not use a pole that he can bend beyond the maximum recommended limits, regardless of the weight of the vaulter or the rating on the pole.

(4) A pole that is too large for the vaulter should not be selected in the hope that he will grow into it.

(5) A pole should not be selected on the basis of hearsay—get the facts before choosing a pole.

(6) Select a pole at or above the vaulter's weight (the best vaulters use poles rated much over their body weight.)

(7) Select a pole long enough to insure a hand hold 12 to 18 inches from the top of the pole. The pole is designed to give the best reaction when gripped here.

(8) Select a pole that the vaulter can use with confidence. If the vaulter weighs 150 pounds and can bend a pole rated at 170 pounds—all the better. Choose a pole strong enough for the vaulter, even if this is 15 or 20 pounds over his weight.

(9) Select a pole that requires the vaulter to work. The more he puts into the pole the more he will get out of it. However, a pole that is too large is of no greater value than a steel pole.

(10) Select a pole based upon the ability of the vaulter and sound vaulting techniques. Read the manufacturer's literature and follow his recommendations when in doubt.

CHART FOR POLE SELECTION

The following chart is offered as a *guide only*. The ultimate choice of a pole must be made by the vaulter and his coach. The weights listed are maximums allowable for the pole listed and should not be exceeded. If

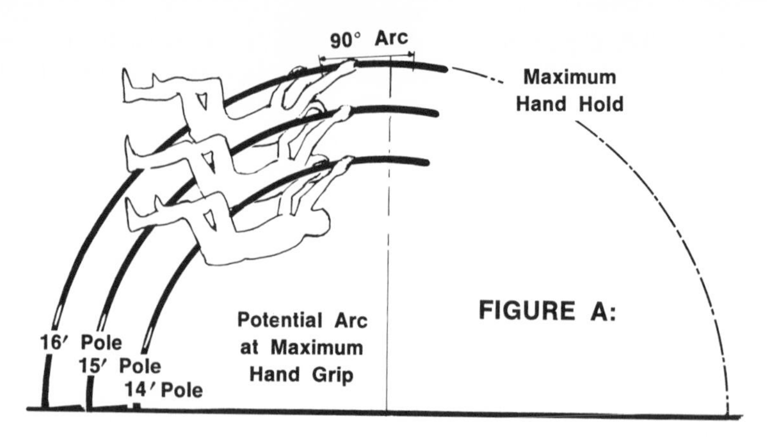

Figure A: This figure illustrates the various pole lengths and their relationship to the 90 degree arc. You will note that the 14 foot pole forms a tighter arc than the 15 or 16 foot pole, although each is bent to 90 degrees. The pole is manufactured this way. A 14 foot model 1460 will not have the same flex characteristics as a 16 foot model 1660 with the hand grip at the same height. When a longer pole is ordered it is assumed that the vaulter will hold higher. *It is necessary to allow for this added stress. Conversely, when a pole is gripped at heights lower than the recommended height the pole may be bent to its maximum arc even though it appears that the bend is less than 90 degrees.*

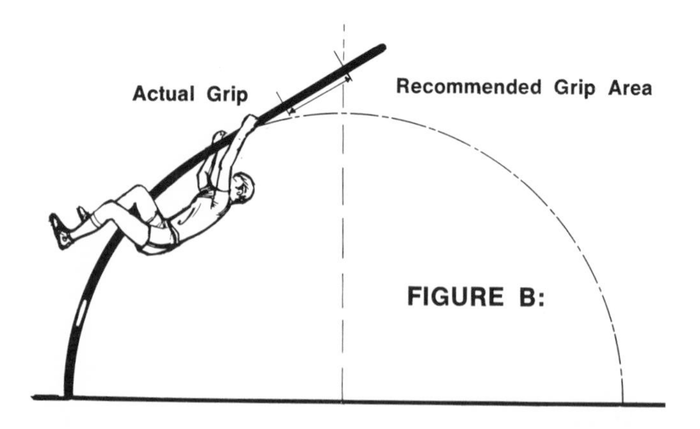

Figure B: This figure illustrates the appearance of a pole bent to its maximum recommended arc when the grip is lower than the average or recommended grip. You will note that the pole bends from the grip to the tip, but the pole extended above the grip remains straight. This gives the appearance of a bend less than a 90 degree arc even though the pole is bent to its recommended limits. The misunderstanding of what constitutes the maximum bend is as much a cause for pole breakage as physical abuse.

Adapted by permission, Pacer American, Inc. (Cata-pole)

a vaulter bends a pole beyond the maximum recommended limits he should change to a stiffer pole regardless of his weight or the rating on the pole. If a vaulter cannot bend a pole rated at his weight when holding in the recommended area, the fault lies in his technique and not in the pole. Never allow a vaulter to use a pole rated under his body weight. A vaulter should work on fundamentals and technique and the bend will come easily.

Guidelines for Pole Care

(1) A fiber glass pole is a unique implement and requires special handling.

(2) A pole should be caught after every vault. Dropping a pole on any hard surface can break fibers and weaken the pole.

(3) A pole should be put back in the shipping tube after every vault. This will protect it from damage incurred by other athletes stepping on it.

(4) A vaulter should not take his frustrations out on his pole. Slamming his pole down because he did not do well can damage it. It's not the pole's fault.

(5) A pole should not be flexed in the box. The pole is not designed to accept this kind of stress, and broken poles can result. This is a poor way to lose an expensive implement.

(6) Do not try to "warm-up" a pole. There is no activity that will change a pole. It cannot be warmed up in any way. The extremes of heat and cold encountered in the normal season will not affect a fiber glass pole. There is no measurable flexibility change between 32 degrees—freezing—and 100 degrees F. Any temperature change may affect the vaulter. Effort should be concentrated on the vaulter—not the pole.

	Vaulters Maximum Weight														
Height of Hand Hold	-100	110	120	130	135	140	145	150	155	160	165	170	175	180	185
10′ to 10′-6″			1210	1220		1230		1240							
11′ to 11′-6″		1210	1220	1230		1240									
12′ to 13′-0″		1410	1420	1430	1435	1440	1445	1450	1455	1460	1465	1470			
13′-6″ to 14′				1530	1535	1540	1545	1550	1555	1560	1565	1570	1575	1580	
14′-6″ to 15′						1640	1645	1650	1655	1660	1665	1670	1675	1680	1685
15′-6″ & over								1750	1755	1760	1765	1770	1775	1780	1785

Four-digit numbers in boxes represent manufacturer's model number. Adapted by permission, Pacer American, Inc. (Cata-pole)

(7) A pole should be inspected regularly for scratches, spike marks, and bruises. These can weaken a pole.

(8) A vaulter should not lend his pole. When a vaulter breaks his pole and then seeks to borrow another of the same weight classification from someone else, the chances are very good that he will break that one also. When a vaulter breaks a pole that belongs to another vaulter, he has eliminated himself and a competitor from competition.

(9) The rubber plug in a pole should be replaced when it shows excessive wear. Vaulting with a worn out plug can cause the end of the pole to split and crack and contribute to irreparable damage.

(10) It is advisable to follow the manufacturer's recommendations concerning weights and hand holds. This information comes from years of experience and intimate knowledge of fiber glass materials and construction.

GRIP AND CARRIAGE

For the advanced pole vaulter, the first consideration in gripping the pole is the location of his *top hand*, the hand he places higher on the pole. For a right-handed vaulter, this would be his *right* hand.

Most good pole vaulters use only one top handhold for all heights. After he has mastered the takeoff, a good high school pole vaulter might start with a top handhold of 12–13 feet. A recent national collegiate pole vault champion started with a handhold of 15 feet in high school and used it throughout his collegiate competition. A pole vaulter, whose execution is correct, should vault 18 to 24 inches over his top handhold before moving it up. Otherwise, he should remain with his original hold and continue working on technique until he can meet this requirement.

A right-handed vaulter grips the pole so that the palm of the top (right) hand is up. Its thumb points diagonally toward the top of the pole and, with the index finger, provides the hand's major gripping force. The left hand, palm down, grips the pole at a point 20 to 30 inches below the right. It grips more loosely and maintains the pole in its straight forward position. Neither hand grips the pole so as to cause tension in the vaulter's arms or shoulders. The exact distance of the hand spread depends upon the individual vaulter. The hand grips on the pole should remain stationary throughout the run, pole plant, and swing up.

ANGLE OF CARRY

Most good vaulters hold the pole so that its tip or point is at shoulder or eye level. Technically this is a medium-angle carry. Experiments have shown that, for a distance of 50 feet, an athlete can run faster carrying the pole in this position than in any other. From this position it can be lowered easily into the plant box. A cross-body pole carry, since it results in lateral movement and whipping of the pole, is not recommended.

THE RUN

The run is the power factor of the vault and determines the amount of kinetic energy available for conversion to body height. Its length will vary according to the vaulter. It should be long enough to build up to maximum controlled speed at a point about three strides from the takeoff. Speed in itself is not essential. In all cases the run should be adjusted to an efficient takeoff and it must be smooth. The pole must be kept steady so that it can be planted correctly. The hands throughout must remain almost motionless.

Many beginners, and some experienced vaulters, particularly at the high school level, do not take a long enough run. To achieve sufficient momentum for efficient vaulting, an approach run of at least 120 to 136 feet should be used. "World class" vaulters use runs of from 148 to 154 feet. Obviously, to maintain steady and proper speed in repeated runs of this distance, the vaulter must be in superior physical condition. His training should include regular and abundant running, with and without the pole.

CHECKMARKS

Since the vaulter must arrive at an exact point in his run for a proper takeoff, checkmarks must be used. If he is to be consistent, he must develop a smooth, even stride, which is the same each time he takes his run. Checkmarks are only a guide. They should never distract the vaulter's attention from his vault.

The number of marks used depends upon the individual. Most good vaulters use one; some, two. If one is to be used, it should be far enough back so that if he finds it necessary, the vaulter will have sufficient distance to stop before reaching the pit.

Assuming a total run of 100 to 130 feet, the average vaulter will use one checkmark seven or eight running strides from his established starting point. Hitting this mark with his left foot, he will take approximately ten to fourteen strides to his takeoff mark. This is adjusted through practice in terms of the speed and stride of the individual.

It is recommended that a vaulter establish and practice an accurate run on some part of the track or field other than the regular vaulting runway. An exact distance, similar to that of the runway, should be measured. Here, free from the distraction of the vaulting box and pit, he may concentrate on perfecting this one important phase of his vault. His checkmarks, accurately measured, can then be transferred to the regular runway.

For vaulters with an even and consistent stride, the establishment of accurate checkmarks is not a difficult matter. Others may require considerable practice. The observation, assistance, and encouragement of a coach is essential in such cases.

It is to be remembered that no matter how accurately checkmarks are established elsewhere, they must ultimately be adjusted to the runway on which the vaulter is to do his vaulting. No two runways are exactly alike. A black top surface is faster than one constructed of clay or cinders. A dry one is faster than a wet one. Wind and temperature conditions vary. All of these factors, in addition to the physical condition of the vaulter, must be considered whenever and wherever he is performing.

Once the vaulter starts down the runway, he should concentrate on driving into his pole plant rather than on whether or not he is going to hit his second check mark. Consistency in the approach stride is vital. The better conditioned the vaulter, the more consistent his approach. Good sprinting action with a high knee lift adds impetus to his approach run. Running over hurdles in practice helps develop efficient and even stride action.

ADJUSTMENT OF CROSSBAR STANDARDS

For the experienced vaulter, crossbar standards should be adjusted so that the distance from the end of the plant box to a line in the pit directly under the crossbar is 12 to 18 inches. If his technique is correct, a vaulter should use only one crossbar adjustment for all heights.

POLE PLANT

The pole plant is a critical point in pole vaulting technique. Many problems can be traced to its incorrect execution. Here the vaulter, who is driving at top speed, must shift the pole from its horizontal position to a vertical one without losing momentum or balance. To do this requires the finest timing.

Methods of planting the pole vary; the important thing in that the plant must be *smooth*. Good vaulters emphasize that it is important to keep the pole close to the hip. The pole must be slid into the box and

The Pole Plant

Note vaulter's straight top arm, hand spread and bent left arm in line with pole. Take off (left) foot is directly under top (right) hand. Vaulter's body in excellent alignment with pole.

not jabbed. Some vaulters, during the last 4 or 5 strides before the plant, ease the pole forward until the top hand is on the hip. This, it is contended, allows for a slow and gradual lowering of the pole preparatory to the plant.

The vaulter must come into his plant driving hard, but relaxed, keeping his eyes on the plant box. At this point he must not slow down. As the pole is planted three essentials must be emphasized: (1) the pole must be well in front of the vaulter's body, (2) hands and the pole must be squarely in front of his eyes, and (3) takeoff foot must be exactly in the middle of the runway.

For smoothness and consistency a *side arm curl type* pole plant is utilized by many good vaulters. When using this technique the vaulter starts elevating the upper end of his pole two strides from the plant. This is accomplished by lifting the pole with the upper hand, curling it up close to the side of the body to a point above the shoulder, and then pressing it above the head to a full arm's length. This action should be completed by the time the vaulter's takeoff foot has been placed down on his last stride.

THE TAKEOFF

As the vaulter starts his takeoff his body weight should be directly over his takeoff foot. His body is perpendicular, with his top hand positioned at a point directly above or slightly back of his head. Shoulders are square, directly over the vaulter's hips, which in turn should be over the takeoff foot. The end of the planted pole hits the plant box at the same time the takeoff foot is placed down.

In fiber glass vaulting there is no hand shift at the time of takeoff as in the more traditional hard-pole vaulting. The vaulter simply plants the pole with the same hand spread with which he grips it at the start of his run. The wider spread of the hands enables the vaulter to bend the pole and take advantage of the added whip which the pole provides.

At takeoff the vaulter's top arm should be straight, but relaxed. The bottom arm should brace firmly against the pole to keep the shoulders and upper body's center of gravity well behind the pole. As the takeoff (left) leg leaves the ground it should be swung up rapidly, with a pendulum action, attempting to catch up to the lead (right) leg. As it catches up to the lead leg, the takeoff leg should also be flexed. At this point the vaulter should hang from the pole supporting his body weight with his top hand. This keeps his shoulders low preparatory for the "rock-back."

THE SWING-UP

A vigorous forward and upward lift of the right leg starts the swing-up action. This is important in helping get the left foot off the ground, adding momentum to the vault. The vaulter must not hurry the action at this point because he wants the momentum already attained to run its full course. In other words, the vaulter must *stay with* his pole. He must not start his pull too soon, but rather he should delay it until his legs have swung past the pole. At this point the upper arm, from which the vaulter hangs, must remain well extended overhead with the elbows close to the body and not pointed outward.

If planted correctly, a fiber glass pole will, itself, lift the vaulter off the ground. The athlete must stay with his pole as it hits the front of the box and be prepared to bring his knees up to his chest in the "rock-back" position which almost immediately follows.

When the vaulter starts his swing, his body hangs from the pole in an elongated position. This is sometimes called his "long pendulum" swing. As his body in this position swings up and meets the pole, it starts to slow down somewhat. At this point, which the athlete must learn to feel from experience, he simply drops his head back, arches his back, brings his bent knees in close to his chest and rolls back to a "half-tucked" position. This action is usually referred to as the "roll-back" or "rock-back" position. Others call it the "hammock." It is fundamentally the same position the vaulter practices in executing the "pop-up."

It is to be emphasized here that in this stage the vaulter should take complete advantage of the momentum of his swing by *delaying* his pull-up. While in this more compact position he does not flex his arms at the elbows. The average vaulter pulls as soon as he leaves the ground. In contrast, the experienced vaulter allows his body to swing well up the pole into the pre-pull-up position before executing his well-timed pull-up. He must keep his body pointing straight forward through this phase of the vault.

THE "ROCK BACK"

A well-executed "rock-back" is essential to correct vaulting technique. To execute it successfully, the vaulter must stay close to the pole,

The "Rock-Back"

Vaulter hangs from straight top arm. Hips elevated. Legs extended up and back toward top of pole. Shoulders are square. Vertical position of body in line with true axis of pole. Vaulter waits *for pole to straighten before starting pull-up and turn.*

keep his upper arm straight, and brace himself back with his lower arm to keep his upper body's center of gravity behind the true axis of the pole. The pivotal point, as he rocks back and swings his legs and hips forward and upward, is his shoulders. This shortens the length of his body and speeds up the rock-back action.

In executing the "rock-back," it is important that the vaulter flex his knees as well as bend his hips. His lead leg is driven forward, upward, and then backward toward the head in a continuous action. Failure to bring the trailing leg up fast enough may cancel the action of the lead leg and delay the "rock-back." As the vaulter brings his knees in close to his body he sights his feet above his top hand on the right side of the pole. At this point his hips should be above the level of his head and shoulders. Just before the pull-up starts, the vaulter reaches skyward with legs and feet, elevating his hips upward toward his top (right) hand. This action starts the pull-up.

PULL-UP AND TURN

The pull-up and turn follow the "rock-back," starting as the bent pole returns to a straightened position of approximately 75 degrees. *It must not be started too early.* Beginners do not delay their swing long enough, and they lose the added force that a fiber glass pole releases as it approaches a perpendicular position.

In executing the pull-up, the vaulter must stay close to his pole. His straight upper (right) arm, which provided much of the force of his pull-up, should be kept parallel to it.

The pull-up combines a vigorous pull of the vaulter's upper right arm and a continued upward elevation of his hips and legs. Legs are straight and held fairly close together. This action starts a lift and 180-degree turn of the body. The pull of the upper (right) arm *precedes* the body lift and turn. As the pull of the right arm is executed, the vaulter should avoid pushing with the lower (left) one. A push with the lower arm will move the vaulter away from the pole, slow down his turnover action, and affect the direct alignment of his body which is so vital to successful execution.

A high right foot during the pull-up and turn is the key to good balance. It assures an effective pull, a well-timed turn and an effective landing. It is suggested that a 180-degree turn of the right foot, without lateral action, will automatically encourage the other parts of the body to follow.

At the completion of the turn-over, the vaulter is ready to add further force to his upward momentum by pushing down on his pole. The push-off is an important refinement of successful vaulting. It must

Completion of Pull-Up and Turn

Pole is stabilized. Vaulter's head and shoulder *of top arm are directly above his top hand. Vertical alignment of vaulter's shoulder and arm through pole into plant box provides* solid *rod for push-off. Hips and shoulders remain in excellent alignment.*

be accomplished while the vaulter's hips are still moving upward. He must stay "over" his pole so that he has a firm base from which to push as he executes the remaining part of his vault. During the push-off the vaulter must concentrate on going *up* and not *away* from the pole. The emphasis is on continued hip elevation, pushing, and turning. When using a fiber glass pole, the final push-off must be carefully timed since the body already has considerable momentum resulting from the pole's excessive bend. Some vaulters use a slight push; others let the pole do the work.

While the pull-up, turn, and push-off are distinct phases, all must be put together in a continuous, smooth, and well-timed action if the vaulter is to achieve the best results in their execution. As the pole is released, the vaulter may throw his head slightly backward to assist in carrying the chest away from the bar as he starts down. Ideally, he should land on his feet, but this is rarely the case. Most vaulters land on their backs, making it essential that a modern landing pit, which is soft and safe, be provided.

Release of Pole

Pull up of arms and shoulders add to vaulter's momentum. Hands, chest and arms are lifted *in push-off action.*

COMMON FAULTS

(Best observed by coach at a position 90 degrees to the side of and 20 yards away from the runway. A second effective observation point is at the end of the runway.)

(1) Swinging body away from the pole. *Cause*: Vaulter does not stay directly behind pole in pole plant. Body not in line with pole in hang from straight top arm. Vaulter does not pull shoulders toward top hand.

(2) Kicking feet into bar or clearing bar in sitting position. *Cause*: Insufficient lift of lead knee and rock-back. Vaulter extends feet toward bar in swing up rather than *up* and *back* over head *toward top of pole*. *Correction*: Practice "pop-ups" and "rock-back" *without* bar on standards.

(3) Pulling up too soon. *Cause*: Vaulter does not hang from straight top arm in rock-back position and *wait* for pole to straighten.

(4) Vaulter attempts to bend pole excessively on takeoff. *Cause*: excessive push on pole with left hand and pull down with right.

Bent rather than straight top arm. *Correction*: Use pole plant described under four fundamentals. *Principle*: The greater the angle between pole and ground at plant, with vigorous lead knee lift, the more effective the transfer of approach speed into vertical speed. Pole is not bent by vaulter; with proper plant, pole bends itself.

(5) Whipping and lateral movement of pole in carry. *Cause*: Cross-body carry. *Correction*: Use straight forward carry described under fundamentals.

(6) Coming down on bar. *Cause*: Incomplete pull-up. Releasing pole too soon. Pulling with arms before feet are up. Lack of push-up in releasing pole. Vaulting standards too close to box.

(7) Falling to the right side of pit. *Cause*: Pole not straight over head at time of takeoff. Running to right at end of approach.

(8) Falling to left side of pit. *Cause*: Leaning to left at time of take-off. Running down left side of runway. Kicking lead leg to left on takeoff.

(9) Jerk at time of takeoff. *Cause*: Takeoff too close to box. Jabbing pole in box rather than smooth pole plant. Jumping at box at time of takeoff.

(10) Insufficient swing up. *Cause*: Taking off too far from box. Top hand not fully extended over head at time of takeoff. Insufficient lead knee lift.

(11) Rubbing pole against chest or side. *Cause*: Takeoff too close to box and usually not in center of runway.

(12) Clearing bar sideways instead of feet first. *Cause*: Takeoff not in center of runway. Kicking lead leg to left and around pole instead of straight ahead.

(13) Hitting bar with hands, arms, or chest. *Cause*: Insufficient or poorly timed push-up and pole release. Poor coordination of arms and legs on push-away.

TRAINING

Most good vaulters recommend year-round training. Weight training and other types of resistive exercises are recommended. Those which develop the abdominal arm, and shoulder muscle groups are stressed. All actions in vaulting are executed quickly. Speed and quick reaction time are therefore emphasized in performing these exercises. Rope climbing is highly rcommended. It has excellent conditioning values. It provides a medium for work on form, particularly the "rock-back" and the pull-up. Push-ups, pull-ups, walking on the hands, parallel bar and trampoline exercises all provide excellent training. Where training is done the year around, a variety of activities should be used to avoid monotony. Where indoor facilities are available the vaulter may actually be vaulting most of the year, but it should be remembered that too much vaulting, particularly without competition, can result in a loss of interest. Participation in other sports should not be discouraged if the vaulter is qualified for and enjoys them. Running of all kinds is beneficial, both in season and out. It is best for the athlete to maintain reasonable fitness throughout the year. This will keep the vaulter psychologically fresh and enthusiastically ready to bring himself to a peak of condition as the competitive season approaches.

During early season, before competition starts, the athlete vaults at least 5 days a week to develop technique. Pole vaulting requires stamina and endurance. An athlete who vaults 15 times during practice with a full run should be able to do so without tiring. Fatigue affects his

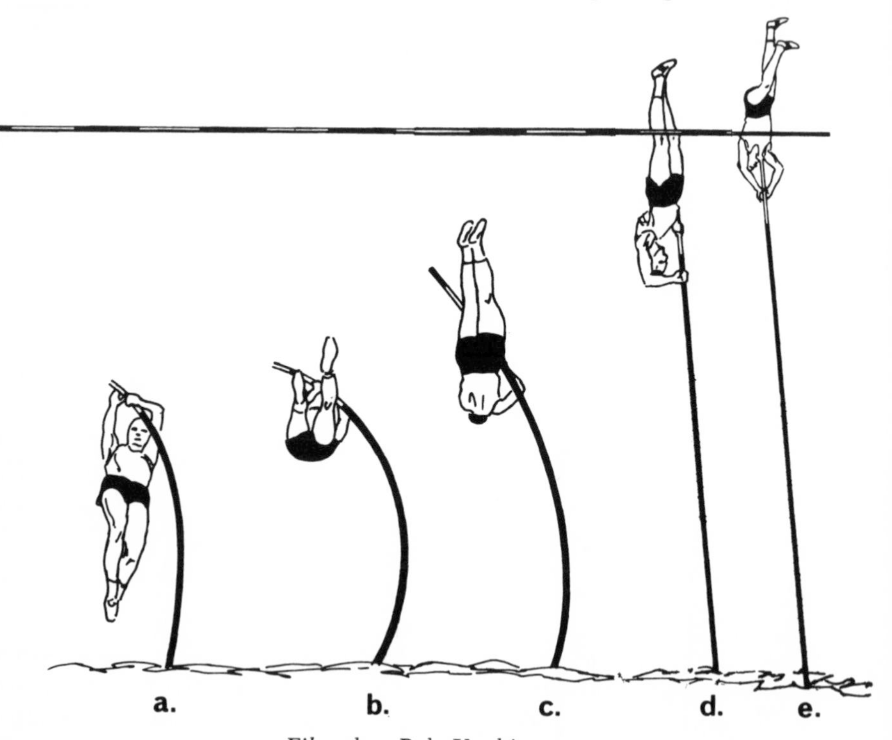

Fiberglass Pole Vaulting

a. Energy in pole lifts vaulter off ground. Right (supporting) hand high. Elbows flexed. Forward momentum continues.
b. The layback, with head back and knees in half-tucked position. Back parallel with ground. Center of gravity in line with lift.
c. Pole straightens. Note vaulter's excellent vertical position (c, d, e).
d, e. Pole stabilized. Hands, spread wide, are directly over center of gravity. Late turn enables vaulter to get legs over bar.

timing and coordination. Practice of technique, therefore, is accompanied by considerable sprinting, hurdling, and continued weight training.

As the season progresses, the number of days devoted to vaulting with a full run, depending upon competition, is decreased to 2 or 3. A day of hard training is usually followed by a lighter one. Ordinarily, a vaulter does not train hard the day before competition. Some do, however, particularly when the next day's competition is not too demanding.

The pole vaulter's training schedule should be *individualized.* His warm-up and vaulting continuity on days of training should be as similar to that of competition as possible. Time spent on vaulting with a full run is devoted to a practice of technique. During this part of the training

f. Completion of turn. Vaulter leaves pole with slight downward push.
g. Release of pole. Hands, chest, and head lifted.
h. Descent, with body well balanced. Rotation of arms keeps elbows from hitting cross-bar.
i. Vaulter prepares to land on both feet.

period, the vaulter works on correcting one weakness at a time. Many vaulters waste time and energy repeating mistakes. Others train at half effort because they are not in good physical condition. For this reason, a coach's observation and advice, at least twice weekly, is essential.

Training for plexiglass pole vaulting should be done *with* and *without* a crossbar. Part of each day's training is conducted on this basis. "Pop-ups," as well as a limited number of vaults with a full run, are practiced without a crossbar.

The height at which the vaulter does his training is important. The basis for establishing the height of the bar for practice depends upon the ability of the individual. A general rule followed by many good vaulters is to practice with the crossbar at a height 6 inches *below* the vaulter's best competitive record. Thus, a vaulter with a best competitive vault of 14 feet would practice with the bar at 13 feet 6 inches. If for some reason the bar is set below this height, he still attempts to clear it with maximum effort.

One or two times weekly, it is recommended that the vaulter take two or three vaults with the bar set 6 inches *above* his best competitive height. Such vaults are an incentive for improvement and help develop the all important *delayed action* timing which characterizes the skilled vaulter.

GUIDELINES FOR TRAINING

(1) Be regular and systematic. Have a daily training pattern and follow it closely. Make practice as close to competition as possible.

(2) Always inspect the vaulting pit and test your pole for safety before vaulting.

(3) Do not start vaulting until your run is accurately measured and takeoff point established. Make sure your takeoff is exactly in the center of the runway. Most common faults can be traced to this point.

(4) Learn to execute a "pop-up" correctly and include it as a part of daily warm-up.

(5) When practicing at low heights, try to clear the cross bar as high as possible.

(6) Develop a correct top hand hold and stay with it.

(7) Stay directly behind your pole and keep it in proper vertical alignment at all times.

(8) Practice planting the pole from a short run to get full extension of top hand over head.

(9) Don't try to bend a fiber glass pole. Work on correct technique, and the pole will bend itself.

(10) Constantly work on drawing lead knee toward the chest on your takeoff. Practice this part of technique on high bar in combination with "swing-over" and "leg-shoot."

(11) Think of slow, deliberate, and continuous action rather than rushing your swing up.

(12) Work for perfection on each vault correcting *one* mistake at a time.

(13) Include sprinting and running as part of your training.

(14) Study illustrations and moving pictures of leading vaulters and get a good mental picture of correct technique.

MIDSEASON TRAINING SCHEDULE

(Adjust to individual age and ability)

The following schedule assumes that the vaulter has established correct check marks and can run with the pole under control.

DAILY WARM-UP PROCEDURES

(1) Jog 4 laps (1 mile).

(2) Calesthenics (10 minutes). Exercises same as for sprinters.

(3) Accelerated running. Short wind sprints without pole (3–4).

(4) "Pop-ups" (6–10). Use approach distance one-half length of full run.

Monday

(1) Warm-up.

(2) 2 vaults without bar (full run).

(3) 10–12 vaults (full run). Cross bar 6 inches *below* best vaulting height. Concentrate on correcting one weakness in technique *only.*

(4) 2–3 vaults (full run). Cross bar 6 inches *above* best vaulting height.

(5) Interval sprinting. Run at best relaxed sprinting effort. Select one of following:
a) 110 yards (10–14 repetitions).
b) 150, 220 (8–10 repetitions).

(6) Weight training (see procedure page 232).

Tuesday

(1) Warm-up.

(2) 8–10 vaults without crossbar. Practice all phases of technique. Concentrate on weakest part.

Wednesday

(1) Repeat *Monday's* schedule, including *weight training.*

(2) Change distance of sprint interval.

Thursday

(1) Warm-up.

(2) Repeat *Tuesday's* schedule.

Friday

(1) Rest or light training. No vaulting.

Saturday

Competition.

Sunday

(Training optional.)

(1) Long runs; relaxed pace.

(2) Weight training.

Weight Training Procedure

(Follow general instructions page 127)

Exercise	Weight	No. of Sets	Rest Interval	Repetitions
Military press (Barbell)	110–195 lbs	2–3	3–4 min	7
Bench press (Barbell)	110–195 lbs	2–3	3–4 min	7
Two arm curls (Barbell)	55 lbs	2–3	3–4 min	7
Reverse curls (Barbell)	55 lbs	2–3	3–4 min	7
Single arm curls (Dumbbell)	10 lbs	2–3	3–4 min	7

Early Season Weight training may be included every other day (Monday-Wednesday-Friday; Sunday optional).

Mid Season Weight training 2 days only (rest one day between). Include Friday on days when competition is not strong.

Late Season Weight training 2 days (rest one day between). None two days before competition.

COMPETITION

(1) Preparation for competition starts the *day before.* Make sure all equipment is ready and if meet is away from home, know how it is to be transported. You are responsible for your own

equipment and do not depend upon others for its presence or return. Make sure you have measured and written down, if necessary, your accurate checkmark.

(2) Be ahead of time on days of competition both at home and away. Check and become thoroughly familiar with vaulting conditions.

(3) Measure and mark checkmarks carefully. Adjust according to weather conditions and surface of runway. With coach or partner observing, take 2 or 3 full runs without the crossbar, to make sure checkmarks are correct.

(4) Do not hurry your warm-up. Make sure you are thoroughly warmed up before vaulting.

(5) Do not take too many warm-up vaults. This is an important advantage to an experienced vaulter. Know exactly how many vaults it *usually* takes to prepare you for the height at which you expect to start vaulting. Do not start vaulting until the bar is at the maximum you can clear *confidently*.

(6) Stay off your feet between vaults. Save energy for vaulting. Concentrate on clearing the bar on your first attempt at each height.

(7) Once you are on the runway, do not delay your vault too long.

(8) Avoid repeated balks or false approaches. This exhausts you mentally and physically.

(9) Make necessary adjustments as vaulting progresses. On all misses, check with vaulting partner or coach on cause. If the cause is the takeoff mark, checkmark, or location of standards, do not take next vault until correction is made. Remember—the higher the bar, the closer the standards are moved *toward* the box.

(10) Do not change height of top handhold as height of cross-bar is raised.

(11) Know the rules and be alert to announcements from officials.

(12) Be courteous to officials and other competitors, but avoid excessive conversation.

Index